Will Rogers

A Photo-Biography

Will Rogers

A Photo-Biography

Bryan B. Sterling and Frances N. Sterling

Taylor Publishing Company
Dallas, Texas

Designed by Hespenheide Design
All photos courtesy of the authors unless otherwise noted.

Published by Taylor Publishing Company
1550 West Mockingbird Lane
Dallas, Texas 75235
www.taylorpub.com

Library of Congress Cataloging-in-Publication Data:
Sterling, Bryan B.
    Will Rogers : a photo-biography / by Bryan B. Sterling
  and Frances N. Sterling.
      p.   cm.
    Includes bibliographical references.
    ISBN 0-87833-249-9
    1. Rogers, Will. 1879–1935. 2. Entertainers—United
States Biography.   3. Humorists, American Biography. I.
Sterling, Frances. N. II. Title
PN2287.R74S75   1999
99-36016
792.7'028'092—dc21
[B]   99-36016
                                 CIP

10 9 8 7 6 5 4 3 2 1

Printed in the United States of America

"That would be a wonderful thing, wouldent it, if a man could pick his own biographer? Trouble with a lot of these biographers is, they go and lower the moral of a character with a lot of facts. Nothing will spoil a big man's life like too much truth."

Will Rogers's Weekly Article #566,
October 29, 1933

Other works by these authors:

Bryan B. Sterling:
> *The Will Rogers Scrapbook*
> *The Best of Will Rogers*
> *Will Rogers, USA (play historian, editor)*
> *Will Rogers, USA (TV-CBS)*
> *Bully (Theodore Roosevelt program)*
> *Eleanor (Eleanor Roosevelt program)*
> *Appomattox (play)*

Bryan B. and Frances N. Sterling:
> *A Will Rogers Treasury*
> *Will Rogers in Hollywood*
> *Will Rogers' World*
> *Will Rogers & Wiley Post: Death at Barrow*
> *Will Rogers Speaks*

Acknowledgments

We owe much to Will Rogers and to those who have carefully fostered his memory over the years. None of our books could have been written or researched without our coming home to the Will Rogers Memorial and Birth Place in Claremore and Oologah, Oklahoma. But buildings are merely construction material and furniture, books and papers. The Will Rogers Memorial has not only the treasures which that unique man left behind, but it miraculously retains that rare spirit of Will.

The warmth and compassion that meet you as you enter, the assistance with any problem, the natural friendliness of everyone from Joseph H. Carter, the director, to the volunteers who greet you at the door, all speak of the past, when those attributes were considered just common courtesy.

We, who are often in need of detail or background information, could not be more supported than by the cooperation we receive from Greg N. Malak, the curator, or Mrs. Patricia Lowe, the librarian, an inexhaustible fountain of Will Rogers lore.

We first walked into the Memorial almost forty years ago. We experienced first hand the devotion to Will Rogers then manifested by Robert W. Love, the manager, and Paula M. Love, the curator. They were the keepers of the flame then. If we feared that with their going would also pass all that they had labored to preserve, we need not have worried.

Our friend Joe Carter has performed miracles by bringing the past to meet the next century, and Will Rogers will live as long as there are dedicated people like Joe, Greg, and Patty.

How can we ever thank them enough?

Bryan and Fran Sterling
June 1999

"A great tradition is that of Will Rogers. He ought to be taught in the schools because of what he embodied of the best of the Constitution and the Declaration of Independence. He was as homely as a mud fence and yet, as beautiful as a sunrise over an Oklahoma field of alfalfa."

Carl Sandburg

Introduction

Dear Reader:

We would like you to meet Will Rogers, quite possibly the most beloved, multitalented phenomenon of twentieth-century America. Born in the Indian Territory—which later became the state of Oklahoma—Will loved the unfenced prairie of his boyhood. He learned to swing a lariat and came to adopt the life of a cowboy, much to the despair of his father, who expected his last surviving son to follow in his footsteps and become a rancher.

Will never received much formal education because he disliked school and was dismissed from several. At the age of eighteen, he fled his last school in the middle of the night. It was then that his education really began. Some have said that the rebellion within Will Rogers was caused by the loss of his mother when Will was ten years old. Perhaps. We know that the little boy loved his mother dearly, yet in the two million words he would write in his lifetime, he wrote "my mother" on only eight occasions. Possibly it was his Indian blood which evoked such stoicism. Will Rogers never explained.

Will Rogers rose from his Indian/cowboy background to such stature that he was called "America's Unofficial President"; "the voice and conscience of America." He became the most widely read and quoted columnist, the most listened-to political radio commentator, America's foremost humorist, and the number one male box-office leader in America's filmdom. He walked with presidents, kings, and heads of state, and he played polo with the famous. Yet all his life, he considered himself to be a country boy.

All his life, in his prolific writings, he would retain his unorthodox style and capitalization, his unique grammar, his haphazard punctuation, and his inventive spelling. The editors of the *New York Times* had strict instructions never to correct Will Rogers' articles. They were unmistakably Will's, and his readers enjoyed them just that way. We hope that you, too, will appreciate them, printed here exactly as Will wrote them. Paula McSpadden Love, Will's niece and the first curator of the Will Rogers Memorial in Claremore, Oklahoma, maintained that it was impossible to write American history of the twentieth century without studying Will Rogers. It is true. For Rogers was an unbiased observer who saw through the sham of it all and made it clear that "all politics is apple sauce." He aimed velvet-tipped arrows at this country's sacred cows, hit the mark every time, yet never left a scar. He traveled extensively, and was so attuned to his various audiences that he was called before congressional investigating committees to testify on conditions in America.

But Will did not merely report on conditions; he did something about them. Without hesitation, he went to the Mississippi Valley to conduct his own campaign to raise funds for flood victims. He and a private pilot flew many hundreds of miles to raise funds for those ravaged by the Dust Bowl drought—simply because it was the right thing to do. He was one of the country's greatest philanthropists, giving away hundreds of thousands of dollars to charitable organizations of every denomination, creed, and color. He could have campaigned for any office in the land and would have been elected. Such power in a lesser man could have been misused. But Will Rogers was a man of rare character and intellect—faithful to his Lord, to his country, and to his family.

After more than forty years of research into his life, we have found nothing to tarnish Will Rogers's image. It would be heartening if that could be said of others we venerate.

Bryan and Frances Sterling

Will Rogers

A Photo-Biography

Will Rogers, age eleven.

Born in a Log Cabin

"My folks dident come over on the Mayflower—
they met 'em at the boat."

Will Rogers's Cherokee roots in both paternal and maternal lines are well documented. While there is no record to substantiate the waggish claim that there was a Rogers antecedent in the 1620 reception committee when the Pilgrims landed near what is now Provincetown, there is no doubt that at least one branch of his forebears had been long established and thriving in the area that would eventually become identified as the Carolinas, Tennessee, Alabama, and Georgia.

Existing documents clearly trace Will Rogers's ancestry back into that original Cherokee part of North America, showing numerous intermarriages with pure and mixed-blood natives of either gender. The European newcomers were readily accepted by the Cherokees and granted all rights, except that of holding office. Will Rogers's family tree bears not only Cherokee names like Sonicooie, Wa-Wli, and Ghe-no-he-li, but those of a variety of western European origin. There is the Scottish or Irish "Trader" McSwain; the Welsh, Dutch, or German Schrimsher and John Gunter (who was one of the first white men to settle in what is today Tennessee); the English Nancy Downing; and the probably anglicized French "Cordery." Will, aware of his racially mixed background, was very comfortable with his Indian heritage. "You know I am an Indian. My folks are Cherokees and I am very proud of the fact," he said at a time when Americans were not too far away from a stated feeling that "the only good Indian is a dead Indian!"

Will Rogers never forgot his background, and on many occasions he reminded his listeners and readers. When, for example, in 1930, his persistence and influence finally made the United States government build the first Indian hospital in Rogers's chosen hometown, he chided:

> Do you know that Claremore, Oklahoma, is going to open the only Indian hospital in the United States? That is no lie, no kidding or anything. It isn't boosting Claremore. But we have the only one, built by the Government entirely for Indians. You know Columbus discovered this country about 400 years ago or

Will's "Grandma Schrimsher" (1804–1877), who was ¾ Cherokee, from an old daguerreotype in the family. Her youngest daughter, Mary America, was Will's mother.

A historic sign commemorating Robert Rogers, Will's grandfather, near Westville, Oklahoma.

something, and it took 400 years for the Government to build a hospital for the Indians. Look what the Indians have got to look forward to in the next 400 years. They are liable to build us a cemetery or something.

In his radio broadcast of April 27, 1930, he touched the conscience of his millions of listeners by restating the shameful treatment accorded the original inhabitants of the land:

Our record with the Indians is going to go down in history. It is going to make us mighty proud of it in the future when our children of ten more generations read of what we did to them. Every man in our history that killed the most Indians has got a statue built for him.

The Government, by statistics, shows they have got 456 treaties that they have broken with the Indians. That is why the Indians get a kick out of reading the Government's usual remark when some big affair comes up, "Our honor is at stake."

And just possibly the most pointed remark on that subject was Will's reference to the general homage and importance Christopher Columbus enjoyed as America's "discoverer":

Being an Indian, I don't mind telling you personally, I am sorry he ever found it. The discovery has been of no material benefit to us, outside of losing all the land. And I am proud to say that I have never yet seen a Statue in Oklahoma to him.

Will Rogers, as usual, was right when he spoke of the dishonorable fate his Indian ancestors had to endure at the hands of the Republic. In 1830, the U.S. Congress, with the full support of President Andrew Jackson, passed the Indian Removal Act. It decreed the displacement of all eastern Indian tribes and their relocation in the Indian Territory west of the Mississippi and Missouri Rivers. At first, several tribes and most Cherokees attempted to oppose the forcible removal, claiming their right to stay on their native soil. Yet a surprisingly large number of Cherokee families—mostly of mixed blood—foresaw the inevitable, signed a treaty selling their land to the government, and moved west. Deciding on their own travel arrangements, they relocated in style and comfort. Arriving in the Territory ahead of the others, they had, of course, far better opportunities to select choice homesteads and lush grazing sites. By 1835 some two thousand Cherokees had already moved west, joining even earlier arrivals, like the Rogers family. These Cherokees and their descendants would later be referred to as the "Old Settlers."

Clem Vann Rogers, Will's father.

In 1838, the federal government began the exacting compliance with the Indian Removal Act in earnest. The great majority of the Cherokees were forced off their tribal lands and escorted westward under military guard. This guard was to ensure that those rounded up would indeed move west. A sizable number, though, being wise in the ways of the forest and its caves, could not be found in time and returned to their land after the armed convoy had departed. The main body's route led some 800 miles along the Tennessee, Ohio, Mississippi, and Arkansas Rivers to the area of Little Rock and from there northwest. The armed soldiers, under the command of General Winfield Scott, accompanied the Cherokee trek by wagon and keelboat. The forced marches, a shortage of food and the lack of even the most basic official concern for health and welfare took their toll. The prodded speed of the transport is demonstrated in that despite the harsh fall and severe winter weather conditions, the journey took only some ninety-three to 139 days—stretched between the first arrivals in the Indian Territory and the slowest stragglers. The last contingent did not reach its destination until March 25, 1839. The average daily distance covered ranged between 8 to 9 miles for the fastest to just under 6 miles for those slowed for whatever reason.

More than a quarter of those who had left the east—some four thousand—died on the way. Small children and the elderly were the first victims of the rigor. Their deaths, so the reports explained, were caused by measles, whooping cough, pleurisy, pneumonia, tuberculosis, and pellagra. Nowhere did it mention that a shortage of food and medical facilities and the inhumanity of the forced march in the midst of winter conditions in any way contributed to the massacre. This appalling episode and others like it have been vividly memorialized forever in Cherokee lore and American history as the "Trail of Tears."

Will's mother, Mary America Schrimsher (1839–1890); married Clement Vann Rogers in Ft. Gibson in 1858.

This photo of Clem Vann Rogers was probably taken in 1906 or 1907, while he was attending the constitutional convention.

The Cherokees were robbed of their land and one-quarter of their nation was killed by the Indian Removal Act of 1830. It is not surprising that President Andrew Jackson, who had endorsed the inhumanity fully, was considered the archvillain. Almost a century later, Will Rogers, a $^9/_{32}$ Cherokee, still carried the open wounds. Being in Washington early in February 1928, Will was asked to address the Democratic Party's annual Jackson Day Dinner. Fully aware of its significance, he pretended:

> They call it a Jackson Day Dinner. I made the mistake of my life. I went there with a speech prepared about Jackson, telling how "He stood like a stone wall," and here it wasn't that Jackson that they were using as an alibi to give the dinner to. It was old "Andy" Jackson. Well, to tell you the truth, I am not so sweet on old Andy. He is the one that run us Cherokees out of Georgia and North Carolina. I ate the dinner on him, but I didn't enjoy it.

Even now, more than 170 years after the indignities and ill-treatment accorded their forebears, the story of the "Trail of Tears" is told and dramatized in Oklahoma. The Cherokees tell it all—how the men, women, and children, worn from the exertion of the degrading journey, arrived in the Indian Territory exhausted and dispirited. Instead of the expected joyful reception, a reunion with friends and family members, they found the "Old Settlers" already well established, prospering and indifferent. The late arrivals felt that they had been betrayed; left behind to wage the honorable fight alone, they were now ignored. Under the leadership of the newcomers' Chief John Ross, the rift between the recent arrivals and the earlier homesteaders threatened to explode into open internecine warfare. As it was, it did result in bloodshed and multiple assassinations.

Will Rogers's grandfather, Robert Rogers Jr., a quarter-blood Cherokee of the Blind Savannah Clan, was one of the victims of that feud. He was killed by Chief John Ross's followers just twelve days before his twenty-seventh birthday. At the time, his wife, Sallie Vann, a mixed-blood Cherokee of the Wolf Clan, was twenty-four; their daughter, Margaret Lavinia, was six; and their son, Clement Vann Rogers, was three-and-one-half years old. Left with two small children, Sallie Vann married again after two years of widowhood.

Young Clem Vann Rogers did not get along well with his mother's new husband. Clem attended the Baptist Mission School and later the Male Seminary at Park Hill. He had great dreams of the future. Young Clem did not really remember his father, yet his father's last words—so he was told repeatedly later on—had been to "tell Clem to always ride your own horse." And that was exactly what Clem intended to do.

In 1856, when the Cherokee Nation organized a new sector on its western border, it was named the Cooweescoowee District, using Chief John Ross's Cherokee name. It was here, to a branch of the Caney River, that a seventeen-year-old Clement Vann Rogers brought a small herd of cattle and two black slaves to start the first "Cow Ranch and Trading Post" in the District. He prospered in the next two years. By 1858, now being nineteen years old, Clem felt that he could

The depot at Claremore, Oklahoma.

Appraisal of the assets of Robert Rogers (1815–1842), Will's paternal grandfather, 1856.

afford a wife and raise a family. He married Mary America Schrimsher, the daughter of a prominent Cherokee family. She was well educated, having attended Cane Hill Female Seminary in Arkansas and later the Cherokee Female Seminary in her native Tahlequa. Will Rogers would refer to his parents in his writings. He said of his mother:

> Mary, the name alone means something don't it? Always helping someone. My mother was named Mary.

As for his father, Will would be somewhat more reserved:

> My Daddy fought with Stand Watie in the Confederacy, but you couldent get much war news out of Papa. I sho dident inherit this continuous flow of blathering around from him.

The first child of Clem and America Rogers was Elizabeth, born September 11, 1861. By that time the War between the States had begun. As the Rogers property lay fairly close to the Kansas state line, federal forays and marauding bands of irregulars often crossed into the Indian Territory, plundering all that could be carried off, trashing that which could not. Clem Vann Rogers sent his wife and firstborn to what was thought at first to be a safer location, the Goingsnake District along the Arkansas border. Little Elizabeth, barely three months old, died there. At Clem's urging, Mary America went farther south and settled at Bonham, Texas, where the Rogerses' second child, Sallie Clementine, was born in 1863.

Clem Vann Rogers's sympathy had always lain with the South, and he joined its cause immediately. He saw duty as lieutenant, later as captain, of Company G, the First Mounted Cherokee Volunteers, under Cherokee General Stand Watie. Clem served the entire four years of the war and distinguished himself in numerous engagements. Stand Watie had the distinction to be the last Confederate general to surrender, two weeks after Grant and Lee had met at Appomattox to end the conflict.

Will's birthplace on the Verdigris.

Will Rogers's birth room. Notice the hand-hewed walnut and oak logs, characteristic of frontier log cabins.

Returning at war's end to the Cooweescoowee District, Clem found what he had expected—the house destroyed, the herd gone, his slaves freed. Rather than rebuild on the same site, he moved a few miles farther east, this time closer to the Verdigris River. There was a small log cabin on the property, which Clem purchased. It was a primitive beginning, but in 1870 Clem decided to bring back the family, which now included, in addition to Sallie Clementine, his first son, Robert Martin, and another daughter, Maud Ethel.

Being an excellent manager and a shrewd businessman who knew land and cattle, Clem Rogers prospered. Every spring he would buy longhorn cattle in Texas, then drive the herd north to his ranch. There the steers would fatten up on the rich bluestem grass of the Indian Territory prairie. Though he did not own the land, as a Cherokee it was his right to use as much of the open range as he needed for his purpose, and it has been said that Clem Vann Rogers controlled some sixty thousand acres. With low labor costs and no expense for feed, the profit margin was substantial. Each year Clem sold range-fed cattle to the markets in Kansas City, St. Louis, and points east. This was indeed the land and the time of the cowboy and horses, of the big roundup and branding. Life was still simple and nature undisturbed.

Clem's fortunes increased and the family grew. Clem and Mary decided on a new home. By 1875 the columned, seven-room "White House on the Verdigris" was finished. It was an imposing two-story log house with plastered walls on the inside and white-washed siding on the exterior. There were four open fireplaces, and airy porches on both floors, offering an unobstructed vista of land and river.

Col. William Penn Adair, commander of the Cherokee Regiment, Stand Watie's Confederate brigade. Will Rogers was named for Adair.

The mansion—or such it appeared to be on the still-primitive western frontier—was not only a landmark by which to set one's course, but a warm haven for many a weary traveler. Located on one of the routes between Texas and Kansas, many travelers stopped in to relate news or to gather it. The nearest city to the north was Coffeyville, Kansas, some 40 miles distant. To the south, some 12 miles as the crow would fly, was a budding Claremore, I.T. (Indian Territory).

Mary America Rogers, ever the perfect hostess, welcomed friend and stranger alike to the "White House." She had a most engaging personality with a fine wit. She was a talented pianist, enjoyed parties, and hosted frequent dances at her home. She was also a most valuable help as Clem began to take a more active position in the politics of the Cherokee Nation, the Indian Territory, and the state of Oklahoma that was to follow it. He held important public offices. In 1877 he was elected judge for the Cooweescoowee District, and served two years. In 1879 he was elected senator of the Cherokee Council, a position to which he was reelected in 1881, 1883, and again in 1889. Clem served on several commissions preparing the Indian Territory for the relinquishment of the title held by the Cherokees to their land, readying both land and people for the distribution of so-called individual Indian allotments of 40 acres each. He also served on a committee to certify claimants for the Dawes Commission. In 1907 he was elected a delegate to the Constitutional Convention which was to form the state of Oklahoma. As the eldest delegate, and in recognition for his work and devotion to the state, his fellow members insisted in naming Rogers County in his honor. From 1894 until his death in 1911, he was vice-president of the First National Bank of Claremore.

His leadership qualities, finely honed by his service in the Civil War; his management of a huge ranch and farm; and his years of public service were frequently recognized. As Clem's hometown newspaper noted about him:

Clem Rogers is attending court as a witness at Ft. Smith. Clem is a whole-souled, sound, practical man, honest in his convictions, capable and worthy of any position within the gift of the people of the Cherokee Nations.

Yet while all seemed to be going so well for the Rogers family, adversity was a frequent caller. After having lost their firstborn, Elizabeth, on the flight toward Texas at the Civil War's onset, three more of their eight children died. After Maud Ethel, Mary (May) had been born in 1873. Zoe, born in 1876, lived less than six months. Then came Homer, in 1878, who lived but three months. And lastly, a most earnest tragedy—Robert Martin, a serious, dependable boy who loved ranching and was being groomed to take over the family's business, died of typhoid fever two days before his seventeenth birthday.

The eighth and last child of Clement Vann Rogers and Mary America Schrimsher was still to come:

I was born on November 4th, 1879, that was election day. Women couldn't vote in those days, so my mother thought she would do something, so she stayed home and give birth to me. That's why I have always had it in for the government.

I was born at our old ranch, it was a two story log house, but on the back we had three rooms made of frame. Just before my birth my mother, being in one of those frame rooms, had them move her into the log part of the house. She wanted me to be born in a log house. She had just read the life of Lincoln.

So I got the log house end of it O.K. All I need now is the other qualifications.

On the authenticated roll of the Cherokees, Willie, as the boy was usually called, is entered as being $^9/_{32}$ Cherokee and a member of the Paint Clan. That is the sole record of his birth. Will Rogers explained that matter years later when he tried to obtain a passport:

Well I said I would like to get a Passport to go to Europe; "Here is the application and here is an affidavit that someone that we know will have to swear that they know of your birth and you will have to produce your Birth Certificate."

Well, I told her, Lady, I have no birth certificate; and as for someone here in New York that was present at my birth and can swear to it, I am afraid that will be rather difficult. You know the old-time Lady of which I am a direct descendant, they were of a rather modest and retiring nature, and being born was rather a private affair, and not a public function.

You see, in the early days of Indian Territory, where I was born there was no such things as birth certificates. You being there was certificate enough. We generally took it for granted if you were there you must have at some time been born.

The earliest photograph of Will Rogers, taken in 1880.

Willie loved the interesting life on the prairie, the activities of a big, busy ranch, the horses and cowboys, the roundups and branding. It was a full, yet so much simpler life. Willie's favorite place away from home was at the cabin of Big Dan Walker and his wife, Babe, both former slaves who still worked for "Uncle" Clem. (In the Indian Territory, as in many places in the South, it was the practice to respectfully call older men "uncle" and older women "aunt.") Dan and Babe took to little Willie and raised him like their own children. As Will would later recall the experience:

Darkies raised me. I wasn't only raised among Darkies down in the Indian Territory, but I was raised by them. And,

Will at age eleven, 1891.

"Aunt" Babe
Walker.

Will's sister Mary,
called May
(1873–1909).

*Lord, I was five years old out at the ranch before I ever knew there
was a white child . . .*

*[Now] one [of those white children] showed up about the
same time that Hereford cattle come in. I thought [for sure that]
this white child and this bald-face Hereford was the same breed.*

What Dan and Babe Walker also taught Willie would serve
him in later life. Both Walkers were excellent ropers and they
introduced the boy to the lasso. They not only taught him to

Will's sister Maud.

catch calves and stationary
objects, but introduced him to
simple trick roping. From then
on, Willie would practice with
the lariat, whether it was to
catch a waddling duck or
merely a fence post. Once he
caught a fleeing turkey and
broke the bird's neck. He was
disconsolate and would not
touch the rope. It was Babe
who finally persuaded him to
be more selective next time in
his choice of targets. The lariat
became Will's companion and
would take him into show
business and unparalleled
stardom.

Clem Rogers nearly lost
his life shortly after his son's fourth birthday. It is doubtful that
either little Willie, or the adult Will, even knew about the serious
accident that almost took his father. It was in February 1884.
Winter was well entrenched, but there had been a short period
when the daylight hours were clear and a returning powerful sun
had thawed some of the frost in the earth. Clem was coming
home and decided to cut through the fields and cross the
Verdigris close to his home. There were no bridges spanning the
river near the Rogers's spread, and during the warm months the
Verdigris could only be breached at fords. This being February, ice
had covered the river for weeks and the few children of the area
had been skating on it. Now that it was later in the day, Clem was certain that the
setting sun had allowed the ice to harden even more, if indeed the mild rays of
the weak winter sun had softened it during daylight hours.

Partway across the Verdigris, he heard the unmistakable crack of breaking ice
under his feet. He tried to turn and retrace his steps. It was too late. A large piece
directly under him gave way and Clem sank into the water. He spread his arms to
catch himself and keep his head above water. But as he tried to pull himself back
onto the surface, the edge of the ice sheet crumbled under his weight. To make
matters even worse, his weight kept increasing as his clothing soaked up more

and more water. At last he was able to reach more solid ice and pull himself up on it. He lay there, panting from the enormous effort. Now prone, he tried to slide along toward the riverbank, not wishing to stand and concentrate his weight on the small area of one foot. It was reported in the area's important newspaper that Senator Clem Rogers's clothing froze solidly on him before he could walk the remaining quarter mile to his house.

Willie's carefree days at home came to an abrupt end when he was old enough to attend school. For his sixth birthday he received his first pony, which made the transition bearable. But for the boy who was used to the unrestricted life on a seemingly endless prairie, the confines of a one-room schoolhouse were like a jail. Miss Ida McCoy, his schoolteacher, was considered an excellent educator; to Willie she was simply the warden. He hated the classroom and tried every way to get out of it. If water needed to be fetched, Willie would volunteer; if an errand needed to be run, Willie's hand shot up first. He did enjoy the horse racing that pitted the various boys against each other. Most of the students arrived daily on their horses, and after school was out the competition began. Willie's pony won most of those races. It is difficult to check whether what Will Rogers later said about those days was factual, or just his way of making a point. He reminisced in *Story of a Misspent Boyhood*, a weekly article filled with his unique grammar, arbitrary spelling, random capitalization, and eccentric punctuation:

> *I was just a thinking what I would have to do if I was to start out to help out my old school. 'Drumgoole' was a little one-room log cabin four miles east of Chelsea, Indian Territory. It was all Indian kids went there and I being part Cherokee had enough white in me to make my honesty questionable.*
>
> *We graduated when we could print our full name and, name to the teacher the nationality of the last Democratic President.*
>
> *. . . the school went out of business. We wasent able to get football games which was profitable.*
>
> *I looked like a promising End. I could run pretty fast. In fact my nickname was and is to this day among some of the old timers "Rabbit." I could never figure out if that referred to my speed or my heart.*
>
> *Mind you, you wouldent believe it, but we dident even have a Stadium . . . Well, you see as I look back on it now, a school like that dident have any license to exist. It had to perish. It just staid with books, such as Ray's Arithmetic, and McGuffy 1st, 2nd, (and two pupils in the 3rd) Readers. We had even a Geography around there but we just used it for the pictures of the cattle grazing in the Argentine and the wolves attacking the sleighs in Russia.*
>
> *They just had the old fashioned idea that the place must be made self-sustaining by learning alone, and you see where their ignorance got them. Now the weeds is higher than the School house was. They won't switch and get to the new ideas that it's open field running that gets your old College somewhere and not a pack of spectacled Orators, or a mess of Civil Engineers. It's better to turn out one good Coach than ten College Presidents."*

Young Willie Rogers and school, any school, just did not seem to be destined for each other. It was not that he was not interested; he just did not like to conform to the type of structured tuition then practiced. His report cards were not

Old Oologah,
Oklahoma.

Main Street,
Oologah,
Oklahoma.

exactly indicative of a poor scholar, yet—so his teachers complained—the boy did not apply himself. There were subjects in which he excelled, such as history and public speaking, but otherwise he developed his own, inimitable system of getting by.

In those days, the most important schoolbooks were the series of McGuffey's Eclectic Readers. A student's progress was not measured by the time he had been attending school, but by the edition of McGuffey he would be studying. Thus the student was not in the fourth grade, but might be on McGuffey's Fourth Reader. This then became young Rogers's strategy:

W. E. Halsell of Vinita gave a school to that country in the early days, called Willie Halsell School, and I went there awhile, in fact quite a while. I was four years in McGuffy's Fourth Reader there, was in Ray's Arithmetic three years and couldent get to fractions. Well, I saw they wasent running that school right, so I just got out. That's the way I have always done with schools; the minute mine and their plans dident jibe why I would get out, or sometimes they would ask me. I would generally always do it if they did; I was an accommodating boy.

My father sent me to about every school in that part of the country. In some of them I would last for three or four months. I got just as far as McGuffey's Fourth Reader, when the teacher wouldent seem to be running the school right, and rather than having the school stop, I would generally leave. Then I would start in another school, tell them that I had just finished the Third Reader and was ready for the Fourth. Well, I knew all this Fourth Grade by heart, so the teacher would remark. 'I never see you studying, yet you seem to know your lessons.' I had that education thing figured down to a fine point. Three years in McGuffey's Fourth Reader, and I knew more about it than McGuffey did.

But I don't want any enterprising youth to get the idea that I had the right dope on it. I have regretted all my life that I did not at least take a chance on the Fifth Grade.

Willie Rogers was ten years old when his mother died, in 1890. The Rogers children had come down with typhoid fever and Mary had nursed them. Her final illness was diagnosed as amebic dysentery. At her funeral and burial, only daughter May had sufficiently recovered to attend. Mary America Schrimsher Rogers was only fifty years old. Decades later Will would reminisce:

My own mother died when I was ten years old. My folks have told me that what little humor I have comes from her. I can't remember her humor but I can remember her love and her understanding of me.

For little Willie the world changed once again. With his adored mother gone, Willie was mostly ignored and underfoot. His sisters, all being older, had their own lives. Sallie was married and had moved away. Maud was now twenty years old and very popular, while May was seventeen, an age when younger brothers are rarely appreciated.

And with a father who personally ran the ranch, negotiated sales, handled all the day-to-day problems a large ranching and farming venture presented, and was politically active, a young boy could not expect to receive much attention. And yet it was with this cool and distant father that Willie wanted most to find favor. For the rest of Clem's life Will tried to prove to his father that he, too, was "riding his own horse."

The year 1889 had also been significant. It marked the coming of the Missouri Pacific Railroad to the Verdigris country. Clem Rogers was violently opposed to it. He was one of the few who could foresee the radical changes ahead. He realized that the railroad, making access to the West so much easier, would bring settlers to the Territory. It would mean an end of "the wide open spaces," an end of his cattle empire and its change to a diversified farm. Surely, these new families would need food and that meant agriculture—the destruction of the prairie's priceless bluestem grass, the advent of small family farms, the building of fences, of communities, and even towns. Indeed, it was the establishment of a railroad switch stop on the Missouri Pacific Railroad line some 6 miles southwest of the Rogers ranch that served as the beginning of the village of Oologah, the community that retroactively would claim to be the birthplace of Will Rogers. It never grew to be a big city; even around 1900 all it sported was a railway depot, a church that doubled as a schoolhouse, a two-story frame hotel, a livery stable, and a few one-story wooden buildings scattered on each side of the two-block-long rutted "main street," which, beyond the last house, withered away into the rich growth of the prairie. In spots there was a rickety plank sidewalk that, in the rain, was partially effective but fully hazardous in the dark.

With considerable power Clem tried to stem the advancing rail lines which planned to cut his holding in two. As the plowing of the prairie by "sodbusters" would destroy his free grazing land, Clem felt forced to enclose the area he absolutely needed. He was the first rancher to bring barbed wire to the Territory, signaling forever the end of the open range there.

When it was obvious to Clem that there was no way to halt the encroaching railway, he accepted the inevitable and converted part of the land he controlled to agricultural use. Having reduced available grazing space, he changed his livestock from longhorns to shorthorns and added wheat farming to his operation.

Will riding a bicycle
in front of his home.

By 1892, the yield of wheat in his section was so great, as the newspaper the *Indian Chieftain* reported in its issue of August 18, that people had to use their dwellings for granaries. Clem's wheat output also made news in local newspapers, which reported a harvest of 10,000 bushels in 1894 and 11,000 bushels the following year. Obviously that was so impressive that the *Claremore Weekly Progress* of Saturday, July 27, 1895, arbitrarily crowned Clem Vann Rogers "the Oologah Wheat King."

During the week of January 15, 1893, the *Coffeyville Journal* and the *Indian Chieftain* carried the news that "Judge Clem V. Rogers and Miss Mary Bibles, both of the Cherokee Nation, were united in marriage at Claremore, I.T." This may have solved some problems for Clem, such as the seeming impropriety of having a widower share his home with a young, single, female live-in housekeeper. But the puzzling issue of what to do with adolescent Willie merely magnified. Mary Bibles, now the new Mrs. Clem Vann Rogers, could never replace the vivacious, outgoing Mary America, nor take her place in Willie's heart, even if she had tried. That there was no trace of emotional identification between the boy and Mary Bibles is clearly shown: Although Will Rogers would go on to write more than two million words, and speak millions more, he never mentioned her.

Even a preoccupied Clem was disturbed by the increasing tension in the house and he realized that a solution had to be found. It was finally decided that the best arrangement—at least for Mary Bibles Rogers—would be that Willie be sent to a boarding school. In fact, Willie attended a number of schools in the area. There was the Presbyterian Mission School in Tahlequa for a year. Then in 1892, it was the Willie Halsell College in Vinita, a town some 17 miles northeast of Chelsea. The *Indian Chieftain* of October 13, 1892, offered some insight into the school's extended curriculum:

> *The calisthenics exercises for the cultivation of physical strength and muscular elasticity . . . given to the pupils . . . at the close of each day's work, by Miss Croom, and the vocal training given at the opening of school by Miss Selleck.*

The same newspaper, the *Indian Chieftain*, of December 29, 1892, had news from Vinita about Willie Rogers:

> *Willie Halsell College . . . fall session closed . . . Willie Rogers was inimitable in each of his declamations and never failed to receive a hearty round of applause.*

What was somewhat less complimentary, though, and appeared in the same issue, was the Honor Roll report, in both Academic and Collegiate Departments. There "Will (note the more formal name here) Rogers averaged in daily grade for the month of December 90 2/3, . . . the average for the entire school on examination was about 93."

In addition to riding, roping and horse racing, Willie played football. That is, he did play, and yet he did not.

Will (left) and pal Charlie McClellan.

You know I used to play me a pretty good end, that is a substitute end. I don't think they ever used me, but the rough way they was playing in those days, that dident hurt my feelings any, not getting in there. I played what you might call a "Wide End." I would play out so far that the other 21 would be pretty well piled up before I could possibly reach 'em.

I think it was along about in our days when the first thing come in the way of a shift. It was called "Tackles Back," "Tackles Right," or left, "Guards Back." They would move everybody over to one side of the line, that is everybody that could remember the signals. Kinder the way it was worked was the fellow that was going to lead the interference would just holler for all the help he could get, then everybody fell in behind and pushed, so you see when I picked this deep end job, I kinder figured that I would arrive a little late for most of the festivities. So that's why to this very day I don't carry any football scars, or bruises. I was pretty fast as a runner. But I never seemed to be fast enough to get there in time to get into one of those massacres. Well in those days if I remember substitutes dident get in games much anyhow. You either played or you dident play. You wasn't allowed to run in and out like a bell hop.

Will (seated) with teenaged friends.

At the closing ceremony of the 1893–94 school year, nine gold medals for scholastic excellence in various subjects were to be presented. The gold medal for elocution was awarded to a Miss Josie Crutchfield. But Will was also honored, as the *Indian Chieftain* of Thursday, June 14, 1894, told its readers:

The recitation of Willie P. Rogers was rendered so well that the Judge decided he was also entitled to a medal, and the privilege of a duplicate was given him.

In March 1895, an organization called the Christian Endeavor was formed at the Presbyterian Church. The *Claremore Weekly Progress* reported under the dateline of March 20 that "Willie Rogers" had been elected president and that "meet-

S.C.I. Team of 96.

ings will be held every Wednesday evening at the church." It is one of the few records that Will Rogers was actively involved in church activities.

At the start of the school year in the fall of 1895, Will, now almost sixteen, moved once again, this time to Scarritt Collegiate Institute in Neosho, in western Missouri; the following year the *Joplin* (Missouri) *Globe* ran a picture of Will Rogers, matriculating from the Institute.

The search for yet another school for Willie continued. All the nearby schools in the Territory and nearby Missouri had already been tried, and found ineffective. The circle widened. Clem made inquiries and finally, in 1897, he sent his only remaining son to central Missouri. "I have my hard-to-manage son in a military school," he told a friend, "the Kemper Military School in Booneville."

Willie P. Rogers arrived at Kemper on Wednesday, January 13, 1897. He was a strange sight to behold. He wore a ten-gallon hat with a braided horsehair cord, and a flannel shirt with a red bandanna handkerchief. His trouser legs were stuffed into his boot tops. He came straight from having escorted a herd of steers from his father's ranch to Kansas City. He had sold the herd and, per instructions, used the cash to pay his tuition at the Kemper Military School.

While Clem Rogers thought his son just "hard-to-manage" at home, Willie pulled his usual pranks and entertained the students at school. He was very well liked, at least by his fellow cadets, if not exactly by the teaching staff. He had arrived with a full complement of lariats, which he used at every opportune—and inopportune—occasion. As usual, he would rope everything that would move. It's told that one day he threw his loop at a large dog and caught it. Terrified, the hound took off. Will now had the option of either releasing the rope and letting the dog run off with it, or keep holding on and be forced to follow. It was quite a show, watching that terrified cur, darting first one way then another, with cadet Rogers in uniform trying to keep pace. Off they went, heading for the private section of the officers' quarters. It was Monday, laundry day, and the lines had been strung holding the freshly washed sheets and clothing. To keep the heavily laden lines from sagging, slim wooden poles had been used to support the lines. With the dog racing wildly around, with an almost fully grown Will following, those supports got in their way. Poles were dislodged and lines sagged, dragging the larger pieces of laundry on the ground. Some of the lines snapped under the heavy, now unsupported weight.

Severe penalties followed. At Kemper, as at most military institutions, punishment consisted of demerit points. Each point was equal to one hour of either additional guard duty, or an hour of marching, fully packed and carrying a rifle, between the farthest ends of the parade ground. While his fellow students would be at play, Will Rogers would walk off his demerits, come rain or sunshine, snow or piercing winds.

It is no wonder that Will amassed an impressive number of demerits. The boy was the class jester; he wanted to entertain, make others laugh. His scholastic average was just a minor fraction above 90, allowing him to stay on, yet somehow the notion persisted that surely, any such "undisciplined" cutup could not possibly be a good student and would never amount to very much.

What everybody agreed on was that Willie cut an exceedingly fine figure in his cadet uniform. Home on leave in June of his first year at Kemper, he intended to impress his friends, and especially the local girls. Taking his father's Winchester rifle from the house, he went through the manual of arms—the prescribed drill in the handling of a firearm. A small crowd gathered to view something none of them had ever seen. Willie went through the performance flawlessly, just as he had been taught at Kemper. He concluded it with the required slamming of the butt on the ground. Since this was not his gun, he could not have known that it was loaded. It discharged straight up, with the bullet passing through his hat, causing a slight scalp wound. As Spi Trent, Will's cousin, would later say: "A old bullet whizzed up and grazed the front part of his forehead and believe me, a quarter of an inch more would a tore the top of his head off. As it was, it just took away a little skin leaving a small scar which remained with him thru life." After this experience Will Rogers never again liked firearms, be they rifles or handguns.

It was back to Kemper, but not for long. This is how Willie looked at his entire stay at the Kemper Military School in Booneville, Missouri:

Will Rogers and friend John Houston Payne.

> Boonville, one of the finest Military schools any-
> where. I was two years there, one year in the
> guard house, and the other in the fourth reader.
> One was about as bad as the other.

Will Rogers (seated at the right) with teenaged friends.

In later years, Willie must have thought about Kemper often, because he reminisced about it from time to time in his columns in a lighthearted manner, as if the experience—in retrospect—was really not as unpleasant as it had seemed at the time:

In 1898 Kemper Military School was not being run in accordance with the standards that I thought befitting a growing intellect. I was spending my third year in the fourth grade and wasn't being appreciated, so I not only left them flat during a dark night, but I quit the entire school business for life. Billy Johnston of Canadian City, Texas, was also an inmate and a ranch boy like I had been in Oklahoma, so he advised me of a friend's ranch at Higgins, Texas.

I, not wanting to face my father with what little I knew by going back home, landed in Higgins. . . .

Will arrived in Higgins, Texas, just across the border from the Indian Territory, on Tuesday, March 15, and checked into room 12 at the Johnson Hotel. Here he waited to meet P. W. Ewing, the rancher he hoped would have a job for him. Will obviously had to wait, as the hotel register shows him still staying in room 12 the following day. Ewing ran a 13,000-acre ranch and knew Clem Rogers well. He hired Will and without the boy's knowledge sent a letter off, advising Clem of the whereabouts of his son. When C. V. Rogers heard that his troublesome offspring had once more run away from a school, he was angered and replied that if Ewing could get any work out of Willie, it would be more than he had ever been able to do.

Just what made me leave Kemper Military Academy in the winter of 98 . . . there is always quite a controversy as to whether I jumped, or was I shoved. Well I can't remember that far back. All I know is that it was a cold winter, and old man Ewing's' ranch on the Canadian River at Higgins, Texas wasent any too warm when I dragged in there. Kemper was my last school.

When Willie P. Rogers left Kemper Military School abruptly, he still had some 150 demerits marked against his name. It was the only assessment against him he would never discharge. The name Willie would be retired until his adolescent children would refer to their father as "Pa Willie" to differentiate between him and the eldest son, who was "Brother Willie." But to the rest of the world the man was "Will Rogers," except for his closest friends. They simply called him "Bill."

Even the happy life of a working cowboy and a couple of cattle drives could not keep Will away from his family forever. By the spring of 1899 he finally decided it was time to return to Claremore. Clem was pleased to see his son. Almost forgotten were the times Willie had changed schools, had caused problems, had acted irresponsibly. If Will really wanted to be a cowboy, that was just fine with him. After all, that's what he had always wanted, a son and heir who would take over. It is true that Mary America, Will's mother, had hoped that her only surviving son would grow to be a preacher, but Clem wanted what a father usually wants: a son to follow in his footsteps. Besides, all the changes of ranching life in the Cherokee Nation had come to disillusion Clem. What he saw ahead was the end of an era and the beginning of an entirely new one he did not like. With the arrival of the railroad, there would be no need for cattle drives. With a station at Claremore and one at his front door, in Oologah, cattle would arrive by boxcar and could be shipped east the same way. Where before unsophisticated consumers readily accepted any grade of longhorn beef, Eastern establishments now began to insist on better quality. No longer was the tougher meat of range-fed cattle as acceptable, and prices had begun to drop. Ranchers had to improve breeds, to cater to the demands of the consumers. Then, of course, another problem had developed. With grazing areas becoming scarcer as homesteaders illegally infiltrated the Indian Territory and staked their claims, it became ever harder to com-

Kemper football team. Will is seated second from the right.

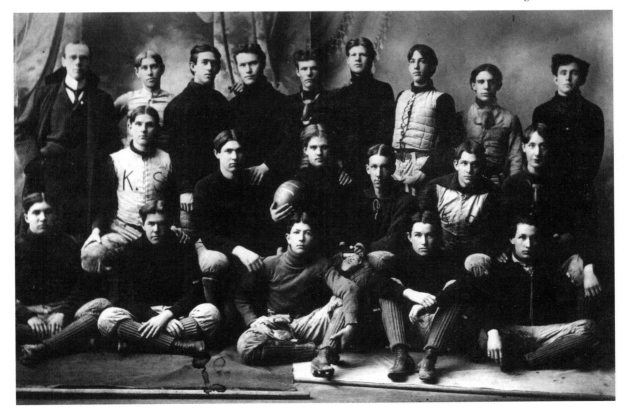

Will Rogers in his
Kemper military
uniform.

*Courtesy of the Will
Rogers Memorial
Commission*

Kemper School
monthly report for
Will Rogers.

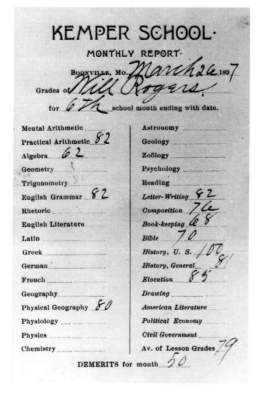

KEMPER SCHOOL.
MONTHLY REPORT·
Boonville, Mo. *March 26* 189*7*
Grades of *Will Rogers*
for *6th* school month ending with date.

Mental Arithmetic		Astronomy	
Practical Arithmetic	82	Geology	
Algebra	62	Zoölogy	
Geometry		Psychology	
Trigonometry		Reading	
English Grammar	82	Letter-Writing	82
Rhetoric		Composition	74
English Literature		Book-keeping	68
Latin		Bible	70
Greek		History, U. S.	100
German		History, General	81
French		Elocution	85
Geography		Drawing	
Physical Geography	80	American Literature	
Physiology		Political Economy	
Physics		Civil Government	
Chemistry		Av. of Lesson Grades	79

DEMERITS for month *50*

Will home on
furlough, probably
spring 1898.

pete in production and price with the huge ranches of Texas and the West. Clem saw the handwriting on the wall. He was getting older and he decided that it was time to retire to the relative comforts of a home in Claremore. He rented the "White House on the Verdigris" to an Illinois family and bought a home in town. He would occasionally visit the old house, but he would never again live out on the open prairie.

When Will now suddenly showed up after his adventures in Texas and Kansas, Clem made his son an offer. If Will was really serious about ranching, Clem would stake him to a herd of his own. The best part of the offer, so Will thought, was the fact that his father never mentioned anything about having to go back to a school. Will accepted and called the new operation the "Dog Iron Ranch," after his own registered brand. All went well for a short time, though the house brought back too many memories of both happy and sad times, and Will did not like having to share it with the Illinois family. With the help of his cousin Spi Trent and Hayward, a black man who for years had worked on the ranch, he built his own 12-foot-square cabin out on the range. It was as fine-looking a cabin as cabins built by amateurs go, except that in their haste, the three men had forgotten to put in windows. The door had to be left ajar if they wanted any natural light at all. The cabin also had only a bare dirt floor. It was, however, equipped with one double bunk, a wood cookstove, one oil lamp, two boxes used as chairs, and cooking utensils. With a horse corral nearby, Will and Spi had their almost typical cowboy camp.

Will left the management of the farm part to the Illinois farmer, while he took on the ranch operation. But the routine of running a ranch was not quite as exhilarating as the cattle drives had been. Soon Will became bored by the sameness of the work and he began to neglect his duties. When he needed money, he would sell a steer or two, go into town, or hop on a train to go to nearby cities. He found it far more entertaining to attend dances or socials, to ride the first rubber-wheeled buggy in the territory, or just go visiting, than to plan the provision of feed for the coming winter.

It was obvious that Will had to grow up some more to assume the tasks expected of a mature, responsible adult. Clem had tested his son, and the son had not yet overcome the heedlessness of youth. Henceforth Will would have to learn everything for himself. He did not know it yet, but there were many more lessons to be learned. School was now out for good and the easy part of life was over; from now on life would exact payment for every new lesson taught.

Will Rogers, the fashionable teenager.

Courtesy of the Will Rogers Memorial Commission

Page 1, "You know I am . . . ," broadcast, April 27, 1930.

Page 1, "Do you know . . . ," broadcast, April 27, 1930.

Page 2, "Being an Indian . . . ," Weekly Article #190, August 1, 1926.

Page 4, "They call it . . . ," Weekly Article #267, February 5, 1928.

Page 6, "Mary, the name alone . . . ," Weekly Article #530, February 19, 1933.

Page 6, "My Daddy fought . . . ," Weekly Article #600, June 24, 1934.

Page 8, "Clem Rogers is attending . . . ," *Claremore Weekly Progress*, January 10, 1894.

Page 9, "I was born . . . ," Will Rogers notes.

Page 9, "Well I said . . . ," *Letters Of A Self-Made Diplomat to His President.* © 1926.

Page 9, "Darkies raised me . . . ," broadcast, January 28, 1934.

Page 11, "I was just a thinking . . . ," Weekly Article #353, September 29, 1929.

Page 12, "W. E. Halsell . . . ," Weekly Article #242, August 14, 1927.

Page 12, "My father sent me . . . ," lecture notes.

Page 13, "My own mother . . . ," broadcast, May 11, 1930.

Page 15, "You know I used to play . . . ," Weekly Article #627, December 30, 1934.

Page 17, "Boonville, one of the finest . . . ," Weekly Article #523, January 1, 1933.

Page 18, "In 1898 Kemper . . . ," Weekly Article #169, March 7, 1926.

Page 18, "Just what made me . . . ," Weekly Article #627, December 30, 1934.

Will in his costume as the Cherokee Kid.

Plum Ruined
for Manual Labor

"Once you are a showman you are plum
ruined for manual labor again."

July 4, 1899, came with all the festivities with which a United States birthday celebration is usually identified. That those same United States had dealt ignobly with most of the inhabitants of the Indian Territory would not dampen the spirit of Claremore's planned celebration. There was to be a parade, a concert by the town band, the obligatory political speeches, and—of course—a grand barbecue with all the trimmings, concluding with homemade cakes and pies topped with hand-churned ice cream. There were games and contests for children and adults, and—this being the West—a rodeo. Among the ten who entered the steer-roping contest was one Will Rogers. It was all for fun, but as it turned out, it was a significant event in his life:

> It was at a little Fourth of July celebration at Claremore on July Fourth, 1899, they had a steer roping, and I went into it. It was the first one I ever was in; the very first thing I ever did in the way of appearing before an audience in my life.
>
> Well, as I look back on it now I know that that had quite an influence in my little career, for I kinder got to running around to 'em, and the first thing I knew I was just plum 'Honery' and fit for nothing but show business. Once you are a showman you are plum ruined for manual labor again.

In his modesty Will omitted to mention the most important part of the story—the fact that he had won that steer-roping contest. The first prize money he received was eighteen dollars and ten cents. While the amount was not inconsiderable in 1899, it was the fact of winning first prize that would prompt Will to try to build on his initial success. From then on, he entered most rodeos in the area. It is hard to say whether it was the excitement of the competition that was the attraction, or whether it was simply Will's passion for travel, to be on the move, to learn what others were doing, or simply to see for himself what lay beyond the horizon. Most likely it was all of these, for as the rest of his life would clearly demonstrate, it was simply impossible for Will Rogers to live life as a mere spectator, standing uninvolved along the sidelines. One thing is certain, the prize money was never an enticement. He was a rich man's son, and money meant little to him. It was simply a case, as Will admitted freely, that show business had bitten him and he was infected for life.

Toward the end of July 1899, several of the young ladies in the Cooweescoowee District met and decided to form a club of their own, a "pastime club." The name they chose was The Pocahontas Club. It was to be exclusively for girls of Indian ancestry, but in August, Will Rogers was one of very few young men allowed to join as honorary member. The young ladies would meet alternately in each other's homes, and spend time in reviving ancient Cherokee traditions, keeping their language alive and exchanging information about their customs. At their regular meetings, they would sometimes perform some traditional dances, or retell details from their history as they had learned it from their elders. It was a worthy effort by the younger generation to keep alive the language and writings of the Cherokees, their Indian history and traditions.

In late September 1901, for example, "An Evening with Hiawatha" was arranged. For this occasion the usual crowd of local girls and boys were invited, and it was a time for general merriment. There were contests such as "Pin the Arrow on the Heart" with prizes for the most accurate attempts. As the *Claremore Weekly Progress* reported in its issue of September 21:

Claremore's
Pocahontas Club,
1901.

Mr. Will Rogers appeared in full Indian costume of war paint, tomahawk and other paraphernalia, and favored the company with several excellent songs, which were highly appreciated.

Will loved to sing and often entertained with either the old favorites or some of the latest popular tunes he picked up. He had an Irish tenor voice which was on pitch and could reach surprisingly high notes. In his inimitable way he described it:

I've got a voice, it's what you call a fresh voice. You know, I've got resonance without any reason, and I've got tone without any tune, and volume with practically no control whatever. You can just go wherever you want with it.

I'm kinda like a crooner. I've got an ideal voice for everything—outside of a satisfied listener.

Half-heartedly Will kept attending to the management of the ranch/farm that his father had entrusted to him. He realized the obligation he had assumed, but there was another pull, strongly tugging him in an entirely different direction. There were many steer-roping contests in nearby communities, since watching cowboys perform their work routines had become a most popular form of public entertainment. Whenever there was an announcement that such an event was planned, whether it was in Oklahoma City to the west, or Springfield, Missouri, to the east, Will would ship his horse there and send his entry. Quite often he was in the company of his cousins Spi and Tom Trent, and a close friend, Dick Parris. All of them, too, had grown up in the saddle, and riding and roping had always been part of their lives. Actually, the steer-roping contests were as much enjoyment for these young men as it was for the spectators. They could hardly wait for the next rodeo to pit themselves against each other again, as much as against the other entrants.

Will may have been a local rodeo celebrity to his friends and neighbors, but he had no idea that his fame had spread beyond that small circle, or that he was about to embark on a successful show-business career. His entering various roping contests had been getting him used to appearing before a crowd, but he was still far from being at ease when he had to perform.

To Will's surprise, his name had reached Colonel Zachary (Zack) Mulhall, one of the Indian Territory's premier cowmen, who had gathered a traveling Western show of cowboys displaying their various work skills.

My show career kinder dates from the time I first run into the Col. [Zack Mulhall]. It was in 1899 at the St. Louis fair, (not the World's fair) just the big St. Louis fair they held every year. They had decided as an attraction that they would put on a Roping and Riding Contest. They were not called Rodeo's, or Stampedes, in those days they were just what they are, a "Roping and Riding Contest."

Well I was pretty much of a Kid, but had just happened to have won the first and about my only Contest at home in Claremore, Okla., and then we read about them wanting entries for this big Contest at St. Louis.

Well some one sent in my name, and the first thing I knew I was getting transportation for myself and pony to the affair. Well I went and Col. Zack Mulhall had charge of it. He was then, and had been for years the General Live Stock Agent for the Frisco Railroad System. That was a very important job in those days, for it took in all the live stock shipments on their whole line. He knew every big cattleman in the Southwest, and almost everybody else.

I dident get very far in this St. Louis Contest. I made the serious mistake of catching my steer and he immediately jerked me and my Pony down for our trouble.

Having only recently turned twenty, Will celebrated the turn of the century in grand style:

Well, I had a great time this Xmas myself, have not been home three nights in a month, taken in every ball in the Territory and everything else I hear. I was in Fort Gibson last week to a masque ball.

Will, obviously, had not yet found himself, and was still behaving like the rich man's son he was. There was no indication about his ambitions nor what he thought his future calling to be. There is no record of Will ever expressing any concern about his own future. True, he had "ridden his own horse" for barely half a year when he worked as a cowboy, but he certainly was not applying himself now to the steady routine of either a rancher or a farmer. He had implied his undying love for certain aspects of the life of a cowboy, but that *affaire d'amour* had lasted six months and had given way to partying and roping contests. Will had done little so far to reassure his father that his only son would ever amount to anything. In fact, Will's cousin Spi Trent quoted Clem's concern:

I'm awful worried about Will. It just looks like he has a yen for this show business.

Certainly that was the last thing Clem would have wished for Willie to take up. Perhaps Will, like Clem, saw the futility of expending a lot of energy on something that was destined to terminate soon. There was already the controlling limitation of the range brought by barbed wire and the "nesters," a cowman's pejorative for farmers. And if that was not threatening enough there was the certainty of the end of the open range, the knowledge that within the foreseeable future the once wide open spaces would be cut into forty-acre parcels and distributed to each Cherokee on the official roll. Gone forever would be the lush bluestem grass, gone the open prairie where huge herds could graze undisturbed. Not only did the century end, but a chapter in the biography of America was about to close forever.

The 1900s started on a somber note. At two o'clock in the morning of January 17, 1900, Mary Bibles Rogers died at Claremore. Services were held the next day at the M.E. Church (south), conducted by the Reverend Vick of Chelsea. Mary was buried at the City Cemetery in Claremore. (Eleven years later, when Clem, her husband of seven years, died, he was buried in Chelsea. Later, the body of his first wife, Mary America Schrimsher, was exhumed from the Rogers family burial ground on the Rogers ranch and buried next to him. The couple's three surviving children wished it that way.)

The following month, an epidemic of what was diagnosed as "a variety of smallpox" put Oologah under quarantine. Will, who lived nearby, ignored the

Oologah's railway station, 1902, where Will Rogers met his future wife, Betty Blake.

posted signs and went into town. He was promptly arrested, taken before the town magistrate and fined five dollars for passing the quarantine line.

Clem Rogers, perhaps more prompted by a concern for his son's future than just looking for something to make himself useful, decided to travel to Roswell, New Mexico, to see whether he could find a site for a stock ranch for his son. The thought could have been that in New Mexico there were no barbed wire fences— at least not yet—and there was to be no apprehension of a distribution of land. A ranch established there had a good chance of lasting more than just one lifetime.

Three weeks later Clem was back in Claremore. He had found nothing he liked as a site for the future home of a Rogers Ranch and Trading Post. There was obviously no simple solution to the problem of the future, and Will carried on with his haphazard management tactics and continued to be the life of many a party.

There were an increasing number of roping contests—so many that there was hardly any time to look after the ranch. Clem could see the end coming sooner than Will did, but it seemed that the latter did not mind. Leaving the ranch in the hands of hired help, he took off for New Mexico himself. He too was looking for

Betty Blake at the age of eighteen.

conditions that would remind him of his youth—the open range and the grazing herds, unlimited space, independence, and the carefree life of a cowboy. In New Mexico one of those novel drives by rail needed help to deliver a small herd of Diamond A ranch cattle to winter grazing land around San Luis Obispo, California. Will signed on.

Once in California, he would have liked to have stayed on the Pacific coast for a while, but was unable to secure a job. He and another cowboy named Billy Connell decided to make a little side trip to see San Francisco, which neither had ever visited before. They checked into a hotel there. Will, being tired, called it a night early, while Billy, determined to start his sightseeing right away, went out on the town.

What happened next has remained an unsolved puzzle, though various theories abound. What Will remembered was that he left the gas light on when he went to sleep. Maybe he turned it down low to darken the room, and a sudden draft from an open window or an opening door simply blew it out.

What Billy remembered when he came in much later has never been quite clear. Maybe Billy had a few drinks during his exploratory tour of San Francisco's famous places of entertainment. A possibility suggested was that Billy, only familiar with kerosene lamps then used in prairie homes, simply blew out the gas flame and went soundly to sleep, accidentally allowing gas to fill the room.

The two men were found unconscious the next morning when gas from their room seeped into the hallway and alerted other guests. A medical team worked four hours to revive Billy, while Will was believed beyond help. As Will told the story later, he owed his life to the persistence of some young doctors who worked over him for nine hours before he fully revived. The near asphyxiation left young Will so weak that he could barely make it back to Claremore, where he had to be helped off the train and into the buggy. When Clem saw his son, he insisted that he go immediately to Hot Springs, Arkansas, and take a cure to recuperate. Will was there for several months and returned home only in the middle of March 1901.

Several weeks later, Clem thought his son well enough to take a load of cattle to Kansas City to see how successfully he could sell them. Will was anxious to do well. It also meant that he could travel again. While In Kansas City, Will learned of the big Confederate Veterans' Reunion scheduled for Memphis, Tennessee, later that month. It gave him an idea. Why not put on a riding and roping contest as part of the festivities?

Will, now the impresario, went to Memphis and conducted all the business arrangements. By May 22, the necessary cattle and horses were on their way south. The cowboys, nearly forty of them from the Indian Territory, followed a couple of days later. The kindest report one can make on the financial end of Will's first show-business promotion is to say that artistically it was a success, but the high costs of transportation and feed made him just about break even.

Will would attempt a couple of more times to produce Western shows, but never successfully. It would take some time, and the loss of considerable sums of money, before Will abandoned all thoughts of being a producer, to focus on what he could do best—be a star performer.

Back home, Will continued to take part in every roping contest possible. At nearby Vinita, he placed third and shared in a $100 purse. Then it was on to Springfield, Missouri, and the big Elks convention, where Will took second money.

Two weeks later Will was off for Kansas City again, and from there on to Des Moines, Iowa, for the roping championships of the world. On the second day the Des Moines Humane Society stopped the roping contest, claiming that the treatment of the steers was inhumane. Rather than enter into a lengthy legal dispute, the promoters of the contest packed up and transferred the entire show to St. Louis, where it played to a more appreciative audience and a less "animal rights"-oriented bureaucracy.

No matter in which direction Will would dash off to enter contests, there was only one way into, or out of, Oologah. Of course one could come and go by horse, but if you wanted to get there sooner rather than later, it had to be via railroad. Just two passenger trains of the Missouri Pacific Railway would stop at the small village of Oologah, one from Fort Smith going north in the morning, and one coming south from Kansas City and Coffeyville, at eight o'clock in the evening. Both occasions were major high points in the daily lives of the area. While only rarely did anyone arrive or leave on them, those trains were the lifeblood of the small community, bringing mail and most needed goods from an outside world.

There was, of course, the standard railway depot, which served as ticket office, waiting room, storage space, and family home of the station agent. In Oologah, this was the domain of one Will Marshall and his wife, Cora Blake. Mrs. Marshall had originally come from the town of Rogers, in northern Arkansas. In the fall of 1900 they had a visitor staying with them. She was Cora's younger sister Betty Blake. Betty had just recently survived a severe attack of typhoid fever and her mother felt that a change of scenery would be most beneficial. Betty had lost a lot of weight and her usually long hair, which had been cut short during the illness, had just now begun to grow back to the length of a boy's haircut.

Will Rogers stepped into the station agent's office to pick up a banjo he had shipped from Kansas City. Will Marshall was out on the platform, attending to some formalities. Only Betty was there. Will took one look at her, turned without uttering a single word and left. Betty, who was considered a beautiful girl, could not help but wonder just what had caused this reaction. Was it his shyness? Was it her short hair? She thought the boy handsome and hoped to meet him sometime when he would speak. Indeed, they met a couple of nights later at the local hotel-keeper's home, where both had been invited for dinner.

All during dinner Will Rogers was shy and spoke little. But then there were the usual after-dinner amusements, like making popcorn and pulling taffy. They sang songs and Will introduced the latest popular numbers he had learned on his trips to Kansas City and St. Louis. Betty, an accomplished musician who could play several instruments, accompanied him on the newly acquired banjo.

Betty and Will saw each other several more times during her stay in Oologah but, as she would write years later, "I don't think you would call our meetings there in Oologah 'incidents in a courtship.' We simply became very good friends."

Betty may have thought so, but Will did not. The campaign to win Betty, which began at that first meeting, would last eight years. They would write to each other, sometimes with long intermissions of silence. Will would stay away, then send small gifts from abroad. It was an uphill battle against local competition and many odds—among them Will's Indian ancestry, which Betty's family did not exactly appreciate. Then, as Will began a show-business career, that too did nothing to enhance his status as reliable husband material. But the courtship went on.

Late in February 1902, the *Claremore Weekly Progress* reported the sale of part of Clem Rogers's holdings northwest of town. Another fragment of Indian Territory history had thus passed and would fade from the memory of the land. It also meant the end of the Rogers family's large agricultural development, the ranching done by self-reliant, fearless men and women. The twentieth century had arrived and had brought with it the seeds of immutable changes. Will saw what the pioneer and his so-called progress and civilization brought to the Indian Territory. He had the wisdom of his Indian heritage, which teaches that man is to live *with* nature, not simply *off* it:

You know, we're always talking about pioneers and what great

Program from Texas Jack's Great American Circus.

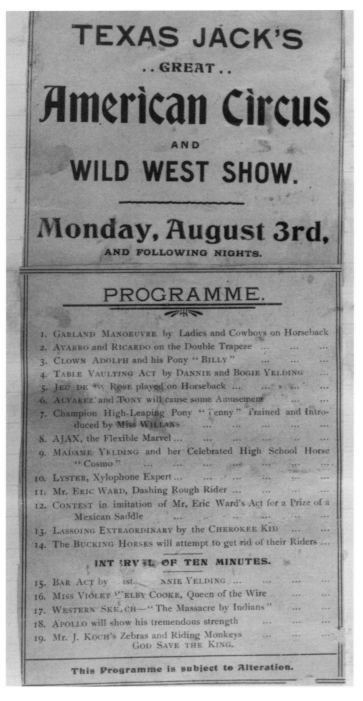

TEXAS JACK'S

..GREAT..

American Circus

AND

WILD WEST SHOW.

Monday, August 3rd,

AND FOLLOWING NIGHTS.

PROGRAMME.

1. GARLAND MANOEUVRE by Ladies and Cowboys on Horseback
2. AVARRO and RICARDO on the Double Trapeze ...
3. CLOWN ADOLPH and his Pony " BILLY "
4. TABLE VAULTING ACT by DANNIE and BOGIE YELDING
5. JEU DE ** ROSE played on Horseback ...
6. ALVAREZ and TONY will cause some Amusement ...
7. Champion High-Leaping Pony " Jenny " Trained and Introduced by Miss WILLANS ...
8. AJAX, the Flexible Marvel ...
9. MADAME YELDING and her Celebrated High School Horse " Cosmo " ...
10. LYSTER, Xylophone Expert ...
11. Mr. ERIC WARD, Dashing Rough Rider ...
12. CONTEST in imitation of Mr. Eric Ward's Act for a Prize of a Mexican Saddle
13. LASSOING EXTRAORDINARY by the CHEROKEE KID
14. The BUCKING HORSES will attempt to get rid of their Riders ...

INTERVAL OF TEN MINUTES.

15. BAR ACT by 1st ANNIE YELDING ...
16. Miss VIOLET WELBY COOKE, Queen of the Wire ...
17. WESTERN SKETCH—" The Massacre by Indians " ...
18. APOLLO will show his tremendous strength ...
19. Mr. J. KOCH's Zebras and Riding Monkeys ...
GOD SAVE THE KING.

This Programme is subject to Alteration.

folks the old pioneers were. Well, I think if we just stopped and looked history in the face, the pioneer wasn't a thing in the world but a guy that wanted something for nothing. He was a guy that wanted to live off of everything that nature had done. He wanted to cut a tree down that didn't cost him anything, but he never did plant one, you know. He wanted to plow up the land that should have been left to grass. We're just not—I don't know, we're just now learning, you know, that we can rob from nature the same way as we can rob from an individual. All he had was an ax, and a plow, and a gun, and he just went out and lived off nature. But really, he thought it was nature he was living off of, but it was really future generations that he was living off of, you know.

Texas Jack.

The same newspaper that had reported the sale of the Rogers ranch later reported that "W. P. Rogers has sold his herd of cattle and all his feed and announces his intention of going to South America to look into the matter of going into the cattle business there."

After paying his father for the start-up herd he had provided, Will had the sizable amount of $1,300 left. He had announced his desire to go to the Argentine, because he remembered the pictures he had seen in his first school's geography book. There had been the gauchos, herding cattle feeding on native grass on the seemingly limitless pampas, and there had been no barbed wire fences, just as it had been on the prairie of his earliest youth. Perhaps there still was a place where time had stood still. He was going to the Argentine. But something in him did not want an absolute break from home and the Territory. He invited cowboy pal Dick Parris to come along, offering to pay all his costs. When Dick agreed, Will bought a fine saddle, took out a life insurance policy, prepaid $140 as a year's premium, and the two were off.

Since the two knew that the Argentine was in South America, it seemed perfectly logical to them to head for a southern port—New Orleans. As neither had ever been there they did some sightseeing first and watched "them unload and load big ships on the wharf."

Unfortunately for the two travelers, they learned that no ships were scheduled to leave New Orleans for the Argentine. They were informed that they would have to go to New York City, and try to obtain passage from there. The best way, so they were told, would be to go there by ship. When the steamship *Comus* weighed anchor at nine a.m. on March 18, 1902, heading for New York City, Dick and Will, with his saddle, were aboard.

When the *Comus* arrived in New York City six days later, a new disappointment faced the two young men: no ship was scheduled to leave for the Argentine. They were advised to go to London, which maintained regular traffic with Buenos Aires. As if it had been arranged by an efficient travel agent, there was an England-bound ship scheduled to leave two days hence, so Will and Dick had barely forty-eight hours to be sightseeing tourists. First, Will, the far more experienced traveler of the two, checked into a hotel. The huge city was far less intimidating to the two men from the serene Indian Territory than one might expect. They found their way about, located the appropriate offices and did not get into trouble. Once they had booked passage on the SS *Philadelphia* to London, there was a call at the nearest commercial bank. Will still had a substantial amount of cash in his pocket and he now converted part of it into a 100 pounds sterling draft, drawn on the London and River Plate Bank Ltd., Buenos Aires. The two young men spent the rest of their time seeing New York's famous tourist attractions.

The SS *Philadelphia* was scheduled to leave New York late on the evening of Wednesday, March 26. Nine days later, April 4, 1902, Will wrote from Southampton, England:

> *Well I landed after eight long days of heaving forth everything I looked at. We left New York at ten o'clock; I ate a hearty dinner and then the thing came off; I went to my little 1½ 3 5 and did not arise till the engineer squalled out Southampton. After that dinner on Wednesday, I could not eat a thing until Monday, then, after various attempts, I got a lemon that never managed to find the way back.*
>
> *Our baggage was searched for tobacco and spirits; they did not find any in mine for I don't chew and my spirits had all left me on that boat if I had any at all I contributed them to the briny deep before I met that officer.*

Here, in Britain, the steamship connection was not quite as fortuitous as it had been up to that point. The next vessel leaving for the Argentine was the Royal Mail steamer *Danube*, scheduled to leave on Saturday, April 12, 1902. This time the two travelers had a wait of almost ten whole days. It gave them ample time to explore the city. Will and Dick visited the Houses of Parliament, read the inscriptions in Westminster Abbey, walked on London Bridge, and were shown through the Tower of London. They stood outside Buckingham Palace with all the other tourists and watched the changing of the Guards. Will even caught a glimpse of King Edward VII leaving the Palace in a coach, but doubted, as he wrote in a letter home, that "the King recognized me."

Will faithfully wrote home to his father and his sisters. His letters invariably—with the deletion of strictly personal news—ended up in several of the local papers. It was easy to follow his travels, as these letters were mailed at every place the *Danube* stopped to discharge commercial goods or pick up passengers, fuel, and food. St. Vincent, Cape Verde Island, was a "horrible place," while Buenos Aires

Texas Jack (left) and Will Rogers (right) with Texas Jack's wife and an unidentified companion.

turned out to be "the prettiest place I ever saw." The boat, he would tell his family, was rocking so badly that he could hardly write the letter. They crossed the equator at four o'clock one afternoon while it rained. There were three hundred Portuguese passengers aboard, most of them emigrants, and on this particular trip he was seasick for just a single day. In one letter, reprinted in the *Claremore Weekly Progress* of May 31, 1902, Will told of seeing sharks fifty to seventy feet long, then reported the ship's arrival in Pernambuco, Brazil. There an outbreak of the bubonic plague barred anyone from going ashore, and no one was allowed to come on board. To the folks back home, who lived roughly 1,500 miles from either the Atlantic or the Pacific and who had never seen an ocean or taken a boat trip, Will's accounts of all those faraway places with strange names were fascinating.

After two days' quarantine, Will and Dick were finally allowed to land at Buenos Aires. They checked into an English hotel, the Phoenix, and made inquiries about transportation into the interior. After all, they had come all this way to be cowboys on the pampas. They were told that they would have to travel about 500 miles by rail and then continue overland. The two American cowboys must have been a strange sight, as Will still carried his saddle with him.

When Will and Dick saw their first gauchos, it was a great disappointment. Will simply had the wrong image in his mind. He had firmly believed that the gauchos would be exactly like the cowboys he knew back in the Indian Territory. The Argentineans were friendly and obliging, but there was a difference. Will would recall years later:

Another cowboy, Dick Parris, and I went down in 1901 [sic] to the Argentine as peace envoys from Claremore, Indian Territory. We was a little disappointed in our reception. We went out on the ranches and those Gouchos we discovered could throw a rawhide lasso further than either of us could throw a green apple. I wrote

**Will Rogers as the
Cherokee Kid.**

*back and said I had never seen such a productive country. You just throw anything
out there and it grows.*

    *Saw the real Argentine gauchos do their stuff right out on one of the big
estancias. These bolos that you hear about 'em throwing they use for ostriches. We
chased ostriches all afternoon. They are the fastest things I ever saw run. I never
got close enough to one to even holler at him. Got the bolos tangled up around my
own neck. These gauchos are sure wild.*

There was no chance for the two Americans to be hired and compete with
the gauchos, nor was there much that could be learned and applied on the
prairie. The trip had been interesting, but little had been gained.

    Less than three weeks after their arrival in the Argentine, Will's character was
to be critically tested. So far the two longtime friends had shared everything.
There had been delays, several long sea voyages, seasickness, a quarantine, an
endless train trip, and now this disappointment. After all that, Dick Parris wanted
to call it quits. He'd had enough, and he wanted to go home. His argument was
valid. They had come to be gauchos, or at least cowboys on the pampas, and that
had not worked out. They thought it would be a great adventure, a job they
would enjoy, and instead they had found that they had nothing to offer and that
the local cowboys were better equipped to handle what was needed here.

It would have been so easy for Will to agree and go ahead and book two passages back with the first available steamship line that would take them back to the United States. The temptation must have been there, but he did not do it.

He paid Dick's passage home and gave his friend some presents that he was to take to Clem Rogers in Claremore and to Will's sisters in Chelsea.

When the two friends parted, Will was left with a major problem. The money that seemed so plentiful at the outset of the trip just a few months ago had dwindled rapidly. The job as a cowboy that Will had envisioned had not materialized. A second trip into the interior in search of any kind of employment proved partially successful in that he found a short-lived job. Fortunately an American battleship, the USS *Atlanta,* had pulled into port and Will "almost lived aboard." He was used to at least three square meals a day even if all three meals were just "navy beans, soupy like." Indications are that he may have missed quite a number of meals. Finally, he had to sell his saddle, the very last thing with which a cowboy will voluntarily part.

By this time getting back to America had become merely a far-off aim. Will no longer could pay for such a trip, and no money was forthcoming from either Clem or the sisters. Will did not want to admit his pitiable financial condition, and none of his folks could imagine that he had spent all his money, even if he hinted at it in his letters. The truth was that Will was now so broke that he was reduced to sleeping out of doors in parks. He no longer had the money for a room in even the shoddiest hotel.

Just when things looked desperately dismal, a job turned up. The task sounded simple enough; it was "to chaperon a bunch of mules and she-cows" on a sea voyage from Buenos Aires to Port Natal, Durban, South Africa. Will remembered from his school days, when he loved to study maps, that the South African province of Natal was on the east coast. That meant that the trip would take him around the Cape of Good Hope. Such a trip was not exactly what Will had been looking for, but this was no time to be too selective. While the job promised a salary and steady meals, several things appeared wrong with it. First of all there was to be another long sea voyage and Will had proven repeatedly that he was not a good sailor. Then, there was the realization that this trip would take him farther away from home, rather than in the right direction. Once this job was over he would be in Africa, and it would be that much more difficult to either get other jobs or to get back to America.

Whether it was his adventurous spirit that wanted to see Africa or the stark reality of an empty stomach and purse, Will decided to take the job and with it the food and the money. His life became changed forever.

I spent six months in the Argentine Republic and inhaled enough Spanish to ask for something to eat, and to cuss.

    Spanish is the language. This old gag of having the children take up French because it's fashionable is the baloney. You don't see anybody in France but Americans, so you don't get any chance to try out your French anyway. But just look at the dozens of countries that speak Spanish in addition to Spain. It's the only one to learn for you can use it commercially the rest of your life.

The trip aboard a ship called *Kelvinside* was to take eighteen days, but due to stormy weather took twenty-five. Most of the mules, sheep, horses and cattle were miserably seasick, but apparently were not quite as tortured as Will Rogers. He lay in his bunk, groaning, unable to eat or even perform much work, but, as he later wrote home, "they couldent fire me." When after three weeks he appeared for the first time on deck, the crew wondered whether he had just boarded the ship.

Recovered from the ocean journey, Will—dubbed "The Yank"—was asked to stay on and assist in driving the mixed herd of mules, sheep, Argentinean thoroughbred horses, and cattle to a place called Mooi River Station, 150 miles from Durban. Arriving at their destination, Will stayed on even longer, to help feed and care for some of the thoroughbreds, take them out for exercise gallops every day, and work with the veterinarian in the hospital.

Will traveled quite a bit in South Africa, as he had to deliver stock to various locations. In a way it was like the cattle drives used to be back home, except for the fact that all this was happening in an area where only recently the Boer War had been fought. He crossed recent battlefields "and passed several English graveyards." He went as far as Pretoria, the capital of the Transvaal, the northeastern province of South Africa.

On Monday, November 17, he wrote to his father about his current delivery and ended that at this delivery's conclusion, he would ". . . then be ready to come home."

A week later, though, when he wrote next, he had a job taking "a bunch of mules to Ladysmith, 250 miles from here." He also reported that he had lost all his luggage on the train, including a new saddle he had purchased, chaps and spurs. Not knowing how long this letter might take to reach Claremore, Will, remembering that his annual life insurance premium would be due early in the new year, enclosed a postal money order for $140, asking his father that it be paid. The check for the insurance premium must have shown Clem that his son was taking his obligations more seriously and was—at least for the moment—riding his own horse. But then came a surprise. In a letter to his father, Will told him of a change in his employment:

> *Monday, December 15, 1902. From W. P. Rogers, South Africa, Potchefstroon: Since I last wrote you I left Durban with some horses that were shipped 600 miles up this way, and to the town where Texas Jack's Wild West Show was and I went to him for work and as soon as I showed him what I could do with a rope [he hired me]. . . I get $20 a week and sleeping cars to sleep in but have to pay for my meals which are very dear at least 75 cents a meal.*

For Christmas, as Will wrote later to his sisters from Standerton in the Transvaal, he had gone visiting to a nearby Canadian soldiers' camp and had seen a baseball game. He had taken supper with the fellows and had what he called "an enjoyable evening," singing for the men. Concerning his new employment, Will merely pointed out that he had now been with Texas Jack for "almost a month," that "we have shown at 7 different towns, stay 2 and 3 nights in a place," and that they would be playing at Standerton for two weeks. There was no further mention of returning home now, or any time soon.

Will had left home almost a year previously for the Argentine with the publicly stated intention of establishing and operating a cattle ranch. He had ended up quite broke, and now was with a traveling Wild West Show. Clem Rogers, back home, could hardly have been pleased with his son's progress.

Will had mentioned that his weekly salary was twenty dollars, or its equivalent in pounds. He probably mentioned that because it may have seemed an impressive figure at a time when the American cowboy might earn thirty dollars a month plus his keep. While twenty dollars was certainly more than the average 1902 worker was being paid in the United States, Clem would not have been impressed. He could have easily made that much on the sale of a single steer.

Eventually Will would write the story of how he had lost out on a $250 reward. It seemed that when he first went to see Texas Jack and applied for a job, he really thought that at best he would be hired for some menial task, like looking after the animals. When Will mentioned his dexterity with the lariat, Jack wanted to know whether Will could do certain catches and tricks. Will was familiar with all of them and proved it easily. Finally Jack asked whether Will could perhaps do a "Big Whirl," usually called the "Crinoline," in which a lasso at least fifty feet long is spun out into a huge circle. The longer the lariat, the greater the strength and ability needed to keep the large, heavy circle in motion without letting it hit the ground. Will said that he had done it many times and demonstrated. Texas Jack hired Will on the spot. It was only later that Will learned that whenever Texas Jack performed the "Crinoline" he would turn to the audience and offer a prize of fifty pounds, or about $250, to anyone who could duplicate it. As an employee, Will was no longer eligible to compete.

Advertised now as "The Cherokee Kid, Champion Roper," Will immediately became a star member of the show. Years of learning and practicing with the lasso suddenly seemed to pay off.

He wrote regularly to his father and to his sisters, and periodically, he would send postcards, photos, and memorabilia he thought would interest them. He did not know that his hometown area's newspapers in Claremore, Chelsea, Oologah, and Vinita would get to print some of those letters. If Clem

Poster for the Cherokee Kid, the World's Champion Lassoer.

TEXAS JACK'S CIRCUS.
THE
CHEROKEE KID
THE WORLD'S
CHAMPION LASSOER.

He will perform the following feats with the Lasso:

Catching a Horse by One Leg, Two Legs and Four Legs.

Throwing the Rope with his Foot and Catching the Horse.

Forming a Loop in front of his body, carrying this behind him and catching the Horse.

Holding the Lasso by one end, jerking the rope through the air and tying single and double knots during its flight.

Several Varieties of the "Crinoline," making it on Horseback, forming a circle round the Horse with a Lasso 65 feet long.

THE MOST WONDERFUL FEAT KNOWN.

Holding a Lasso in each hand, throwing both at the same time and catching Horse and Rider, each by the neck, while going at full gallop.

Program for Texas
Jack's Wild West
Show & Circus.

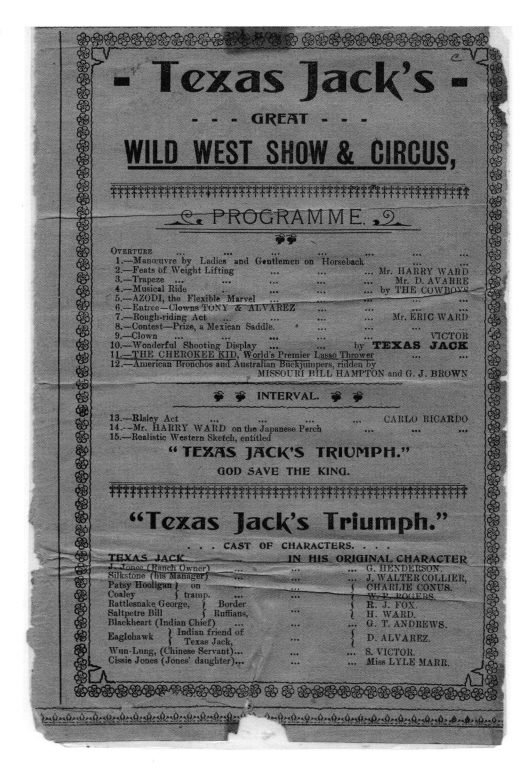

Program for Texas Jack's Wild West Show & Circus.

received a letter he would, with suppressed paternal vanity, relay most of the latest information to one of the Claremore newspapers. He would never have admitted it openly, but he began to take more than just a little gleam of pride in his only son's accomplishments. And every time there was another letter, Clem saw to it that the local newspapers would have the latest news and that all his neighbors knew about Willie. The Chelsea, Oologah, or Vinita newspapers would immediately spy these interesting tidbits about a local boy, and copy the news in their very next issue. The same was true when either sister Sallie or sister Maud received news from Will. As they lived in Chelsea, their local newspaper would be the first one to break their story and the other three papers would copy it later. Of course, these newspapers had a different readership and in 1903, the local newspaper was an essential part of everyday life. It was the only means of disseminating local, national and—in case you were interested—some international news.

A typical example of such shared news was the item in the January 9, 1903, morning edition of the *Claremore Messenger*:

> *C. V. Rogers has just received some interesting photo cards from his son, Will Rogers, who is still in South Africa. One photo shows a Zulu wedding, another a lot of Zulu warriors in their war dress, while another shows a collection of shells used by the Boers in their war with England.*

Texas Jack's Wild West Show and Circus covered a lot of territory. Since most of the towns where he "showed" were relatively small communities, he could not expect to draw a large enough audience for more than two or three performances. It took time to set up the tent, unload, and get ready for the performance. It was the typical nomadic life of any circus.

If Will Rogers had thought that he had seen much of South Africa while on his various deliveries of horses, mules, and cattle, his tours with Texas Jack's Wild West Show and Circus were far more interesting and instructive.

While Will was pleased with his African adventure, problems were magnifying back home. The ranchers of the Indian Territory had immediately foreseen the problems that the allotment distribution of acreage to the Cherokees would cause. Clem, as well as the other ranchers, knew that it was obviously the end of the era of the cattle barons in the Indian Territory. Forty-acre allotments, too small to sustain but a few head of cattle, would soon become the fields of the "sodbusters" who would plow the land and forever kill the sea of grass. What no one could know, however, was that within a generation the topsoil which had provided nourishment for millions of buffaloes and thousands upon thousands of steers would be blown away until it darkened the sky of that area, turning day into night, and night into nightmare. No one foresaw it, least of all the lawmakers, the theoreticians who had believed that they were really dividing up the wealth of the land.

Now the time had come when the government's plan was about to be put into effect. On February 9, 1903, Clem Rogers wrote to his son:

> *Willie, if you don't come home this fall you will have to send me a power of attorney to take your allotment for you . . . me, you and Spi [Trent] will take the old home place.*

Will promptly sent the requested document, though he had not yet made up his mind whether he would be back in the United States by the fall. In the meantime he learned his craft as a performer. When he approached Texas Jack, he was already an expert "lasso thrower," but showmanship was an art that needed fine

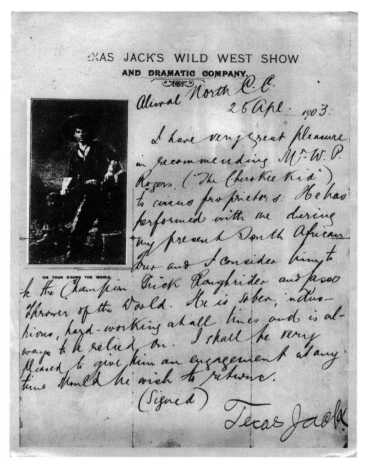

Will's letter of recommendation from Texas Jack.

honing. Will claimed that he learned most of it from watching Texas Jack, who with less talent than Will, knew more about how to play an audience. Jack taught him how to miss a catch or throw on purpose to heighten the audience's expectation, and to emphasize just how difficult a certain trick was. Jack also instructed Will in the fine art of knowing just how long to entertain and the precise moment when to get off the stage. In the months the show traveled to communities like Potchefstroom, Harrismith, East London, Durban, Cape Town, Bloemfontein, Port Elizabeth, Johannesburg, and back north to Pretoria, Will had become an accomplished showman who could hold an audience with ease. He could act in a drama called "Texas Jack's Triumph," which the newspapers described as "a thrilling circus play," take the part of an Indian in some imitation of the "American Wild West," or perform solo, demonstrating his artistry with a rope. Will became such an accomplished performer that he would fre-

quently take over the starring roll of Texas Jack, when the latter was needed elsewhere. Jack thought of the youngster—Will was only twenty-three years old—as his son and often said that when he was ready to retire someday, he would want "the Kid" to carry on running the show. Will did not look that far ahead into the future. For the time being, he liked this life of entertaining and traveling, meeting new people and seeing and learning something different every day. But as far as making this the occupation for the rest of his life, that was something he did not even consider—though if he had wanted it, it surely was there for the taking.

It became apparent that Will had matured a lot when he began to send back money, asking that it be deposited to a bank account. Clem, who had been so critical of his son's spending habits, must have been pleased at this change. He had written to his son about it, and though they were thousands of miles apart, Will had felt the sting and defended his position in a revealing manner:

> I never cared for money, only for what pleasure it was to spend it, and I am not afraid to work, and so as I am now I feel better than I ever did in my life, and I am in good health, so don't you all worry about me. . . .
>
> I have spent a world of money in my time but I am satisfied as some one else has got the good of some of it. It has not been all on myself and if you will only give

*me credit for just spending my own, as I think I have, I will be as happy as if I had
a million.*

*All that worries me is people there all say: "Oh, he is no account. He blows in
all his father's money," and all that kind of stuff. Which is not so. I am more than
willing to admit that you have done everything in the world for me and tried to
make something more than I am out of me (which is not your fault), but as to our
financial dealings, I think I paid you all up and everyone else.*

I only write these thing so we may better understand each other.

*I cannot help it because my nature is not like other people, to make money,
and I dont want you all to think I am no good simply because I dont keep my
money. I have less money than lots of you and I dare say I enjoy life better than
any of you, and that is my policy. I have always dealt honestly with everyone and
think the world and all of you and all the folks, and will be among you soon as
happy as any one in the world, as then I can work and show the people I am only
spending what I make.*

It is obvious that here speaks a grown-up Will Rogers, defending his conduct
while facing his father on an equal basis. He had been places his father would
never visit, had met and spoken to people his father would never see. Will had
already learned to get along in a world which knew as little of the Indian Territory
as he had known of the Argentine. Will realized that his formal education had
been directed toward a satisfactory life in the milieu in which he had studied. It
had not really prepared him for the international traveler he had become. So far
he had learned another valuable lesson that he only wrote about years later:

*America has a great habit of always talking about protecting American interests in
some foreign Country. PROTECT 'EM HERE AT HOME! There is more American
Interests right here than anywhere.*

*I left home as a Kid and traveled and worked my way all through Argentine,
South Africa, Australia and New Zealand and was three years getting enough
money to get home on. But I never found it necessary to have my AMERICAN
rights protected. Nobody invited me into those Countries and I always acted as their
Guest, not as their Advisor.*

Having stated his lack of interest in money for its own sake, a credo by which
he would live the rest of his years, he was now going to be offered an opportunity
which had to be faced.

In August 1903, in South Africa, the young Will had a serious talk with Texas
Jack. It seemed that Jack had decided to return to America, partly to scout for
new talent, and partly as a well-deserved break in his routine. He now wanted
Will Rogers to take over the management of the show during his absence. Since
he had hinted at times that he would want Will to take over someday, this would
have been a breaking-in period. Stepping into a small but successful operation,
Will might have had an assured future. It is true that he would have been far
away from his family and friends, and all that was familiar to him in the first
twenty years of his life, but had he sought security and a steady income, this
would have been an incomparable gift.

But Will wanted none of it. Almost immediately he quit Texas Jack's Wild West Show and Circus and prepared to leave South Africa. It must remain unresolved whether his intention was to simply distance himself from a troubling decision he was unable—or unwilling—to make, or whether there was some other strong reason, as for example a persistent young lady, whose initials were M. S. One or two of her ardent love letters are still at hand, and more than hint at her desire for marriage.

Texas Jack and Will Rogers parted on good terms, as can be seen by the recommendation Jack wrote:

> *I have very great pleasure in recommending Mr. W. P. Rogers ("The Cherokee Kid") to circus proprietors. He has performed with me during my present South African tour and I consider him to be the Champion Trick Roughrider and Lasso Thrower of the World. He is sober, industrious, hard-working at all times and is always to be relied on. I shall be very pleased to give him an engagement at any time should he wish to return.*

By the beginning of August, Will Rogers was on his way farther east. He planned to go to Australia, but not intending to waste time, he took one of the first available ships, which stopped just briefly at the Island of Tasmania and had as its destination Wellington, New Zealand. It was a 9,000-mile, 25-day trip across the Indian Ocean, skirting Australia to the south. As usual, Will Rogers had a very rough trip. He spent about a week in New Zealand, taking a ship from Wellington to Auckland on the North Island. Then it was another unpleasant experience on the 1,500-mile trip to Sydney, Australia, which took four and a half days.

Will traveled far into the interior of both New South Wales and Victoria, looking at ranches and noting the differences between the management used at home and here, Down Under. In almost every letter to the folks back home he mentioned that his plan called for a visit to Melbourne, that he would only stay a month in Australia, and that he hoped to be home before Christmas.

It was not to be. One night Will got into a card game and lost all his money, including the fare back home. There was only one thing to do: stay on and get a job. The letter of recommendation given him by Texas Jack served as an introduction to the well-established Wirth Brothers Circus. His unusual act fitted in perfectly with the format of a circus and was well received by the public and by newspaper critics.

Touring along the coast towns of Victoria, Will was arrested one night for leading an elephant through the streets of Warrnambool at midnight. When brought before a local magistrate the following day, Will explained that the elephant's keeper at the circus had become intoxicated. Fearing that the animal might wander about and do some damage, Will simply had taken it for a walk until he was stopped by a horrified police constable. The amused judge shook his head over the improbable sight of an American cowboy taking a large African elephant for a walk through the deserted streets of a southern Australian town. As there was no specific law or even a town ordinance against taking an elephant for a midnight stroll, and as no damage had been reported and no disturbance had been created, the case was dismissed. Will Rogers was instructed never again to take an elephant on his exercise airings—at least not in Warrnambool. All available records show that Will Rogers kept his word.

The Wirth Circus was next scheduled to tour New Zealand. Another sea voyage, but this time it was at least in the right homeward direction. Will was back in Auckland, and the *Auckland Star* reviewed the Circus:

Auckland, New Zealand . . . one can confidently recommend the two newest acts— Herr Pagel's and the Cherokee Kid's. . . . The other new act is, like most of our New things, American—a lassooing business. The Cherokee Kid is a gentleman with a large American accent and a splendid skill with lassoos. He demonstrated what could be done with the whirling loop by bringing up a horse and its rider from impossible position, once throwing together two lassos encircling man and horse separately. He also showed the spectators how to throw half-hitches on to objects at a distance, and did other clever work with the ropes. It was a very interesting performance. . . .

When the Wirth Brothers Circus tour of New Zealand came to an end in March, 1904, and was scheduled to return to Australia, Will counted his money and found he had just enough to purchase a third-class ticket back to America. He headed for Auckland, and caught a steamer for the USA. After numerous letters guessing when he might be arriving back home, Will Rogers walked in unexpectedly on April 11, 1904. He had been gone more than two years. He had left with a pocketful of money and returned broke. He had sailed around the world and had more than enough adventures and experiences to satisfy every single inhabitant of Claremore, Oologah, Chelsea, and Vinita. There were folks who envied his adventure, but Will saw his travels differently:

You know I never did do much along that line for just pleasure. I was always pretty busy. Done a lot of traveling but it was always working my way. In the early days it was working my way on a boat to try and get back home. I left home first class one time and it took me two years and nine months to get back third class. That's what a clever lad I was, and had to go all the way around the world to do it.

Page 23, "It was at a little . . . ," Weekly Article #499, July 17, 1932.

Page 25, "I've got a voice . . . ," broadcast, January 28, 1934.

Page 25, "My show career . . . ," Weekly Article #459, October 11, 1931.

Page 26, "Well, I had . . . ," letter from Will Rogers (L.III, Memorial).

Page 26, "I'm awful worried . . . ," *My Cousin Will Rogers*, by Spi M. Trent, p 40.

Page 30, "You know, we're always . . . ," broadcast, April 14, 1935.

Page 31, "As neither had . . . ," letter to sisters.

Page 32, "Well I landed . . . ," *Chelsea Reporter*, April 25, 1902.

Page 33, "Another cowboy . . . ," Weekly Article #311, December 9, 1928.

Page 34, "Saw the real . . . ," Daily Telegram #1938 October 20, 1932.

Page 35, "I spent six months . . . ," Weekly Article, #177, April 26, 1926.

Page 35, "Spanish is the language . . . ," Weekly Article #311, December 9, 1928.

Page 36, "Monday, December 15 . . . ," *Claremore Weekly Progress*, February 14, 1903.

Page 41, "America has a great habit . . . ," Weekly Article #133, June 28, 1925.

Page 42, "Touring along . . . ," *Argus*, August 19, 1935.

Page 43, "Auckland, New Zealand . . . ," *Auckland Star*, January 20, 1904.

Page 43, "You know I never . . . ," Weekly Article #639, March 24, 1935.

Betty Blake wearing furs Will sent as a Christmas present in 1906.

Betty

"The day I roped Betty I did the
star performance of my life."

C lem Vann Rogers seemed genuinely happy to welcome his son back home. It
was just as well that neither father nor son knew at that moment just how
short-lived this reunion would be. Clem, now usually called "Uncle" Clem by
those wishing to show him his due respect, notified his daughters and their families and planned a large feast, celebrating the safe return of what he still considered his prodigal son. He surely must have expected that after all the excitement
of a lengthy, adventurous voyage around the world, his son would at last be ready
to settle down and become the responsible community member for which Will's
mother, Mary, and he had always hoped.

Just a few days after the festivities came word from Col. Zack Mulhall that he
wanted Will to come and see him at his ranch. Will went to see Zack rather than
show the expected interest in managing the family ranch.

*It was at this point that Uncle Clem, his patience exhausted, confided to friends
that no boy who wasted his time around Wild West circuses could ever amount
to anything.*

This was 1904, the year of the great Louisiana Purchase Exhibition, which
was to be held in St. Louis. This exhibition was the most ambitious one America
had ever seen. It cost over $40 million to build and assemble and was expected
to attract more than 20 million domestic and foreign visitors. Zack Mulhall had
great plans for his Congress of Rough Riders and Ropers, and he invited Will to
join the crew.

Mulhall, always the optimist, intended somehow to become part of the
attending "Wild West and Indian" show to be held at the amusement section
called "The Pike." However, Frederick Cummins had already obtained the exclusive concession to present an entertainment featuring cowboys and Indians, while
Mulhall had not even a permit. Cummins's Wild West and Congress of North
American Indians had in its group supposedly "750 Indians, squaws and
papooses," including Geronimo, the famous Apache chief. Zack, with the audacity

and confidence that a successful promoter needs, somehow established himself and his group with the Cummins show and was able to draw crowds.

Will Rogers was not even mentioned in the program at first, but his acquired showmanship attracted considerable attention and admiration. There was something that set Will apart even then. Even his competitors had to admit that he had "star quality." Rogers and his sidekick, a fellow named Tom Mixco, being among the youngest of Mulhall's group, had agreed to a relatively small salary when signing on. There was, however, a small problem with that.

> *We didn't get much money; in fact our salary was supposed to be $20 a week. I told Tom in the Theater the other night, that was the only time we were ever paid just about what we were worth. That was one time we were not overpaid Actors, because we didn't even get the twenty.*
>
> *But he was a great old fellow, Mulhall, a typical old time westerner. We would touch him so much at odd times we never had anything coming. He was a very liberal fellow and in those days of Bar Rooms would always order drinks for everybody in the place and hand the Bar Tender a Bill of perhaps $20 to pay for what was a $5 or 6 Dollars check and my great habit was to edge in next to him when the man put the change back in front of him, and I would grab it and duck with it.*
>
> *Well he thought that was a great joke, and so did I. In fact I think it was one of the best jokes I ever pulled. He would laugh and that would make a good fellow out of him with the crowd, and incidentally keep from making a Tramp out of me. I was perfectly willing that they could have the drinks as long as I got the change.*

The members of the Mulhall group believed that once accepted by the other exhibitors, they would have steady employment at the Exhibition until its closing date, December 1, 1904. But Zack and his frequently unpredictable outbursts of temper got them all into deep trouble. The problem arose out of ongoing arguments between Mulhall and a man named Frank Reed, who had charge of the horses used by the Cummins show. It was understandable that there would be fierce competition between the two groups, especially as one felt that it was the main attraction and the only one officially sanctioned, while considering the other a parasitic encroacher.

The incident that followed was set off by Mulhall having Frank Reed arrested for supposedly disturbing the peace. Reed's excuse was simply that Mulhall had tried to take over the management of the horses. On the afternoon of June 18, the two adversaries met. Zack pulled his gun while accusing Frank of having used one of the Mulhall cowboys to help round up the Cummins horses. The yelling contest was quickly settled, but the conflict erupted anew later in the evening on a crowded street of The Pike. This time both men pulled guns, and shots were fired. One of Mulhall's cowboys, trying to act as peacemaker, was shot in the abdomen. Frank Reed, the intended target, suffered minor wounds in the arm and neck, while an eighteen-year-old innocent bystander a hundred feet away also was shot in the abdomen. This young man, identified as one Ernest Morgan of St. Louis, was at first considered as having been mortally wounded, but did recover. Mulhall was arrested, taken to jail and subsequently released on a bond of twenty thousand dollars.

Accounts of the shooting, with varying degrees of accuracy, made most American newspapers. Vinita's *Indian Chieftain* of June 23, quoting from the *Kansas City Journal*'s story "Shooting on The Pike," reported that Ernest Morgan had been killed. Even the *New York Times* carried the story but got it wrong, headlining it: "President's Friend Slays." The allusion here was to Mulhall's oft-claimed but most likely imaginary friendship with President Theodore Roosevelt.

Will Rogers, who was present on the street and quite close to the shooting, somehow missed witnessing it. The excuse was said to be that having just crossed the very muddy street, he was leaning over to clean his boots at the very moment the shots rang out. It is also feasible that Will did not wish to be called as a witness against a man he considered his benefactor and so consciously chose to miss all the action.

Before the case ever came to trial, Mulhall was made to feel some immediate consequences. He was officially barred from The Pike. The *Claremore Weekly Progress* reported an interesting sidelight on this ban. It claimed that the Indians of the Cummins show had held a protest meeting, demanding that Mulhall be barred, and had threatened that if he were allowed to remain active, they would take vengeance for the wounding of one of their fellow workers.

Will Rogers remained Mulhall's devoted friend. For the next month, Will worked for several shows on The Pike, including Mulhall's former rival, the Cummins show. As Mulhall was mostly inactive, Will saw no disloyalty in his need to earn a living. There were smaller outfits, too, that used his talent, and he appeared with Zack when Mulhall and his group gave weekly performances at a nearby racetrack. After appearing at a burlesque theater, the Standard in St. Louis, Will was off for Chicago to try this new direction: big-city vaudeville. He performed at the Cleveland Theatre in Chicago, being billed as Wm. Rodgers (sic) World's Champion Roper. He was so successful that he was held over a second week, the sign in vaudeville of a great attraction. During that second week at the Cleveland, something happened that Will immediately realized as a most fortunate incident. While he was on stage as a solo, demonstrating his dexterity with a lasso, a small dog from one of the trained animal acts on the program escaped and ran across the open stage. The audience laughed, thinking it part of the act, especially when Will successfully roped the dog and returned him to its owner. The applause that followed gave Will the idea that he should not be just standing there and doing an infinite variety of arm and neck rolls, Butterfly Spins, Texas Skips, or Merry-Go-Round Loops.

Instead of trying to keep on with this single roping act I decided that people wanted to see me catch something. So I went back home and marked me a place of ground about as big as a stage and started to work on the horse act. . . .

As Will envisioned the act, he would have a horse and rider gallop across the stage so he could demonstrate a variety of catches on either, or both. There would, for example, be the figure-eight catch, in which the upper loop would catch the horse by the neck, and the lower loop would delicately hobble the horse's forelegs. Or another loop, again forming the figure eight, would end up encircling both the rider's and the horse's necks. And a throw of two ropes at the same time, each catching a different target, would be a sure showstopper every time. Yes, he decided, that was the way his act would have to be.

Will on horseback.

But Will also realized that in addition to his own dexterity, much would depend on selecting the right horse and the right rider. He had the perfect animal in mind—a small pony, dark bay with black mane and tail, that he had seen on the Mulhall ranch, back in the Indian Territory. It had been offered to Will once before for $100. He now bought it and named it Teddy, in honor of President Roosevelt. He also realized that on the hard, wooden floor of a stage, a hoofed animal would slide and easily lose its footing. He ordered felt buckled boots for Teddy to wear on stage. Next, he started looking for the right rider. Before he found one, a surprise visitor re-entered his life after an absence of over four years.

Betty Blake, the young girl he met and courted in Oologah, was visiting the St. Louis Exhibition with one of her sisters and Mary Quisenberry, a friend. Somehow the name of Will Rogers came up, and Betty was kidded and teased by the other two girls into sending Will a note, wondering whether he would like to see them. In her book—*Will Rogers, His Wife's Story*—Betty recalled that Will answered her note and invited the girls to that afternoon's show. While a girl's approach of a onetime beau may have seemed forward behavior for that time, Betty was really a very conservative girl. In her book she remembered:

> *Though I wanted to see Will very much, I had a streak of conventionality in me, and I was not particularly thrilled about Will's profession. But I hid my misgivings and tried not to hear the teasing and joking. Finally Will entered the arena for his roping act. To my horror, he was decked out in a very tight-fitting red velvet suit, bespattered with gold braid. He looked so funny, and I was so embarrassed when my sister and Mary gave me sidelong glances and smiled at the costume, that I didn't hear the applause or find much joy in Will's expertness with the rope.*

It was the very suit Mrs. Wirth had especially made for him with her own hands when he appeared in Australia and South Africa in the Wirth Brothers Circus; but then he had been billed as "The Mexican Rope Artist." Betty wished she had never sent that note and that she were safely back in Rogers, Arkansas. But it was too late for that now. Will had asked the girls to wait for him after the performance. He was late joining them, explaining that he had just quit the Cummins Wild West Show and had been chasing the manager to get his back salary.

Will and Betty had dinner together and then listened to John McCormick, the famous Irish tenor, who years later would become a friend of the family. Will and Betty toured the midway and when they parted, they promised to write to each other—again. When the St. Louis Fair closed, Will went home, ostensibly on a visit. He found his father in poor health. "I am here I guess for the winter," he wrote to Betty, "as my father is in very bad health and I am the only one who can stay with him." By the following spring Uncle Clem had recovered sufficiently to be left in the care of a housekeeper. Will decided to accept Zack Mulhall's invitation to be part of a Wild West Show that was to be an added entertainment feature of the annual Madison Square Garden Horse Fair in New York City. Will gladly went, but he had more in mind than being merely another cowboy on a two-week job. He had tasted success in vaudeville, and he felt that New York was the place to start a permanent career.

As so many times in Will Rogers's life, just when he was in need, opportunity came looking for him. Years later he would write:

Everything I have done has been by luck, no move was premeditated. I just stumbled from one thing to another. I might have been down. I dident know at the time, and I don't know yet, for I don't know what "Up" is. I may be lower than I ever was, I don't know. I may be making the wrong use of any little talent (if any) that I accidentally have. I don't know.

The opportunity that came looking for Will Rogers arrived suddenly, unexpectedly during a performance in Madison Square Garden. It was during Lucille Mulhall's starring moments when the steer she was chasing to rope became agitated by the crowd noises and the strong lights, climbed the guardrail into the loge seats and headed straight into the panicking crowd. Ushers and spectators scattered in fear. Will and Tom Mixco tried to catch the animal. According to the report in the *New York Herald*, Tom ran up one aisle, threw his lasso and "caught an usher by the leg, bringing him down with a thump on the stairs." Will stood at the next aisle, swinging a rope. He caught the steer on his first toss. Somehow he was able to steady the spooked animal and lead it back into the arena to appreciative applause by relieved spectators.

The Horse Fair at Madison Square Garden was covered by every newspaper in the city and several national wire services. The runaway steer, which could have caused considerable harm to lives and property, having been subdued by just one slight man, was newsworthy. Will's bold act was duly reported in the New York City newspapers and was a topic of conversation for several days. Will even cut out one of the columns reporting his deed and sent it to Betty Blake in Arkansas. She had been constantly in his thoughts and he had written, asking her to marry him. The answer had been a "no"; an amiable no, but a no, nonetheless.

Having had this New York City publicity, Will finally found a sympathetic agent at the William Morris Agency who attempted to get him vaudeville bookings. Even though Rogers's name was in the news, and his act commended by the public, New York City vaudeville theaters, always known as a tough lot, were not exactly eager to have some cowboy on their bill just because he had lassoed— What was it? Some cow? And what was he going to do now? Play with a rope? What's that idea of trying to catch a galloping horse on my stage?

Finally, on June 11, 1905, after numerous rejections, the agent found a manager willing to at least give Will an audition. The theater was the prestigious Keith's Union Square Theatre, and the trial performance was to be the notorious "supper show." Despite its imposing sounding appellation, it was an unimportant fill-in show, squeezed in between the Matinee and the Evening performance. It usually had scarcely an audience, as most people would be home for supper at that time. Will and Teddy, the pony, knowing little about such fine points, walked confidently down to the theater for the show. Jim Minnick, a fellow cowboy from the Mulhall group, who had rehearsed with Will, would ride Teddy during the performance.

It was 6:30 on a hot afternoon, when the ten or twelve people that were in there laid their afternoon papers down and kidded us into a pretty good hit.

The manager was impressed with the startling novelty and dexterity of the performance and offered a standard, three-performances-a-day contract, starting

**Will taking a rest
out on the range.**

the very next day and paying $75 per week. Keith's Union Square Theatre, on 14th Street near Broadway, had three performances a day, starting at one o'clock in the afternoon and finishing at 10:45 p.m. Each performance featured eleven acts, with Will being number eight. Seats were twenty-five cents and fifty cents, reserved seats one dollar.

Will would remember clearly the start of his full-time vaudeville career. That first week at Keith's Union Square Theatre was surely important, but it was Hammerstein's Victoria, where he was booked the second week, that placed him firmly on the path to future stardom. Hammerstein's Victoria, in the heart of Times Square, New York, was run by William Hammerstein, one of the great theatrical producers and managers.

Keith's old Union Square on Fourteenth Street was the one where I made my first stage appearance. But it was at the Theatre where they sent me the second week where I made my best hit and stayed at it all summer. That was at the greatest Vaudeville theatre of that and all time. That was Hammerstein's. I stayed on the roof one whole summer. We played on the roof at nights and down stairs at Matinee. We have never produced another showman like Willie Hammerstein, and the old man himself was living in those days and with what that Theatre made he was able to indulge in presenting Opera.

Hammerstein's Victoria on 42nd St. and Broadway was the peer of them all in those days, they and the Percy Williams' houses in New York. But Hammerstein's had a following and a type of audience that no theater before or since ever had. It knew its Vaudeville like a cow knows its calf.

Throwing three ropes at once.

I used a horse on the stage then and had a Cowboy ride him across at a run and made catches on him as he run by. I had Sheriff Buck McKee with me.

Buck trained the pony for the stage. He wasent any trick pony, he just worked on a smooth board stage, with felt bottom boots bucked on his feet like goloshes, and run for my fancy roping catches. But Buck trained him to do on a slick stage just about what as good turning cowpony can do on the ground. We started the act in the spring of 1905. He was with me for I think it was four or five years.

We stepped on the stage togeather, only he was on horseback. He always said, 'I can get away if anything happens, but the audience can get you.' I was married too in 1908. And sometimes the salary wasent any too big to ship Buck and his wife and Teddy, and my wife and self, to the next town. In fact I think Buck rode some of the short jumps.

Those were great old days, (but darn it any old days are great old days. Even the tough ones, after they are over, you can look back on with great memorys).

On Hammerstein's old Roof Garden that summer they had an old lady that he dug up. They called her "Sober Sue." She was supposed to never laugh. He sat her in the box every night and the Vaudeville act among us who made her laugh was supposed to get a raise in salary.

We tried all summer and never got a wrinkle out of her, and, mind you, he had acts that he was paying a lot more than $1,260 to.

Of course, incidentally, in our case on the last night after the roof closed she confided to us that she was deaf, and was short sighted, and had never seen or heard any of us all summer. She laughed when she told us this, but that was too late to do us any good.

Despite deaf Sober Sue, by the time Will had been a couple of weeks at the Hammerstein, his salary had almost doubled to $140 a week.

Now that the Hammerstein's Roof had closed, Will was booked into other theaters and other cities. Engagement followed engagement; even Sundays were not rest days for the trio. After New York City followed Philadelphia, and Boston, and then it was back to New York City.

Will, who had not missed a single week's work, was offered an engagement in Europe the following year. He signed the lucrative contract and immediately wrote to Betty Blake, once more proposing marriage. He even suggested that the trip to Europe could be their honeymoon. Betty turned him down—again.

Accepting an offer from the Manhattan Beach Theatre in Coney Island, Will asked for, and received, $150 a week. He was now making money faster than his mystified father could have foreseen. Clem was even more astonished when Will began to send larger amounts of money home, asking that it be put into an account at the First National Bank in Claremore, where Uncle Clem was an officer now. His father neither acknowledged receipt nor sent a written statement. It was a stubborn man's way of showing either his disapproval at the way the money was earned or his unwillingness to admit that he might have been wrong about Will ever amounting to anything. Still, Will kept sending money and asking in practically every letter whether his father had received the previous transmittal.

By September 1905, when Will appeared in Brooklyn, his salary had dramatically risen to $250 a week. In just three months he had become a major vaudeville attraction. Local theater managers practically bid for his services, yet Will really was using New York City as a break-in trial for his vaudeville act. It is astonishing that almost every other vaudeville act had years of traveling the circuits, playing "small time," polishing and changing their routine, learning their craft, all in the hope of having another booking next week, or at least the week thereafter. Yet here was Will Rogers, having practiced roping since he was a child, learning showmanship in South Africa, Australia, and New Zealand, stepping right into the number-one spot in America. Will's popularity was only possible because he did what no one else had done as well. In this "try-out" period he had made one major change in his act—he had added some talk. Mostly it was small talk, almost as if to himself, with the audience only an unintentional eavesdropper. If he missed a catch, often on purpose, he had a number of ad-libs ready he could use.

It has long been argued just who should be credited for Will's transformation from what was called a "dumb"—meaning a silent—act, to his identification as a roping humorist. Many serious people have taken credit for offering the advice that Will should display his humor in his roping act. Actually it was a most natural evolution. Will liked to joke, and he had the extraordinary gift of expressing his thoughts and observations in a humorous manner. As the reviews and reports of the time indicate, this was first seen in his act when Will started introducing some of his catches. Betty later described this:

Will did no talking whatever, and at first used no special music. A few weeks later someone suggested to Will that it might be a good thing for the act if he announced one difficult act from the stage. Without preparing what he would say or deciding how he would say it, Will stopped the orchestra and announced the trick. The audience started laughing. Will was embarrassed and angry. He had no idea that his Southwestern drawl was either pleasing or comic. Not meaning to say anything funny, he thought the audience was making sport of him, and he wanted to quit then and there. Will was always joking and clowning with his friends and with members of the other acts; but laughter coming from a crowd of strangers was something else again. Will didn't like it. Other performers on the program tried to tell him that it was fine, that a laugh was the best thing for his act and by all means to leave it in, but Will took his roping seriously and he was a long time getting used to being laughed at.

Even *Variety*, the most severe, yet respected critic, recognized Will's special talent:

> *. . . he has about him a western breeziness that marks him as the real thing from the cowlands. His indescribable faculty of communicating his feeling to the audience is his chiefest asset. . . . besides his clever handling of a lasso he has a sense of humor and style which aided in making his act a success. . . .*

Life settled into a routine. With the success in and around New York City as a basis, Will's new, more powerful agency, William Morris, had little trouble booking his act into theaters farther away. Cleveland; Rochester; Washington, D.C.; Buffalo; Detroit; and Toledo were now all on the list. It was an easy life, with only two or three performances a day, each lasting about fifteen minutes. Will had much time for other activities everywhere he played. His inquiring mind used some of that time to study other acts that interested him; he learned to juggle and how to play several musical instruments, though none too well.

Will demonstrating the art of throwing a bola.

Despite the easy life, Will was not happy. He was making more money than ever before, but there were his own expenses, Buck McKee's salary, and the feeding and steep costs of transporting Teddy. And something else kept nagging at Will. He kept thinking of Betty, and he would write to her. He thought that perhaps he should return to his roots and go back to the land. On Thursday, October 26, 1905, he wrote his sister Maud from Rochester, in upstate New York: "I want to restock the farm . . . this is nice work but I am not in love with it." Yet he would keep at it for almost ten more years.

**Will doing a reverse
Ocean Wave catch.**

The months went by, with bookings coming in steadily. When there was an occasional split week, or a hiatus, Will would try to get home to visit with his father and sisters. He also called on Betty at Rogers, Arkansas, when an occasion arose, but felt that while she was genuinely glad to see him, her citified family was not exactly welcoming of the "smell of horse liniment." When Will proposed marriage again, Betty was still reluctant.

On November 1, Will was "showing" at the Chase Theatre in Washington, D.C. Doing some sightseeing, he wrote home telling of having climbed up all the way to the top of the Washington Monument. After a week there it was on to New York. Will was again booked into Hammerstein's Victoria, and then into upstate New York and New England theaters. He continued to send more money home. By the end of the year he had saved $1,750 in just twenty-seven weeks. This was quite a considerable amount, especially at a time when, for example, the latest Cadillac automobile was advertised for less than $800.

As Christmas neared, Will became ever more homesick. He had not been home for the Yuletide in several years, and this year it was certain that he would not be able to be there either: "Sunday night, Xmas eve, you can think of me boarding a train after the show for Pittsburgh, Pennsylvania."

From the Hotel St. Cloud, in Syracuse, New York, Will wrote a Christmas letter to Betty. He enclosed a fancy handkerchief he had bought in the Argentine
with her in mind, saying that it had "sentimental value" for him.

Dearest Betty

*As it is Xmas and you are "one best fellow" I want to send you a little token that I
have carried with me and which I prize very highly (although not of much financial value) for I do believe you will receive it and appreciate it accordingly.*

*Now Betty I got this Hdkf. in South America it is supposed to be very fine work
done by the Paraguay Indians who are noted for their needlework. . . .*

*The old Indian Lady I bought from then gave me this asking me if I was mar-
ried. I said NO. she said then give it to the wife when you do marry. I have kept it
carried it all through Africa at time when I dident have a cent and was actually
hungry. then to Australia most of the time in an envelope in my pocket then back
home and on all my travels. I did intend always to do as the old woman said but I
guess theres nothing doing for me. I will just give it to you as I kinder prize it and
you might do the same.*

Hoping you a grand Xmas and a Happy year
I am always the same to you Betty

Yours Will.

Obviously Will felt lonely and sorry for himself. Even if he had reminded
himself that here he was, pursuing a calling he had chosen—nay, created—for
himself; that he was making more money than most people in America; that he
traveled, which he loved; that he was riding his own horse, it would have meant
little. His family was far away; the girl he loved had turned down his numerous
proposals of marriage; he was in a strange city, in an impersonal hotel room
which gave no indication of the celebration of the birth of Christ, which the rest
of the world was observing. He was not a religious man, at least not one who
demonstrated religiosity by high-profile tithing and attending church services in
style. But he had been brought up in a Methodist home, instilled with the foun-
dation of the Bible, the Ten Commandments, and the Golden Rule. He did not
wear his belief for all to admire; he quietly lived it. This joyous season, Will
Rogers—alone in a wintry hotel room in Pittsburgh—had reason to weigh the
value of his life against the advantages of spending the holiday season among
family and friends. In a letter to his father, written from the Hotel Boyer in
Pittsburgh, Will ended: "This is a pretty poor Christmas. I wish I was at home."

The year 1906 may have started on a low note, as Will wrote to his sister
Maud: "I am mighty homesick for I have been doing the same old stunt for 35
weeks," but it promised much. There were still some preliminary bookings in the
East to be fulfilled, but beyond that lay the month-long engagement at Berlin's
world-famous Wintergarten. Performing there immediately gave any act international recognition. While it was most prestigious to appear there, Will approached
the engagement with uneasiness. First of all, as he spoke no German, he would
not be able to use his usual accompanying banter. Second, it meant another two
ocean voyages, and he'd had ample evidence of just how bad a sailor he was. He

worried about the whole idea, even though everyone else envied him the opportunity.

In Washington, D.C., Will at last succumbed to one of the affectations of successful vaudevillians by buying two outward symbols of their status: a diamond scarf pin for $208, and a diamond ring for $400.

Not until March would Will have a chance to visit home. It was just before he had to catch the ship that would take him to his German engagement. He had barely time to see Betty in Arkansas.

Will left for Europe on March 17 aboard the SS *Philadelphia*, the same ship on which he and Dick Parris had crossed four years before, and headed straight for Cherbourg and Paris. He

Will and Teddy.

Courtesy of the Will Rogers Memorial Commission

was impressed by the open-air cafes: "And how they do sit and drink at cafe's with the tables right out on the sidewalk—they seem to have nothing else to do." Another complaint was "there seems to be no laws and especially of morality." He did, however, like the food: "It is the best cooked stuff I ever eat . . . they do know how to cook."

In Berlin, audiences raved about one of the most unusual acts they had seen. For decades German boys had grown up with the fascinating stories by author Karl May, recounting the adventures of an Indian brave and the experiences of his German friend on the North American prairie. May had written a whole series of these adventure books, all of which featured the Indian as the hero who instills in his friend the wisdom of his people. Since then German boys had play-acted the episodes so vividly told by May, vying with each other to be either the Indian or the young German. Karl May, who influenced generations of boys, had never been to America when he wrote those adventure stories. He visited the United States only after he had written the last of his books. But for most German boys growing up, reading about this great friendship between an Indian and a German was forever etched in their memory as a lasting thrill of their own adolescence.

Suddenly, here at the Wintergarten, there was a real live Cherokee Indian and a cowboy. Part of the Wild West had come to Berlin—fantasy and reality had met. It had all come to life. One just had to go to see it.

One of the German reviewers wrote:

> *A brilliant program in April. A very excellent number are the two lasso throwers, Mr. Will Rogers and Buck McKee, 2 gentlemen cowboys who work as Rough riders and who bring to you a part of the Wild West. When the lesser [assistant?] gallops across the stage, on his fiery runaway and Will Rogers, with unimaginable dexterity lets his rope fly catching horse and rider you might compare it with a brilliant summarization of a Buffalo Bill Play. Will Rogers is a master of the Crinoline.*

Will Rogers with Buck McKee and Teddy.

Courtesy of the Will Rogers Memorial Commission

Life in Berlin was exciting. Will was the star of the April program at the Wintergarten, and he lived the life of a star.

> *They talk of Gay N.Y. Why N.Y. sleeps more in one night than Berlin does in one week. Honest, I havent had my eyes closed here while it is dark what sleeping I have done was in the day.*
> *Oh, I have met the <u>Kaiser</u> when I was out exercising my pony in the park and he rides every day he always <u>salutes</u> as he gallops past, oh he is a dandy good fellow.*

During the Berlin engagement two events occurred that changed Will's perception of Germany and of Germans. In Berlin, as in most cities, the fire prevention safety laws stipulated that a uniformed fireman be on duty during all performances. As Will could not use his usual humorous remarks, he decided to do some sight gags. During one performance, while demonstrating his artistry with the lar-iat, a loop suddenly shot out and dropped over the surprised fireman, who stood just in the wings offstage. Will pulled the surprised man onto the stage, but instead of the laughter and applause he expected, there was a gasp of sheer shock.

Will, as most Americans, had never heard of "Majestätsbeleidigung" or "lèse majesté," the crime of high treason, or violation of the dignity of a sovereign. It is thought that in early times, when there were few transportation systems and the distances to the nearest safeguarding law enforcer were measured in days, this law protected hated local administrators or loathed officeholders—like tax collectors—from the rage of insurgent citizens. The idea was simply to designate all bureau-crats and civil servants as personal representatives of the ruler, thereby declaring any offensive act against any one of them as being a direct attack on the sover-eign. Thus when Will Rogers roped the "imperial" fireman and made him an object of humor, Will, de facto, held Kaiser Wilhelm II up to that same ridicule, an act which German law considered high crime and treason.

A timorous manager hurried on stage and profusely apologized to the most indignant "imperial" fireman, claiming that the foreigner's rope had "slipped." The stage manager next apologized to the audience and finally asked Will to at least feign some expression of contrition. This Will did, though he still did not know the reason for it all.

On April 30, 1906, at the end of his otherwise highly successful and lucrative engagement in Berlin, he reluctantly accepted another booking to appear in Leipzig, some 90 miles to the south. Having packed his belongings in haste, he hurried to the railway station. There the porter he called refused to move his trunk, because, as he pointed out, the corner of a shirt had been caught in the closure and was plainly visible. It was against official rules to accept for transport any piece of luggage not properly closed. Obviously, so the porter insisted, this trunk was not properly secured. He demanded that Will open the trunk and prop-erly stow the offending garment. An irate Will refused. It became a standoff between the German porter, insisting on his interpretation of the law, and a free-spirited, equally determined Will, insisting on his right to pack his own belongings any way he saw fit, even if two shirts were to protrude.

After a lengthy confrontation, an exasperated Will finally realized that if there was to be any progress, he would have to be the one to make the first move. He opened the trunk, repositioned the offending garment and secured the closure. Then, to the porter's astonishment, he ordered that the luggage not be put on the south-bound train to Leipzig, but instead on the northwest-bound train for the deep sea harbor city of Hamburg. Will simply canceled the booking in Leipzig and took a ship for England. Any place just to get out of there, and England had been good to him—and he spoke their language. The Berlin episode merely reinforced his opinion, voiced on a postcard to Betty: "I dont like it here at all and am book-ing no more work." And he never did.

Accounts of the act's Berlin success had preceded Will in the British trade papers. Once in England, he had no trouble in immediately booking a week's run at London's premier Palace Theatre. His unusual act proved such an attraction that he was not only asked to extend each performance time, but to stay an extra four weeks. If Will had wanted, he could have accepted a number of additional appearances throughout the provinces. But his agent had a full season of thirty-

A giveaway card advertising "The Greatest Catch in Vaudeville."

Courtesy of the Will Rogers Memorial Commission

The Greatest Catch in Vaudeville

Manipulating 90 ft of Rope.

COMPLIMENTS OF **WILL ROGERS,** THE LARIET EXPERT

six weeks booked for him in the United States, starting in September. Besides, both Will and Buck were eager to get back home.

During the run at London's Palace, an invitation was extended to Will Rogers to favor the highly exclusive Ranelagh Club with a private performance. Will not only duplicated his entire stage act, but demonstrated some of his fancy trick riding. The members were duly impressed and at the end of the exhibition, Will was presented with a silver cup. It was only after the performance that Will and Buck were made aware of the presence of King Edward VII during their show.

Will had come a long way in the four years since 1902, when he and Dick Parris had stood outside Buckingham Palace and had watched the same king go by in a carriage. Now the elegant and exclusive Ranelagh Club had invited him to perform for its members and even the king. Nor could Will know that at some future date he would return to play polo at this same Ranelagh Club as an honored guest.

Back in the United States, Will went directly home to Oologah. He was still pursuing Betty, and following strictly observed social customs, he had his sisters extend an invitation for Betty to come to visit. Betty had never met any of Will's family before, and such an invitation was arranged with a possible alliance between the families envisioned in the future. If this had not been in Betty's mind, she could have invented a dozen excuses for declining the invitation, but she accepted. This, in turn, was an indication that, though there was no understanding between them yet, and she had turned down several of his proposals so far, Will Rogers was certainly high on Betty's list of eligible beaux.

Rogers, Arkansas, was hardly 100 miles from Chelsea, Indian Territory, where Sallie and Maud, two of Will's sisters, had their homes. However, traveling from one town to the other was complicated and grueling.

I had to take a roundabout way to get there. Leaving on a slow train at four-thirty in the morning and changing to another slow train at Monett, Missouri, I was due in Chelsea at two o'clock in the afternoon. It was a hot summer day and I had to ride the whole way in day coaches. I was completely bored and weary when the train pulled up at Vinita, twenty miles from Chelsea and still a good hour's ride on the slow train. There, to my great surprise and delight, Will walked into my coach.

His theatrical success hadn't changed him a bit. He was still bashful, and at this particular moment fate played a low trick on his gallantry. For after he had come up to Vinita on an early-morning train to meet me, it happened that the chair next to mine was occupied. Will reached over, shook hands and then found a seat for himself far ahead in the crowded coach. And that was the way we finished the journey.

Maud and her guests were at the station in Chelsea to meet me. When Will stepped down from the train carrying my two bags, the girls immediately started teasing . . . after that, neither of us had any peace.

During Betty's entire stay she and Will had few chances to be alone, and it seemed to Betty that Will was trying to avoid her. The visit was a social success, but when she left to return home, they had still not come to an understanding. They parted and promised to write to each other. It was time for Will to start work again.

The year 1907 came, and when his contractual commitments had been fulfilled, Will, without any planning, took Buck and Teddy, and two more cowboys and their horses, to England. He intended to put on a small version of a Wild West Show, but had neither a show planned nor bookings arranged. While he did manage to stage some appearances, the troop nearly starved. With boarding for the extra men and horses, as well as their own expenses to cover, Will, Buck, and Teddy had to go out into the provinces to raise enough money to pay the return fares. As Will said, "For a while it looked like we all would have to swim back."

Returning to American soil, Will, Buck, and Teddy were immediately booked for a two-week run at the Chestnut Street Opera House in Philadelphia. Somehow Buck and Teddy missed a train connection and did not make the opening performance, but as *Variety* wrote, "Rogers

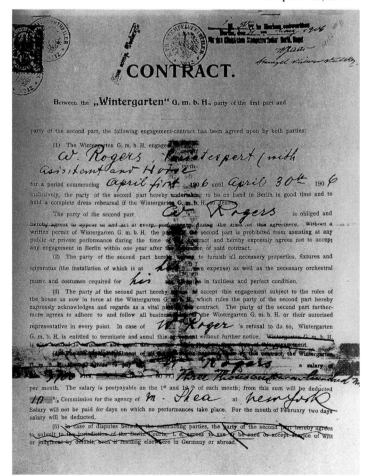

Contract for Berlin's *Wintergarten*, covering the period of April 1–30, 1906.

Will aboard the German steamer *Augusta Victoria*, the biggest ship afloat at the time, April 1907. Will remarked: "I look happy, but I wasn't."

had his lassoo and his wit and made a pronounced impression."

The expertise Will displayed with such ease on stage never revealed how much he would practice every day. For hours every forenoon, he would repeat the various tosses until sweat would soak his clothing and his muscles begged for mercy. What few knew was that by the time he began his workout with the lariat, Will had already exercised for hours at a new pastime—baseball. He would rise early and go out to the ballparks and practice "shagging" balls hit into the outfield. "That was back in 1905–6–7–8. From then on I had got out of my country ways, and was too lazy to get up and practice in the mornings. I was a 'Regular' actor by then."

It has been suggested that Will's habit and trademark of chewing gum was started by watching ballplayers doing it to ease the tension. However, no one proved as steadfast a chewer as Will. It was well known that in the absence of gum, he would chew rubber bands, or any similarly masticable matter. Will became so closely identified with gum chewing that he was asked to be the spokesman for Beechnut Gum.

I endorsed chewing gum one time and almost like to had to take up chewing tobacco, to win my 'fans' back again. Nothing can get you in wrong quicker than an endorsement.

In later years, as Will Rogers and chewing gum became so closely linked in the public's mind, his fans sent him so much chewing gum that he had a hard time just giving most of it away.

Back in the Indian Territory, Clem Vann Rogers, Will's father, had seen the land he had controlled for so long now cut into hundreds of small sections and assigned to Cherokees, who decided either to farm or to ranch, or to sell their allotment to interested buyers. Clem had tried to buy or lease as many allotments as were available, but he knew that the days of the large grazing herds would never return to the Territory.

The clamor of the new landowners for statehood resulted in Congress passing the Enabling Act, which provided for a Constitutional Convention composed of delegates from both the Oklahoma Territory and the Indian Territory. These men were to write the Constitution merging the two territories into the new state. Clem Vann Rogers was elected delegate from his district.

On November 16, 1907, two important events took place concerning the Indian Territory. One was the passing of the various Indian nations, including the Cherokee, Choctaw, Seminole, Chickasaw, and Creek nations; the other was the admission of Oklahoma as the forty-sixth state to the Union. While the individual tribes would, of course, maintain their customs and structure, they lost their status as nations with their respective capitals, their own governments, laws, and schools, their courts of justice, and their elected officials. Henceforth the former Indian Territory, a carefully designated landmass, was merely a part of the new state of Oklahoma, with the same federal laws applying that pertained to the other forty-five states, but also subject to the laws passed by the state itself.

By fall Will had a new—but as it turned out, disappointing—experience. He was to appear as a specialty number between the acts in a "melodrama," called *The Girl Rangers*. As the show had a western motif, the presence of a real cowboy made perfect sense. What did not make sense, however, was the show, which folded after just a few weeks. Will had foreseen it: "It was a beautiful show, but too expensive." He signed a contract to appear in Klaw and Erlanger theaters for the next twenty-five weeks at a weekly salary of $300.

Playing the Tremont Theatre in Boston in November, Will received a telegram from presenter H. B. Marinelli: "Kindly send me your route and mark the time you would accept in Europe." The meaning was quite clear. Marinelli wanted to arrange a European tour. What Will answered is not available, but one thing is certain: he did not go. Once having played in Germany seemed to have been enough. While Will went back to Europe on a few occasions, he never again performed on the Continent. England was a different matter; there they spoke English. To Will the difference between continental Europe and England was about the same as appearing in a silent motion picture and a "talkie." Will's foremost strength was his talk, his serious joking, where he would tell unpleasant facts couched in humor, where he could make an audience look at reality yet see also the folly that lay behind it. As Will's display of humor in his act grew, so did his confidence that he could hold an audience by simply talking common sense, made palatable by injecting laughter.

> *I use only one set method in my little gags, and that to try to keep to the truth. Of course you can exaggerate it, but what you say must be based on truth. Personally I don't like the jokes that get the biggest laughs, as they are generally as broad as a house and require no thought at all. I like one where, if you are with a friend, and hear it, it makes you think, and you nudge your friend and say, "He's right about that."*
>
> *I would rather have you do that than to have you laugh—and then forget the next minute what it was you laughed at.*

Christmas 1907 was approaching and Will was still unsuccessfully courting Betty, and that at long range by mail.

My Own Dear Girl.

Well my pal heres hoping you have a glorious Xmas and a plum good New Years. I know you will have a good time there at home. I am so sorry I could not come out but I only had the one week and I could not get the next week booking set back. . . .

Kid I sent you a little Xmas remembrance in the shape of a coat, and a muff. you should get it as soon as this letter. Now I dont know if it will fit you and that it is just right. but I hope it will suit you and prove serviceable for there is such a skin game in buying furs it may prove to be a <u>lemon</u>. but it is the only thing I could think of that would do you any good and that I thought would please you.

Well Dearie I will jar loose. have a good time and think occasionally of the Kid in the east who loves you best of all in the world.

    By-By. My Darling
        Your loving Kid
        Will
        237 W. 43rd St. N.Y.

Year's end found Will back at Hammerstein's Victoria, the best on Broadway. His vaudeville career had started here; now, a year and a half later, he was again at the same place. Of course, his salary had increased dramatically in the interim, but he was not yet the headliner. Still, the money was good, audiences liked him, and *Variety*, that show-business bible, kept writing favorable reviews:

Rogers attained classification as a comedy talking act, with a good deal more certainty than a host of others who bill themselves that way. His incidental remarks are fresh and breezy as can be and the act runs along entertainingly. Rogers affects not to take himself seriously, and therein lies the novelty of his attitude.

The one thing which would have made Will's life complete would have been to have Betty Blake finally accept his proposal of marriage. Will had now pursued the lady of his choice for almost seven years. True, there were times when the pursuit was less ardent than at others, and most of it had been at long distance via the United States Postal Service, but it was a steady pursuit, nevertheless. Betty had always demurred, yet she had not chosen any of her other swains—and there had been quite a handful. Betty was not only very pretty, but she had charm, a fine musical talent, a sense of humor, and best of all, she had a sensible head on her shoulders. Most likely it was that sensible head that made her hesitate where her heart might have rushed in. There was no doubt, Will was a very handsome young man, well built, athletic, a lot of fun to be with, even if he spoke and wrote ungrammatically and had only a nodding acquaintance with correct spelling. Any good wife could straighten that out in short order. But what she had heard about that Rogers boy hardly made him prime husband material. She even had heard that his own father worried about his wayward son's future. That he loved her, she never doubted; after all, he had declared it often enough and his persistence certainly vouched for it. But what could he really do to support a family, which their union surely would produce? Throwing a rope, even if he was better at it than most, hardly augured a secure future. Show business? What kind of life was that? And what about all those stories one always heard about itinerant show folks? No security, no permanent home, living out of trunks. Was that what she wanted?

And then, there was, of course, the fact that Will was part Indian. You know, "one of those . . ." Surely there must have been pressure put on Betty by relatives and so-called friends. It just was not done. Society, especially small-town society, can be pretty cruel. There must have been talk, but Betty was not swayed by it. She continued their correspondence, she did not break off any contact, she spent the evening with him in St. Louis, accepted his attention and gifts. True, there was never an understanding of exclusivity, of "going steady," but Will was never long enough in one spot. Had Betty been a weak, easily influenced girl, given to living by the dictates of small-town cliques, she would have stopped any contact with Will right at the beginning. If she had listened to the small talk, she would have married one of the local suitors, of which there were a handful. The fact that Will was "a performer," a man always on the go, weighed heavily against Will, for Betty was traditional in that she wanted a home with the man she married, and she wanted that man home for dinner and there for breakfast. And so 1908 started like the year before, with Will working at the Victoria in New York City and thinking about the girl he loved, who was fifteen hundred miles away.

Shortly after the New Year, Will was in eastern Canada, scheduled to play Montreal; Hamilton, Ontario; and Toronto. From Montreal he wrote Betty:

A busy Saturday in Rogers, Arkansas, circa 1908.

Courtesy of the Rogers Historical Museum, Rogers, Arkansas

The Blake home in Rogers, Arkansas, where Will and Betty were married.

Courtesy of the Rogers Historical Museum, Rogers, Arkansas

Well I had my first little sick spell last week in Montreal and it was kinder like a very hard or congestive chill and I went on Matinee then to my hotel and was very bad called a Dr. and he came 4 different times before 12 at night I missed only the one show as I felt better the next day but I shoo got sorter scared and some way I kinder wished for my Betty and would of got well quick. Its all alright away off all the time till you get to feeling bad and then it puts you to thinking and you wish you was home but I feel good now and am all O.K.

Will soon had another scare. *Variety* of March 7 reported that on March 2, after the night performance at Poll's in New Haven, Connecticut, Will Rogers left the show abruptly. The article went on to explain that the reason for the sudden departure was a telegram bringing news that Rogers's father was seriously ill.

Will rushed to Chelsea, where he found his father near death. Only small hope for his recovery was held out, and the family prepared itself for the worst. But after many weeks, the doctor's care and the careful nursing by his children brought Clem back to reasonably stable health. He would have to stay on medication for the rest of his life.

Will returned to the East and vaudeville. He was getting discouraged that he had only been able to get bookings into Eastern theaters, while the whole of the West had been closed to him. But vaudeville was controlled by a small number of feuding companies which had cut out for themselves certain territories and jealously guarded their control over "their" theaters, and who was or was not to appear in them. The same was to be true later, when a few motion picture companies controlled the entire market, each with its own star system.

At last in 1908, after almost three years in vaudeville, Will was able to break out of the Eastern enclave and was booked into several Western circuits. Not only was he able to play for audiences who had never seen or heard of his act, but he was able to visit a part of America he had not visited before. Thus he finished an engagement in Duluth, Minnesota, in June. His next engagement was in Butte, Montana, and because of the time it would take to get there, the following week had been left open for travel. Will consulted railroad timetables and realized that he would not need a whole week to get from Duluth to Butte, even on a slow train. Surely, he figured, there was ample time to make a visit to a place he had heard so much about, Yellowstone Park.

He checked into the big Cañon Hotel. It was opening day for the season, with the first guests expected for the following day.

I seen the Cañon stayed last night at the big Cañon Hotel. The first and only Guest. Oh it did seem funny. A tremendous big hotel. All the clerks and Waiters and servants and all ready as their first bunch will arrive there tonight so I had the whole Hotel to myself. They even had the Orchestra to play while I was in the big dining room that would seat 300. All alone but them.

Oh, I was the "poplar" Kid for fair once in my life.

Unfortunately Will had not taken into account a major washout along the rail line to Butte and he was forced to miss the first four shows of his week at the Grand Theatre there. The house manager was a most understanding man and paid Will for a full week.

Meanwhile, Will's courtship with Betty Blake continued and almost ended. As she had all along, being a practical woman, Betty had wanted Will to abandon show business and settle down. She argued that it would not make for a happy marriage with the husband being lonesome in some cheap hotel room, hating the job that kept him from seeing his children grow up, while the wife was at home having to cope alone with the problems of raising children and running a house. No! A husband and wife belonged together. All around her that was the practice. Men had jobs nearby in their town and came home for dinner. Who ever heard of a husband being on the road for months at a time and suddenly dropping in on his wife and family while on the way to another booking? No, if Will was prepared to settle down, he would present a far better prospect as a husband.

Will made his point of view eminently clear in his response:

My Own Dearest—

Well Sweetheart your letter came yesterday and say you did take your time about writing I thought you had lost the address.

Well I will try and tell you a few of the things you asked me about. Yes it is very lonesome sometimes but as for hating the work and wanting to give it up, <u>NO</u> not as long as you can get booked and get a good salary for there is no work in the world as nice and easy as this business when things are coming right.

It beats that old <u>farm</u> <u>and</u> <u>ranch</u> and <u>store</u> thing.

Now the time to stop is when you have made enough to live without it and when they cant use you any more.

Now I am going this summer and next year to make a good little bit of money out of this—bar misfortune of course and how could I do better at home I will get *there in time enough and have my good place to live and wont have to depend on a business. thats my <u>dope</u> on this thing.*

You are wrong about this trip. this is one of the best <u>paying</u> trips I ever <u>took</u> for the time. I will be $1500 or $2000 ahead of what I was when I left New York. it will keep me away from those <u>cheap</u> <u>summer</u> <u>houses</u> and parks all summer where $200 is the best I could of got.

Betty had to see two things from this debating point: First, there was going to be no way to change Will's mind about show business; second, he certainly had a valid point of view. Offhand, she knew no one who came home for dinner making that kind of money legally.

Along about that time Betty Blake down in Rogers, Ark., had a mental relapse and said "Yes" after several solid years of "Nos," She threw her lot with "Buck" and I, and the pony "Teddy."

At 1 P.M. November 25, 1908, William Penn Adair Rogers married Betty Blake in Rogers, Arkansas, at the home of the bride's mother. After an elegant repast had been served, the happy couple left for New York, or so the *Claremore Weekly Progress* reported in its issue three days after the event.

Page 45, "It was at this point . . . ," *Will Rogers*, by Betty Rogers, © 1941.

Page 46, "Rogers and his sidekick . . . ," Later, as Tom Mix, became foremost cowboy star of silent and early sound motion pictures.

Page 46, "We didn't get much . . . ," Weekly Article #123, April 19, 1925.

Page 48, "Instead of trying . . . ," *Will Rogers*, by Betty Rogers, © 1941.

Page 49, "Though I wanted . . . ," *Will Rogers*, by Betty Rogers, © 1941.

Page 50, "Everything I have done . . . ," Weekly Article #524, January 8, 1933.

Page 50, "It was 6:30 . . . ," *Will Rogers*, by Betty Rogers, © 1941.

Page 51, "Keith's old Union Square . . . ," Weekly Article #563, October 8, 1933.

Page 52, "I used a horse . . . ," Weekly Article #300, September 23, 1928.

Page 52, "Buck trained the pony . . . ," Weekly Article #649, June 2, 1935.

Page 52, "On Hammerstein's . . . ," Weekly Article #100, November 9, 1924.

Page 54, "Will did no talking . . . ," *Will Rogers*, by Betty Rogers, © 1941.

Page 54, ". . . he has about him . . . ," *Variety*, January 20, 1906.

Page 55, "He had not been . . . ," Will Rogers's letter to sister Sallie, December 20, 1905.

Page 56, "Dearest Betty . . . ," Will Rogers's letter to Betty, December 22, 1905.

Page 56, "In a letter . . . ," Will Rogers's letter to his father, December 27, 1905.

Page 56, "The year 1906 . . . ," Will Rogers's letter to his sister Maud, January 26, 1906.

Page 57, "A brilliant program . . . ," translation by Mr. Emil Sandmeier.

Page 58, "They talk of Gay N.Y. . . . ," Will Rogers's letter to Betty, April 17, 1906.

Page 59, "The Berlin episode . . . ," postcard to Betty, April 12, 1906.

Page 61, "I had to take . . . ," *Will Rogers*, by Betty Rogers, © 1941, pp. 94–95.

Page 62, "That was back . . . ," Weekly Article #617, October 21, 1934.

Page 62, "I endorsed chewing gum . . . ," Weekly Article #604, July 22, 1934.

Page 63, "Will had foreseen it . . . ," Weekly Article #632, February 3, 1935.

Page 63, "I use only one . . . ," from notes.

Page 64, "My Own Dear Girl . . . ," Will Rogers's letter to Betty, December 21, 1906.

Page 64, "Rogers attained . . . ," *Variety*, December 28, 1907.

Page 66, "Well I had my first . . . ," Will Rogers's letter to Betty, January 23, 1908.

Page 67, "I see the Cañon . . . ," Will Rogers's letter to Betty, June 12, 1908.

Page 67, "My Own Dearest . . . ," Will Rogers's letter to Betty, June 5, 1908.

Page 68, "Along about that time . . . ," Weekly Article #563, October 8, 1933.

Betty and Will with (from left to right) Will Jr., Mary, and Jim.

Courtesy of the Will Rogers Memorial Commission

Broadway, Hollywood, and in Between

"An actor is a fellow that just has a little more monkey in him than the fellow that can't act."

Traveling in the early nineteen hundreds would usually require a discomforting effort. The only means of long-distance transportation was, of course, the railroad. While there were major lines laboriously crossing the country, connecting primary cities, relatively few so-called feeder lines serviced the small communities. Where there were these local railways, they usually lacked comfort and amenities provided by major lines, but they were essential for the transport of people, goods and animals. Thus the leading problem often was simply how to get to the nearest railway line. As the century aged, the proximity to a railhead would spell the difference between a community's growth or stagnation. Rogers, Arkansas, was fortunate in that it was located on a railway feeder, which connected to the transcontinental system.

The wedding joining Will and Betty was scheduled for 1 P.M., allowing enough time for the post-nuptial repast and meeting the northbound train afterwards. Most of the town's citizens assembled at the little railroad station to see the newlyweds off on their honeymoon. Leaving Rogers, Arkansas, Will and Betty—now Mrs. Rogers—had to travel on a "stuffy local train—all day-coaches," seated in their going-away finery amid a group of curious onlookers. It seemed an eternity until they reached Monett, Missouri, only some fifty miles away. There they could make connections with the "through" train to St. Louis, on which Will had reserved a stateroom. "It was nice then to be reminded that he was an experienced traveler and a man of the world," Betty would recall years later.

November 26, 1908, in St. Louis, the first full day of their marriage, was a busy one. It was Thanksgiving Day and they sat through a 17–0 trouncing inflicted by the Carlisle Indians football team on its Washington University counterparts. Afterwards Will ordered an impressive turkey dinner with all the trimmings, including champagne, to be served in their hotel room. It was the first champagne Betty had ever tasted and she fully enjoyed the experience. Then, to cap the day, Will had reserved orchestra seats for the evening performance of *What Every Woman Knows*, starring the celebrated actress Maud Adams. Betty had been looking forward to seeing her first famous Broadway star. When they were

**Will and Betty on
their honeymoon at
Niagara Falls, New
York, 1908.**

seated in the theater she began to feel strange; she thought at first that it was unpleasantly hot and stifling in the theater. But as the houselights dimmed she felt so feeble that she whispered to Will to take her out at once.

*Will quietly hustled me up the
long aisle of the theater and tact-
fully suggested that we walk back
to the hotel. We walked and
walked—miles it seemed to me. I
didn't understand until afterwards, when Will explained that
he had wondered during dinner
just what sort of a girl he had
married. From the way I drank
champagne, he explained, he had
decided champagne-drinking must
be an "old Arkansas custom."*

The next few weeks Will had engagements booked in and around New York City, which gave him a chance to show Betty the sights. Since this was her first trip to the city, she wanted to see everything she had ever heard of, from Chinatown to the top of the forty-one-story Singer building, then the tallest building in the world. Much to Will's displeasure, music-loving Betty dragged him to several performances at the Metropolitan Opera to hear world famous tenor Enrico Caruso. Years later, so Betty would recall, Caruso roared with laughter when Will told him that "the two things my wife wanted most to do on her arrival in New York were to see Grant's Tomb and hear Caruso sing."

Will and Betty may have started their wedding trip in St. Louis and stopped over briefly in the New York City area, but the two extended their honeymoon all along the Orpheum vaudeville circuit. Years later Will would describe that early episode of Betty's married life perhaps a little more dramatically than it was: "From cheap hotels to dark stage door entrances, she trudged her way."

While vaudeville could be tiresome at times, there were new towns and new acts, there were museums and concerts, there were new sights and joys, and now and then, there were even calamities. One came pretty early in their travel. Will and Betty had decided that after the present tour was over, they would return to Oklahoma and settle down in a house Uncle Clem had given Will some years earlier. While Will's salary was great, so, unfortunately, were his expenses. There were now three people who needed hotel accommodations, and Teddy, who needed a stable. There were travel expenses and food, and sometimes open weeks when there was no salary but the expenses went on. Before his marriage, any clean hotel was acceptable to Will, but now he demanded far better for his bride. Where earlier he was easily satisfied with his favorite bowl of chili in any nearby parlor, his selection of restaurants and menus had to be more discriminating now, with Betty. There was no longer the matter of sending $100 a week back into the bank account in Claremore. Now there was the urgency of trying to stretch the salary to cover expenses. There was many a week when Will's yellow diamond ring had to visit the inside of a pawnbroker's repository only to be temporarily redeemed on the next payday.

It was level-headed Betty—dubbed later by Will as "the balance wheel" of the Rogers family—who instituted a regular savings plan. They bought a metal chest with a slot at the top into which daily, without fail, a single dollar was to be deposited. And they religiously stuck to this commitment. Now traveling out West, where paper money was rarely used, the deposits made were those large silver dollars, popularly called "cartwheels." Week by week the trunk with the metal box became heavier, but the deposits were kept up. Feeling that the box was secure, the couple kept their jewelry in it as well. Checking into the Park Hotel in Butte, Montana, at the end of February 1909, Will and Betty had the trunk hauled up into their third-floor room. Then, according to Betty, they locked the door and went out for dinner. When they returned, someone had entered their quarters, pried open the metal box and removed its entire contents. As there was no sign of forced entry, the police assumed at once that those "visiting actors" had carelessly left the door unlocked. Gone was the jewelry and the savings of many weeks. The theft was never solved, nor was the cash or any jewelry item recovered.

Since Betty needed to have some new clothes made, and just possibly as a temporary economy measure, it was decided that she return for a brief visit with her family. Consulting Will's schedule, the couple arranged for Betty to join her husband when he next played St. Louis, Missouri. In the meantime Will worked his way through the Pacific Northwest.

Life settled into a certain routine. When the season was over and it was time to put into practice what Will and Betty had decided before they were married—namely to retire from show business and settle in Claremore—fate, as it so often likes to do, tested their resolve. The temptation came in the form of an offer from the Percy Williams theater group, offering $300 a week. Even Betty agreed that such a lucrative offer should not be refused, and so the routine continued. Actually, there was a little more to it than just the lure of good money. Betty had begun to like

Betty Rogers with Teddy during the vaudeville days, 1909.

show business. It allowed the newlyweds to spend so much time together, go on sightseeing trips, plan picnics, go horseback riding, sleep late—with the only fixed obligation being just two twenty-minute shows a day. Of course there were daily hours of practice, but what other occupation could compare with Will's?

Will, however, was not satisfied. He was still not a headliner. It seemed that he might never make it, as he was really part of a team. Buck and Teddy each deserved some credit for making the performance what it was. Will gave the matter some thought and decided to expand the act. He hired several contest winning cowgirls and ropers and acted as the master of ceremonies for the show, introducing each member and making humorous remarks about their performance. It was here that he really gained the confidence that he could entertain by just talking. And then, one night at Keith's Theatre in Philadelphia, the house manager, one Harry Jordan, changed Will Rogers's future.

Will twirling a big Crinoline over the Boston Red Sox team, circa 1909.

Courtesy of the Will Rogers Memorial Commission

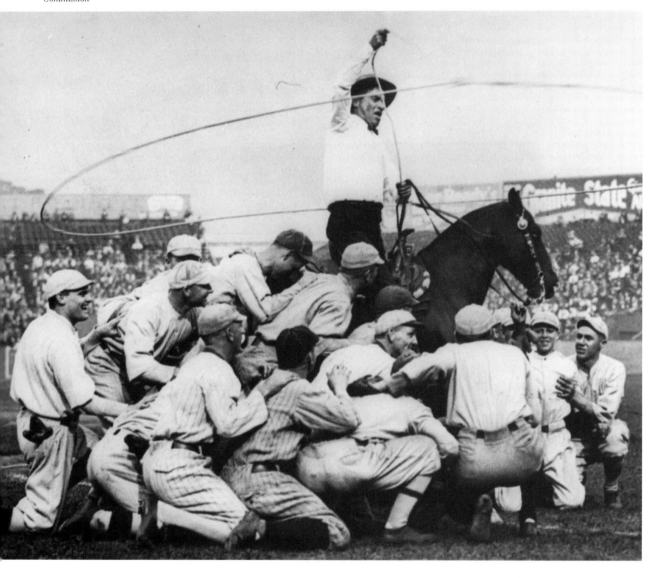

"Tell me, Mrs. Rogers," he said, "why does Will carry all those horses and people around with him? I would rather have Will Rogers alone than that whole bunch put together."

That settled it for Will . . . [he] went back to the original act with which he had started out in vaudeville—just himself and his rope. But now he talked continuously, rambling on about other performers on the bill and the different tricks he was trying to do.

"Worked pretty good," he could confide to the audience when things had gone smoothly, "made my joke and the trick come out even." Or when things hadn't gone so well: "I've only got jokes enough for one miss. I've either got to practice roping or learn more jokes."

Buck McKee went back West again to raise and train horses. Teddy was put out to pasture on the Rogers ranch in Oologah. One day he wandered off through a broken fence and was gone. Will was very upset and sent instructions that no expense should be spared to find the pony. Despite the fact that a reward of $125—"No Questions Asked"—was offered, it took several months before Teddy was found. The little pony that had performed before the king of England and delighted audiences on two continents was hitched to a farmer's plow, turning over a cornfield. He was brought back to Oologah, and a permanent retirement was guaranteed. He lived to a very old age.

There was less and less talk about retiring from show business. Even though Betty longed for a permanent home of her own, where she could have her own china and crystal, where friends, family and neighbors could come to dinner or stay on a visit, moving to Claremore and becoming a farm family rarely came up as a topic.

In 1911, when Betty realized that she was pregnant, she especially wanted a place of her own. It certainly would not do to bring a newborn baby to the Hotel St. Francis, which had been the couple's New York City headquarters. At the beginning of September, Will and Betty found a small, five-room apartment on the Upper West Side of Manhattan, at 203 West 94th Street. Something must have been amiss with the place, because after staying there less than a month, and just two weeks before the baby was born, they moved again—this time a little farther north, just off the Columbia University campus at 551 West 113th Street.

Billy wants a boy of course . . . if it is a boy I am going to name it after Billy. I would name it for you but there are so many Clems in the family I am afraid they would get mixed up.

On Friday morning, October 20, 1911, William Vann, the first child of Will and Betty Rogers, was born. When Uncle Clem learned about it he went out and bought a pair of beaded moccasins and two pairs of stockings. He took them to the post office and mailed them to his new grandson. However, before the reminders of his distinguished ancestry reached little Billy, Uncle Clem had peacefully died in his sleep at his daughter's house in Chelsea.

Will canceled his engagements at Proctor's Fifth Avenue Theatre and Hammerstein's Victoria to attend his father's funeral. The service was held on

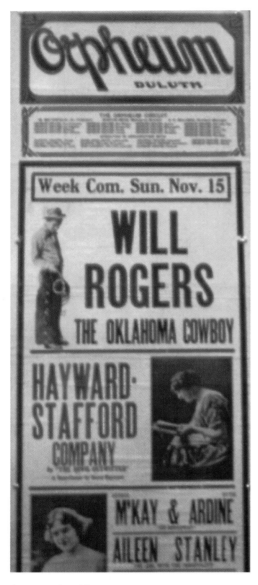

A poster advertising
the Orpheum circuit.

October 31, at the Southern Methodist Church in
Chelsea. Clem Vann Rogers rests next to Mary America,
his first wife, in the cemetery in Chelsea. There on a hill
that offers an unobstructed view of the prairie he so
loved, this leader of his people was buried close to his
children who had preceded him.

Uncle Clem had had a rich life. He was all that a successful pioneer had to be. Tough, resourceful, enterprising, honorable, decent, concerned about his neighbors
and fellow citizens. He had worked hard and never
shunned even the most menial tasks. He had carted
freight and served with distinction as an officer in the
War Between the States. He had ranched and farmed,
been elected senator, then judge, in the Cherokee
Nation, and been a delegate to the convention that created the state of Oklahoma. The county of his residence
was named in his honor. With all his important political
and commercial experience and background, it came as
a most surprising revelation that Uncle Clem died without preparing a legal will.

Will Rogers was mourning the loss of a parent. Yet
he must have felt contented that his father had known
that the son he'd thought a failure had ridden his own
horse to success. Perhaps that father was disappointed
that the son became one of those "actors," rather than a
rancher. That father's innermost thoughts were never
recorded. Clem Vann Rogers was a private man, not
given to effusive praise. Will knew that. Though he did
not expect it, he was certain that he had achieved recognition for his achievements—accomplishments based
not on his father's name, money, or influence, but solely
on Will's own talents and drive. Probably Uncle Clem
never told his son directly that he felt pride in his career.
What is known is that this father had taken his son's let-
ters to the newspaper office to have them published, so that others could share
his son's life and adventures; that this father went around with press clippings
lauding his son's performances in his pocket and showing them around. Clem
Rogers did not understand show business, but he knew business. He knew that if
a theater manager was willing to pay his son $300 a week, that son must be
worth a lot more to that theater manager. Clement Vann Rogers did not have to
say much; his actions unveiled his feelings more eloquently than words.

Betty was slowly becoming reconciled to the fact that any plan of a return to
Oklahoma was an ever farther-receding dream, to be realized perhaps someday,
but surely not soon. She could see that Will was quite content to continue in his
current profession, practicing and working hard to become a headliner. There was
the rare talk about ranching and farming, but only one sign that Will gave a tran-
sient thought to returning someday to the earth of his youth. He purchased 20
acres on "Preparatory Hill" overlooking Claremore, with an unobstructed view

that reached the horizon. He referred to it as the site for their retirement home. Will was only thirty-two years old when he made the purchase, an age when one might speak of retirement but not really visualize it as an inflexible goal.

The year 1912 began with weeklong bookings in Scranton, New York City, Providence, Bridgeport, New Haven, Worcester, and other towns in the Northeast. Betty and little Bill were now well settled in their apartment on 113th Street. Playing in nearby towns, Will could be home weekends before taking regularly scheduled trains Monday mornings to his next engagement. Nothing changed until the spring, when Will was signed to appear in *The Wall Street Girl,* a musical comedy in three acts starring Blanche Ring and featuring Charles Winninger, Harry Gilfoil, Florence Shirley, and William P. Carlton.

Will did not really have a written part in the show, but since there was a Western motif to it, a cowboy with his lasso could easily be fitted into such a story. This kind of theatrical trick is often used to give characters a chance to rush to their dressing rooms and change costumes for their next entry. Years later, working for Ziegfeld, Will would step in front of the drawn curtain and explain his completely unrelated insertion into undraped female sophistication by claiming: "I'm just out here while the girls are changing from nothing to nothing."

Betty in front of a vaudeville billboard.

Broadway was blessed that year with an impressive variety of successful shows and stars. There was George Arliss in *Disraeli* at the Wallack's, the longest running play on Broadway; Otis Skinner in *Kismet;* David Warfield in *The Return of Peter Grimm;* Eddie Foy at the Globe; and Weber and Fields at the Broadway. Any new show would have to be truly extraordinary to compete successfully against such significant competition.

After out-of-town previews for several weeks, flaws in *The Wall Street Girl* had been remedied and weak points strengthened. The Broadway opening was set for April 15 at the George M. Cohan Theatre. That date was an unfortunate choice, as the superliner *Titanic* hit an iceberg during the night of April 14–15, with the news causing banner headlines though details were few and sketchy. More than a dozen New York newspapers were vying to outsell each other without any detailed facts for their headlines. Readers could be certain only that the *Titanic,* supposedly the safest ship man had yet built, had struck an iceberg. Surely, so it was generally assumed, if this was indeed the safest ship afloat, there would be few casualties, if any. Therefore, there was no reason to postpone the opening; the show opened as planned.

It was the following spring that Will went into his first musical show, The Wall Street Girl, starring Blanche Ring. We rode to the opening on the subway and I remember how nervous I was and how anxious for Will's success. I took my seat well down front, and shortly after the curtain went up I began to hear whisperings in the audience and to notice people rising abruptly and leaving the theater. This alarmed me. Then Will came on stage, and interrupting the action of the play announced that the ocean liner Titanic . . . had gone down with a shocking loss of life.

The play went on but rows of seats were empty and those who remained were stunned into numbness which made it impossible to say whether The Wall Street Girl was a success.

While the news of the sinking of the *Titanic* was known when the show began, the cataclysmic news of the number of lives lost became known only with the early evening editions of the next morning's newspapers. Late arrivals for the 8:15 P.M. opening-night curtain had just enough time to read the announcement that 1,250 passengers had perished. They whispered the dramatic news to their neighbors, and the calamitous fact raced through the audience. Men left the theater to buy the early editions and read the horror story for themselves. "The tidings spread through the theater and there was a noticeable change in the attitude of the audience, the spirit of gayety lessened greatly," wrote *The World*.

The *New York Times* review in the April 16, 1912, edition, carried the headline: "Wall Street Girl Is Rather Tame." A sub-headline read: "Two High Spots Struck" and went on to explain:

There were two high spots in The Wall Street Girl, produced with Blanche Ring as the star of the George M. Cohan's Theatre last evening. One of them was the "Deedle-Dum-Dee" song, sung by Blanche Ring herself and the other was that extra-ordinary lariat performer Will Rogers, who did his regular vaudeville act but who undoubtedly scored the success of the evening doing things with ropes and conversing in his quaint way with the audience.

As there was no written part for Will, he had no lines in the musical. He performed his usual vaudeville act while scenery was shifted or costumes were changed.

The Wall Street Girl did not survive lukewarm notices and played only fifty-six performances in New York City. But producers have a way of trying to recoup those huge investments needed to mount a Broadway musical. They take the show and play it around the country, advertising it as being "Straight From Broadway," and "With The Original Cast!" Therefore *The Wall Street Girl*, which played only seven weeks in New York City, closed for the summer and then opened a cross-country tour in Poughkeepsie in mid-September. It played well into the first half of 1913.

By this time, Betty was pregnant again. It was decided that it would be wiser for her to go to Rogers, Arkansas, instead of having her mother come again to New York to be by her daughter's side. At 2 P.M. on Sunday, May 18, 1913, Mary Amelia Rogers was born. The telegram announcing her birth and Betty's well being was handed to Will just as he was about to go onstage.

Will, playing in Houston, Texas, was so overjoyed by the good news that he took the telegram with him onstage, stopped the music, and made an official

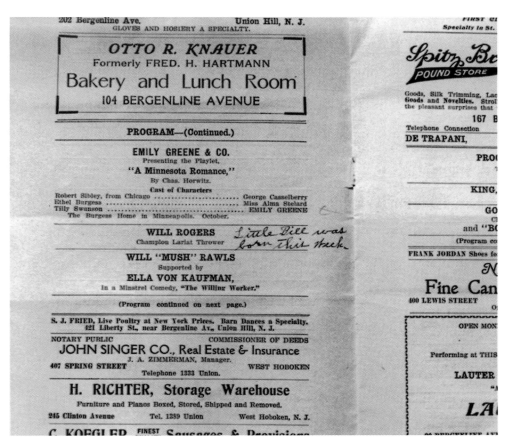

Will's note on the Union Hill, New Jersey, Hudson Theatre program reads, "Little Bill was born this week." Bill was born October 20, 1911.

announcement of the blessed event to the audience. As soon as he could, he raced to Arkansas to be with his wife and the new arrival. But he could not stay; he had performances scheduled in and around New York City.

Early in 1914, Will Rogers found another use for his lariat. Depending on which New York City newspaper one reads, the event occurred either in the Longacre Building at Broadway and 43rd Street, or the Putnam Building. However, there is no argument as to what took place. Fifteen passengers were trapped when an elevator became stalled between two of the upper floors. This happened at the busiest time of day, 5:30 P.M., when various offices had just closed. After one of the men was able to pry open the trapdoor in the elevator's ceiling, Will Rogers found enough room to throw his lasso so that it caught a protrusion on the floor above. Will and several men were then able to pull the elevator cab up to the next floor and open the door, releasing the passengers.

Even though Will felt that his vaudeville career might be nearing its end, he still tried to improve his act. Just as he had taught other vaudevillians to twirl a rope, so Will had picked up the specialties of others. He practiced one especially, learned on a tour during which he had constantly traveled with an entire group of performers. Usually, acts would be contracted separately and might meet by the chance of having been booked into the same theater, but this time the entire show of twelve acts had moved as a solid unit. This had given Will an opportunity to befriend a husband-and-wife team, the Hancocks, who performed cycle tricks.

The gravesites of Clement Vann and Mary America Rogers, Will Rogers's parents, at the cemetery in Chelsea, Oklahoma.

From them Will had learned to ride the unicycle. He had even gone so far as to purchase his own shiny unicycle, shipping it as part of his luggage from city to city. Eventually he incorporated the delicate balancing act into his roping presentation.

In later years James Blake Rogers, the youngest surviving son, had quite a story to tell about the unicycle. Years earlier he had, as kids will do, rummaged around the garage in the old Beverly Hills house. He came across a large case. Curious, he opened it and discovered a unicycle, which he just had to try out. James had been riding horses since he was able to sit up straight on a horse, and he had been falling off them just as long, but the number of falls off a horse seemed small compared to the number of times he fell off that unicycle. He was still trying to negotiate that "overgrown eggbeater" when his father came home from the movie studio. "Dad was now close to fifty," so James said, "but he took that thing and showed me how it was to be ridden. He probably wasn't the greatest unicycle rider, but he was still astonishing. And then, as we were putting that bike back into its box, he told me the whole story."

It seemed that there had been a very strong motivation for Will Rogers to learn to ride a unicycle. In one town along the vaudeville circuit, Will was going through his patter accompanied by the display of his lariat skill, when a drunk in the audience kept tauntingly yelling: "Can you do this on a unicycle?"

All through Will's act, the heckler kept interrupting: "Can you do this on a unicycle?" After Will had concluded his act, he went to see the house manager to find out what the interruption had been all about. He was told that just the preceding week a unicyclist who called himself the "The Greatest Unicyclist on Earth" had been on the bill. During his performance, while riding his unicycle, he had also done a few simple rope tricks.

Will was concerned. While he knew that his act depended on roping, his verbal patter was becoming ever more important. He also realized that in case someone was lessening his act by repeating part of it under more difficult conditions, he, Will Rogers, had better be prepared to perform under similar conditions. And therefore, along with his chaps and ropes, the unicycle became part of his luggage—

and sometimes part of his act. Will would not use it regularly, but if he knew that "The Greatest Unicyclist on Earth" had recently been performing at the same theater, he would introduce the unicycle into his act. And so the tour continued. Somewhere between St. Louis and San Francisco—so Jim Rogers told the story—the two performers were on the same bill by accident. The "Greatest Unicyclist on Earth" and part-time roper had been appearing the previous week; having an open week, while the theater needed an extra act, he had been held over. To make it appear that this arrangement was not one of mutual financial convenience, the unicyclist was advertised as being held over "by popular demand." Along came Will with his ropes and unicycle, suspecting nothing. When he saw the program, he

Betty and little Bill, 1911.

realized that "The Greatest Unicyclist on Earth" was the man who was doing part of Will's act. And, as he was being "held over," he was placed in the honor spot of the show, toward the very end. This placed Will's performance earlier on the program. Opening the week's run on Monday at matinee time, Will did his entire act—roping and gags—riding the unicycle. He did the same for the evening performance, when the audience was larger. When the "star" of that week's show began his display of simple roping on the unicycle, the audience saw an inferior repetition of Will's act and began to jeer and heckle. The unicyclist closed his act as best he could and rushed offstage demanding an explanation from the theater manager. Told that this fellow Rogers had done his similar act earlier that evening, "The Greatest" belligerently confronted Will.

Will Rogers calmly explained that he had been on the stage a long time and that he was primarily a roper, that he had taken up the unicycle merely in self-defense. He further pointed out that "The Greatest" was primarily noted for his intricate tricks with a unicycle, and that if he would just eliminate the roping from his act, he, Will Rogers, would never ride his unicycle again. Thus, so Will suggested, each would have his own specialty for which they were known, and they would no longer compete with each other. And that was the reason Will never again used his shiny unicycle on the stage.

While that may have settled the bloodless unicycle war, it did little to solve the question of Will Rogers's show business future. In fact, Will did not even have any commitments for the summer of 1914, and so, on impulse, he suggested that Betty join him in Atlantic City, New Jersey. Expecting that this would be merely a week's quiet vacation, Betty packed a small case. She left the two children in

The curtain call for the cast of *The Wall Street Girl*, 1912.

mother's care and took the next train east. To her surprise, Will suggested that they take a trip to England and leave at once. He confessed that he had already booked passage aboard the largest and most luxurious ocean liner, the German ship *Vaterland*. Betty had a single day in which to acquire the items she felt she would need on the voyage and in London. As Will had no bookings awaiting him in England, this promised to be a truly leisurely sojourn. But Will Rogers had become too valuable a property to remain untapped.

Sir Alfred Butt, who had managed the Palace Music Hall when Will had last appeared in London, immediately offered him a spot in the musical show *The Merry-Go-Round,* starring Nora Bayes. The theater was the famous musical hall, the Empire Theatre. Will was familiar with the place. It was huge, allowing for a large crowd, and it not only served drinks during the performance but employed so-called percentage-girls. These young "waitresses" constantly moved up and down the aisles, urging patrons to buy not only drinks for themselves, but for the young ladies as well. Will Rogers did not really want to compete with the noisy commercial part of this enterprise and felt that there was no chance that his act would succeed under these conditions, especially since his act now consisted mostly of talk. Will was certain that his quiet talk would be resented by the hostesses as interfering with their trade, and that they would purposely ruin any chance for success. But the more obstacles Will enumerated, the more determined Sir Alfred became, and finally he made a most generous offer: Will would name his own salary.

Will made a counteroffer. He would appear one night on a tryout basis. If the experiment failed, there would be no pay; if it succeeded, Sir Alfred could decide the salary. Will had repeatedly said that money meant little to him, and he had found that Sir Alfred was an honorable man and would not take advantage of the fact that Will had no idea what current star salaries were.

A strange thing happened. The girls Will had feared became intrigued by the American's talk and wit, and not only stopped their travels up and down the aisles but hushed customers wanting to order drinks. Even the lobby bar, usually teeming with thirsty patrons, emptied as customers wanted to find out what it was that had suddenly quieted the house. It was a new experience for patrons of the Empire. Sir Alfred gladly made out weekly checks of $400 for Will. What had started as an impromptu vacation turned into just another engagement for Will, while Betty and her friend, the actress Charlotte Perry, went on a week's sightseeing trip to Paris, and then on to Berlin.

Europe was seething with rumors of war; still, most serious minded men and women felt that the world had outgrown war. Will was not so sure. Even though Sir Alfred Butt wanted him to continue in the show, Will decided to get home as quickly as possible. He and Betty booked passage again on a German ship, the *Imperator,* and barely had reached New York before war was declared in Europe.

It was back to occasional vaudeville engagements, carefully selected so that Will could spend most of his time in and around New York City. It was not a matter of being unable to get bookings elsewhere; it was a matter of either establishing himself on Broadway soon, or calling it quits on a vaudeville career and going back to Oklahoma. Will and Betty had decided that Will had paid his tuition to show business and it was time to graduate, to go on to the next "Reader."

Fred Stone was one of the major Broadway stars of musical comedies. He and his partner, Dave Montgomery, were masters of unusual dance routines, usually choreographed by themselves. Fred was famous not only for his remarkable, audience-stunning opening in the super-musical *The Red Mill,* in which he "fell" down an eighteen-foot ladder, but also for his legendary dance as the scarecrow in *The Wizard of Oz.*

Early in his vaudeville career, while laying over in New York City between engagements, Will had caught Fred Stone's performance in *The Red Mill.* He had marveled at Stone's performance, never thinking that he would ever get to meet such an accomplished performer. Yet, here was Will at the stage door looking for Fred Stone. Stone's daughter, Dorothy, later recalled the story of their meeting:

> *Daddy decided that he wanted to dance inside a lariat, for the show The Old Town. Nobody had ever done this. So he hired an Indian boy, called Black Chambers, to*

go on the road with him during the last part of The Red Mill tour, to teach him roping. Well the following season, when The Old Town opened, that particular dance was one of the highlights. But all the time Black Chambers was with Daddy, he kept talking about another Oklahoman, Will Rogers. He kept saying, "This is a wonderful guy, Fred, and I think you ought to meet, because if you and Will met, you'd get along real good."

One day, Daddy was coming out the stage door when a man came up to the doorman asking, "Is Fred Stone around?" Since Daddy was standing right there, it was obvious to the doorman that the man didn't know my father by sight and he asked, "Who wants to see him?"

The stranger said, "Will Rogers." Daddy remembered what Black Chambers had told him and he walked over and identified himself. "Black Chambers told me about you. You know, he taught me to rope."

And Will said, "Shucks, I would have taught you all the roping you want, just for the fun of it. Shall we go and rope now?" And Daddy and Will went back into the theater, and there, on the darkened stage, they roped together. They roped all afternoon, without dinner, until it was time for the company to come in. From then on these two were just like . . . brothers.

Every day the two men would practice roping. They started to play polo together. Stone, who had a house in Amityville, on Long Island, had his own polo field, and with famous dancer Vernon Castle and Frank Tinney and Will, they had a formidable team. In 1915, when Betty was again expecting, Will thought it best for her to escape the humid summer heat of New York City, so he rented a house in Amityville.

**Mary Rogers's first
photograph, 1915.**

**Will, Bill, and Betty,
1912.**

Will rented a house in Amityville, Long Island, opposite our house, so Daddy and he used to be together all the time. Every morning, Will would come over with his little rope, whistling under Daddy's window. Now Daddy was to sleep till noon, because he was working so hard at night. Mother would stick her head out the window, and she would say softly: "Will Rogers, you go away and come back at 12 o'clock! Fred's asleep."

Then Daddy would stick his head out and say, "I'll be right down!" And the two would ride and rope all day.

It was here, in Amityville, that Will had an accident.

Mary Rogers swinging on the front porch, 1914.

It was that accident that got him to do more talking than roping. Daddy had a little creek back of our house, and it had low tides and high tides. At low tide, you shouldn't dive off the diving board, as there was only little water there. Well, this one day, Will didn't look, and he dived and hit his head and almost broke his neck. His right arm and side were completely para-lyzed. The poor man was stunned. He was still in vaudeville, that's how he earned his living. Now how could he do roping without the use of his right arm? But from that very day on, he started learning every trick he knew with his left hand. It did two good things. True, it was a frightening, horrible thing to happen; but it got him to talking more, which made a star out of him, and it made him an even greater roper than he ever was before, because he learned to rope equally well with either hand.

One evening at Amityville, Will and Fred had a serious talk about the future. The two men talked freely, the way friends will sometimes discuss problems that they might not even mention to their wives. Will was becoming discouraged. He had now been almost ten years in vaudeville, yet he seemed to be still distant from becoming a headliner. He had to admit that he was tasting success; that he was earning a marvelous salary, compared to the average working man; that many would readily trade their jobs for his. But Will felt that he had reached a certain level in vaudeville, and that he just could not get further. He had been in a couple of musical shows, and had personally received excellent reviews, but the

Bill and Mary swinging on the front porch in Rogers, Arkansas, 1914.

shows had failed. He wondered whether the time had not come to pick up his family and move to Oklahoma, settle down as the rancher or farmer his father had wanted him to be. After all, it was a thought he and Betty had discussed at the beginning of their marriage.

Fred, the older of the two men, with more show-business experience, then gave Will the best advice of his career: "You must get into another musical show," he told him. "Do not go out on the road again; stay in New York City where things constantly happen; be ready to step into a Broadway show on a moment's notice."

Betty, Mary, Bill, and Will in Rogers, Arkansas, 1914.

Will promised to give his friend's advice a chance. It would be difficult, for it was on the road where Will earned $350 a week now. There were only so many theaters in New York where he could play and retain the pay level to which he had risen. To play a smaller house which paid a lower wage rate would adversely affect his standing. It could not be done. It would be better not to play at all.

When there were no bookings in the city, or in any of its boroughs, Will would play nearby New Jersey or Connecticut. Several times, when smaller theaters offered Will a job, he would accept the lower salary and appear under an assumed name. It was difficult to try to raise a family and stay intentionally unemployed. But Fred's advice would eventually pay off.

James Blake Rogers, Will and Betty Rogers's third child, was born July 25, 1915. Now that Will had a large family, he felt that he needed a car. Thus the family acquired a secondhand automobile.

> . . . my first car, [was] an old Overland. It had some of the most terrible noises and knocks. People would say, "Will, get that noise fixed," but I wouldn't. I would just keep on and in a few days a worse one would drown out that [first] one.

That Overland automobile was so noisy that the neighbors in the bedroom community of Amityville finally complained to the law. When Will would come home towards midnight after an evening performance, that car would wake up everybody. Finally, one night, the police waited for Will at the county line, barring his way. When Will protested that he lived there and just wanted to get home, he was officially informed that he was most welcome to go home, but not in that car.

In 1915, when the Shubert organization produced *Hands Up*, Will was hired. But it was not for a part in the show; again it was a specialty number and a change of pace. A most bizarre incident took place on opening night. Will Rogers was working in front of the curtain while scenery was shifted. The space between the curtain behind him and the footlights in front was confining, and allowed only limited space for a twirling rope. Will had worked out a routine involving five little dance students encircled by Will's spinning rope. Three times the rope collapsed because it hit the curtain. After the third time, one of the Shuberts ordered the lights turned off, forcing Rogers to withdraw in darkness, after failing to complete the trick:

> *Will Rogers, cowboy, was on hand with a new series of lariat tricks. When he was trying to complete a difficult rope dance, the lights were switched out and he was compelled to make way for a stage full of bathing girls. The audience resented this and although the orchestra played several minutes the singing and dancing number had to be abandoned until Mr. Rogers had returned and completed the dance. Then there were shouts of applause. Five little girls, pupils of Maurice, danced with him in one number. They were recalled again and again.*

What Will did not know was that Fred Stone had been in the audience and, as Dorothy Stone recalled, vigorously resented what had been done to his best friend:

> *. . . they turned the lights out on Will. Now you know, Will could go on and on, as was his wont, he was liable to do that, but he had the audience with him, and he just didn't keep track of the time. So Will just walked off and they started the finale. Well, my father, who was well known to theater audiences in New York, leaped to his feet and turned to the audience and said "Don't let 'em do that to Will Rogers! He's got a great act. We want Rogers!"*
>
> *And going up and down the aisle he got the audience into a frenzy, and they all shouted, "We want Rogers! We want Rogers!" Will didn't know any of this. He had gone to his little dressing room, way upstairs, thinking he had been a flop— that they had turned the lights out on him because he had been flopping. Well, the audience drove the finale right off the stage, and they had to go and bring Will back on stage. Then the audience gave him an ovation.*

Will left the show after two weeks. Again it was back to vaudeville. This time he booked appearances right across the country. The change in tactics was dictated by financial consideration, rather than logic. In August, Will received a call from Gene Buck, Florenz Ziegfeld's trusted general manager, major writer of the *Follies,* talent coordinator, originator of the Midnight Frolic, an after-midnight nightclub atop the New Amsterdam Theatre. It was here that the elite of society came after attending the *Follies,* which was presented in the theater on the ground floor, or after any show on Broadway. There was haute cuisine and the champagne flowed freely, though not inexpensively. At the Midnight Frolic Ziegfeld presented *The Ziegfeld Frolic,* a shorter but more dazzling show than his *Follies.* There was a different cast and different beauties. Buck thought that in this particular production, named *Just Girls,* this Will Rogers would not only provide humor, but would certainly be a sharp contrast to the carefully selected showgirls.

There were two problems: one minor, and one major. Will's salary was about half his weekly fee in vaudeville. The argument against paying him more was that he had only one performance, and that one late at night, which left him time to perform at least two shows elsewhere earlier in the evening. The other problem was far more serious. Too many of the after-midnight guests were repeaters who would show up several times a week. For vaudeville Will had developed an act which he could slowly hone to sharpness. As the performer moved weekly from town to town, he changed the audience without the need of altering the act. Now, at the Frolic, the audiences changed little and could not be expected to laugh at the same jokes more than once. Ziegfeld, who was not exactly partial to comics in the first place, ordered that this cowboy be fired. Gene Buck had the unenviable job of executing the order. It is told that Rogers forestalled the entire unpleasantness. Buck, who had come to fire him, was immediately disarmed by a Will Rogers asking for a raise, and before Buck could sufficiently recover, Will informed him that from now on, following his wife's advice, he would comment nightly on the current news gleaned from the many papers he read every day. Gene Buck stalled the raise by saying that he wanted to await the reaction to the proposed format; he also delayed the order to fire Will.

Betty's advice changed Will's career. Will's shrewd, humorous, yet penetrating comments became the talk of a certain strata of society—the one that could afford the exclusive and high-priced *Ziegfeld Frolic*. But word of mouth spread Will's fame, and there never again was talk of firing Will. In fact, Will Rogers became the most loyal friend of Florenz Ziegfeld Jr. Will never made a joke about him, never called him either by the familiar "Ziggy" or "Flo"; it was always either "Mr.

The seven Blake sisters at the Blake home in Rogers, Arkansas. Left to right: Betty (Mrs. Will Rogers), Waite (Mrs. Arthur Ireland), Theda (called "Aunt Dick," never married), Virginia (Mrs. Bruce Quisenberry), Anna (Mrs. Lee Adamson), Cora (Mrs. Will Marshall), and Zuleki (Mrs. Everett Stroud).

Betty, Will, Mary,
and Bill.

Betty, Bill, and
Mary.

The Rogers family
with Will's sisters,
Sally and Maud.

Seegfield" or simply "boss." Will always felt that it was Ziegfeld who gave him the opportunity to move out of the ranks of the vaudevillians and gain stardom.

But in the fall of 1915, when Ziegfeld saw the early run-throughs of the new *Follies* in Atlantic City, he realized that the show was too heavy on musical production numbers and needed the addition of humor to lighten it. Florenz Ziegfeld Jr.

was still not thrilled by having an ungrammatical cowboy mixed in with his American beauties, but he was convinced by the customers' reactions. There was no doubt that this Westerner did appeal to an audience, even if Ziegfeld could not appreciate the man's humor. And forgetting that he had wanted this man fired only a few months before, he now approached Will with an offer to join the *Follies.*

Will discussed the offer with his wife. Betty was a realist. She pointed at the schedule of every *Follies* show, which played New York City in the summertime and then spent the months until the next spring touring America. It would mean, she contended, that Will would be away from her and the children for the better part of the year. She suggested quite strongly that Will should turn the offer down. This Will did, even though his own preference had been to reach out with both hands and grab what he considered to be a great opportunity.

Opening night of the new *Follies,* Will and Betty were at the theater. As the show unfolded, Will realized that it was beginning to slow down badly and needed a lift. During the intermission, Will and Ziegfeld met in the lobby. Again an offer was made for Will to join the show, and this time Will did not hesitate. He agreed. A verbal understanding was reached the next day at the Ziegfeld office. Will wanted no signed contracts. Legend has it that Will said: "You know you can trust me and I know I can trust you." Ziegfeld, totally unused to such vague commitments, called in a witness to see the two men shake hands.

At first, Betty was not pleased with Will's rash change of mind. As things developed, however, she reconciled herself to the changes brought about and the definite advance in their status. Becoming an almost "overnight" star in both the *Ziegfeld Frolic* and the *Ziegfeld Follies* brought with it fame and fortune. Will rented a house in what is now Kew Gardens, Queens, one of New York's boroughs. All seemed right with the world. He had two steady jobs, a loving wife, and three fine children. He was a favorite with the viewing public, and his father would have been justly proud of his son. But there were still mountains to scale.

One of those mountains resurfaced almost immediately. It should have been foreseen by either Ziegfeld or Rogers. The problem arose out of the practice by many *Follies* patrons, after seeing the show, to take the elevator to the roof of the New Amsterdam Theatre and frequent the Midnight Frolic. Obviously Will could not use the same jokes he had just delivered in the theater on the ground floor and expect the very same listeners to appreciate them again on the roof. It was necessary for Will to send out for the early editions of the morning newspapers and prepare an entirely new, fifteen- to twenty-minute act between his performances. On matinee days, Wednesdays and Saturdays, Will had to devise three different monologues. Perhaps the greatest appeal of Rogers's commentaries was their immediacy. The interval between the latest "Extra" edition of any of a dozen newspapers then in New York City and the corresponding Will Rogers comment on the stage of the New Amsterdam Theatre was often only a few minutes. It happened on some occasions that Will Rogers's comments were made onstage before the audience had even had a chance to read the latest newspaper, so they were not familiar with the basis for the quip. It must have been on one of those occasions that, after one of his appropriate jokes fell flat, Will had been heard to mutter: "I must be two editions ahead of you."

Being in the *Ziegfeld Follies* brought new associations. Eddie Cantor and W. C. Fields were already established performers in the show when Will joined them.

Master showman
Florenz Ziegfeld Jr.
and his wife,
famous actress
Billie Burke.

Yet there was little, if any, rivalry among them. Cantor maintained that Ziegfeld referred to his three funny men as "My Three Musketeers," but Will Rogers never mentioned it. He had first met Cantor touring in vaudeville, when young Eddie was a member of the group called Gus Edwards' Kid Kabaret. They had been friends, though it was more a father and son relationship. Cantor, raised by his grandmother, looked up to Rogers and introduced him to what passes as Jewish gourmet cooking. Rogers ate chopped liver and gefilte fish. Years later, when Rogers had to undergo a gallstone operation, he jokingly blamed Eddie's haute cuisine for it. Eddie also became responsible for Will's single foray into the bull stock market of the 1920s.

W. C. Fields, whose motto seemed to have been "Anybody who hates children and dogs can't be all bad," was a misanthrope. At one point Fields introduced a female visitor to Will Rogers. After spending a couple of minutes, Rogers excused himself. After he had left, the lady rhapsodized about Will and how she just adored his Western twang. Fields could not let her go on. "That son-of-a-bitch is a fake," he said. "I bet a hundred dollars that when he gets home, he talks just like everybody else."

Late in March, *The Ziegfeld Follies* closed its annual tour in Baltimore. This is the way W. C. Fields hazily remembered the story in an interview:

In those days I had a high-powered automobile. Ever since I had been able to afford one, I'd buy the best car on the market. I don't drive any more, and I give my chauffeur a lot of cautious instructions, but then I was a pretty good driver myself. The "Follies" went down to Washington for a performance, and I drove down. Coming back I offered to drive Will Rogers and a couple of other people. We hit a rock or had a blowout, or something. Anyway, the car went careening into a ditch, turned over, and distributed the passengers about the landscape.

I seemed to be intact, and so were the two other fellows, but poor Will had a broken leg. We hailed a passing car and hurried him to a nearby hospital.

Justifiably, Mr. Fields's recollection seems slightly suspect. There is no doubt that there was an accident, whatever its cause may have been. After all, the foregoing version was recounted by the man who had said: "Once in South Africa we went on a safari and they forgot to bring a corkscrew. For two weeks we had to survive on nothing but food and water." But Will's leg was not broken; his ankle was wrenched. Though in great pain, he was able to appear in the *Frolic* two days later.

Part of Will Rogers's rope act at the _Follies._

The United States entered the Great War on April 6, 1917. Will Rogers, though being thirty-seven years old, married, and having three children, registered for the draft. He also pledged $100 a week to the Red Cross. In New York City, Mayor Mitchell issued a wartime measure decreeing that no entertainment may start after midnight. To abide by that order, the Midnight Frolic had to open its doors a half hour earlier, which caused wags to rename it "The 11:30 P.M. Frolic."

Will Rogers became a most popular performer. Every charitable affair asked that he attend their reception or that he speak at their function, and Will obliged them as best he could. This demand for Will's assistance at local fund-raising events indicated recognition of the man as a major attraction. Among the many charities Will Rogers helped were the New Detroit Opera House, the Traffic Club of Chicago, the Jewish War Sufferers, the Salvation Army Drive, the Orthopedic Hospital for Crippled Children in Los Angeles, and the Stage Women's War Relief. Ethnicity, religion, or gender made no difference; Will felt that it was an honor to be asked, never that it was an imposition. If there was an occasional time when other famous people were asked to contribute their talent but he was not, Will Rogers wondered what he might have done to be so singled out. Often, he turned a request for his appearance at a benefit into one of his jests:

> I was called on to speak at the 30th anniversary of the Empire Theatre. I don't know why I should have been there; I had never played in that place. I suppose I really contributed more to its success by not playing there.
>
> The Barrymores and everybody of note in the theater were there, and a lot of critics. I was as much in the dark as to why a critic should be at a theater celebration as I was for being there myself. Their contribution to the success of most theaters is at about the same ration that a fire would be.

Will Rogers's rise to super-stardom seemed dramatic. Overlooked was the fact that he had served a long and hard apprenticeship. For years he had stayed in cheap hotels, eaten in assorted beaneries, moved from town to town, thoughtfully honed his talent for banter, practiced his roping till every muscle ached and his clothing was sweat-soaked. This was no overnight success story. Will Rogers had appeared in vaudeville for ten years, rehearsing for that day when someone like Florenz Ziegfeld Jr. would give him a chance to show what he could do. Even the usually thorough *New York Times* never recounted the years of hardship but made only note of the dramatic emergence of a new star. Repeatedly it would single him out in reviews, and on Sunday, June 10, 1917, it marked the anniversary of Rogers's addition to New York City's premier show, *The Ziegfeld Follies*: "... last season it was not until the middle of summer that Will Rogers, who was amusing Midnight audiences on the New Amsterdam Roof, was given a niche in the downstairs show. One performance showed that he distinctly belonged there, and he remained and now Mr. Rogers's name leads all the rest. ..."

Life now became a new routine. Seasons still changed according to Nature's dictates, but life at the Rogers household was now to be determined by the timetable of the Ziegfeld pro-

A *Ziegfeld Follies* skit.

ductions. Spring and summer were
spent in New York, as that was
where the *Follies* played then.
Come the fall, the *Follies* tour of
America began, invariably, with
Thanksgiving in Pittsburgh and
Christmas in Chicago. Will would
be away for months, with holidays
and birthdays observed without
him. Little Willie was now enrolled
in the local public school and Mary
would go the next year. Jimmy
still played in the backyard. Then,
on July 15, 1918, Betty gave birth
to the last child in the Rogers family. Because of Will's great friendship with Fred Stone, and perhaps
because Fred had talented daughters but no son, the baby was
given the name of Fred Stone

**Will during an early
morning practice
session, circa 1916.**

*Courtesy of the Will
Rogers Memorial
Commission*

Rogers. That was one way that his name would live on.

Will was being asked now to write for various publications. His *Says Will
Rogers* appeared in the *Chicago Examiner,* and his columns and interviews drew
readers across the country. Photographers and reporters followed him wherever
he went:

> *The question that every guy asked who used to come to interview me was: "Did you
> really come from out West?" I got so tired of hearing it that I used to tell them:
> "No, I'm from New Jersey, but don't you tell anybody."*

In 1918 Will added another career. Through his friendship with Fred Stone
and his wife, Allene, the Rogers family socialized with the famous author Rex
Beach and his wife, Edith, Allene's sister. There was talk that Sam Goldfish—who
eventually changed his name to Goldwyn—was going to film Rex Beach's book
Laughing Bill Hyde. The Beaches had seen not only the sketches in the *Follies,*
where Will had to act, but they had also seen the public's reaction to his persona.
There was something in Will that seemed to reach across the footlights and
embrace every member of the audience. It was an endearing quality, which made
him immediately likable and acceptable as a friend, a member of your family. It
was said that if you could design your own perfect uncle, Will would be the ideal.
It was that specific trait of instant affability which Edith and Rex Beach sought for
the part of "Bill Hyde."

> *Rex was responsible for my little toe hold on this eighth science. I played by request
> of Mrs. Rex Beach in one of his stories called, "Laughing Bill Hyde." The part
> was rather that of a crook, who received money under false pretenses. Mrs. Beach
> had seen my little act in the Follies, so she decided that I was the one to do natu-
> rally this crook who obtained money under false pretense.*

Sam Goldwyn obviously agreed with the suggested casting and arrangements were made to star Will Rogers in the silent film *Laughing Bill Hyde*, at the Goldwyn Studio in Fort Lee, New Jersey.

During the week of August 11, 1918, Florenz Ziegfeld Jr. released a stern warning through the New York City newspapers. He declared that he had exclusive contractual control of the professional services of every single member of the *Follies* cast, and that if any member attempted to appear in one of those new motion pictures without his permission, he, Ziegfeld, would obtain an injunction against the producer of any picture involved, and would initiate a lawsuit for damages against any theater exhibiting such a film.

Unperturbed, Will Rogers continued to commute early each morning to the studio. He never missed a single performance, whether matinee or evening, during the filming. He recalled his inauspicious entry into the celluloid world:

> I remember that first day. . . . It was now ten thirty and I thought I was late. We took the first scene at exactly three forty five in the afternoon. The director says: "Now, Will, we are going to take the scene where your old pal dies. You have broken out of jail and he gets hurt and you are bringing him into the Doctors office at night to get him treated and he dies. Its the dramatic scene of the whole opera." I says, "But I havent got out of jail yet." He says, "No, you won't for a couple of weeks yet. Besides the Jail is not built yet."
>
> Thats the first time I learned that they just hop around any old way. We took a scene, the start of a fellow and I fighting outdoors and a lot of rainy weather come and a week later he knocked me down in the same fight.
>
> The Director . . . warned me if I was thinking a thing the camera would show it. I told him I would try and keep my thoughts as clean as possible. He said, "Now we will rehearse the scene and then take it. Now carry your pal in. Ha! Wait a minute, you wouldent carry him in that way, would you? You will hurt him worse than he is even supposed to be in the story."
>
> I told him to change the story around and let me be hurt and him do the carrying, that the other fellow was the biggest. But those guys are set in their ways and wont change anything.
>
> Then we took it, him ballyhooing at me through a megaphone, just what to do. He says, "That's fine, very good!" Then I heard him say to the cameraman, "Mark this N. G." The next take I was really getting along fine on it, I was draming all over the place, holding this pal, a-pleading with the doctor to do something for him. My mind was more on my art than on the load I had and I dropped him.
>
> Well, I want to tell you folks, somebody could of bought my moving picture future pretty cheap right then. The Director kept impressing on me that my only pal was dying. Well, he dident have anything on me. I was almost dying. He looked and he saw I had tears in my eyes, and he says, "That's great!" He thought I was crying about my pal and I was crying about getting into the darn thing.

Yet even after Will thought that he had now learned enough lessons to sail along smoothly in his new craft, there were still the occasional major miscues:

> I went to the barber and got a hair cut right in the middle of the picture and like to spoiled it, I dident know what I was doing, (and here I was going in one door with

*long hair, and coming out with a hair cut). They all like to had a fit. I think yet it
was the best picture I ever made, for I hadent learned to try to act. There ain't
nothing worse than an actor when we act.*

One of the actresses on the film remembered that Sam Goldwyn, himself, had
to call for the makeup department to provide matching hair, which was then cut
to length and glued on the back of Will's head. Sam, contradictory to his public
image, was a perfectionist, and Will would never forget *Laughing Bill Hyde:*

*It was made for Mr. Sam Goldwyn, who has all these years remained the famous
producer. With producers coming and going, and changing, he has held his own
right at the top. He was my first picture boss, and we have remained friends all
these years, a rare combination.*

In August, the *New York Times* took note of the new direction of Will's talent
by musing: "It will be interesting to observe what Rogers can do when he can't
talk." *Laughing Bill Hyde* received both critical and popular acclaim.

The National Board of Review "enthusiastically terms" *Laughing Bill Hyde* "one
of the most powerful and appealing pictures we have ever seen. . . ." The Motion
Picture News wrote: "Will Rogers turns out to be such a fine screen actor that you
would never know he was acting." But as there seemed to be no follow-up, Will
joked about it: "I've been hearing a lot about how good I was," he said, "but I
notice nobody is making me any of those big offers to do another one. So I guess
that's the tip-off."

But the offer did come. Goldwyn proposed a two-year commitment, and on
November 18, 1918, the two men signed a contract under which Will would be
paid $2,250 per week for fifty-two weeks, with an option for his services for a sec-
ond year. Should that option be picked up, the salary would be $3,000 a week for
fifty-two weeks of the second year. There was only one stipulation that could
have caused a problem: Paragraph 7 called for Will to report to the Goldwyn studios in Culver City, California, no later than June 16, 1919.

The money offered was almost three times the Ziegfeld salary, but what
would Betty and the children say about moving to California? Betty immediately
saw that Southern California would be better for the children, that living in a
more temperate climate would be healthier, and she supported the move. It was
decided that Will would go there first, rent a house, and then the family plus
ponies and horses would follow. In the meantime Will gave notice that he would
stay with the *Follies* until the end of the current season. Despite the fact that
there was no written contract between Ziegfeld and Rogers, Will had kept his
word.

On May 31, a Saturday, Will officially gave his farewell performance in the
Follies. When the two men parted, Ziegfeld presented Will with a watch onto
which he had inscribed: "To Will Rogers, in appreciation of a great fellow, whose
word is his bond."

On Monday, June 2, Will made a surprise appearance at the Midnight Frolic,
and though not on the program or paid, he gave an impromptu performance. The
following night, Will was again at the show and pleasantly surprised the guests
with another special performance. The *New York Times* wrote that Will Rogers

Will's portrait from
the advertising
poster for *Laughing
Bill Hyde*, his first
motion picture,
1918.

"enjoyed the distinction of being the only entertainer extant who could even
make the waiters pause to give ear to his drolleries."

It was in 1919 that Harper & Brothers published the first two of Will Rogers's
books. Actually the contract between publisher and author called for a total of six
books. They were smaller than usual books and rather thin, a total of some forty

Filming with director Hobart Hanley (seated) and camera-man A. A. Cadwell, are "escaped prisoners" Dan Mason and Will Rogers. From *Laughing Bill Hyde*, 1918.

A still from *Laughing Bill Hyde*, 1918.

pages each. The price was sixty cents, not an inconsiderable sum in those days. The content was to be categorized funny lines that Will had spoken from the *Follies* stage or on the *Frolic*'s. The first two books—or rather booklets, even though they had hard covers—had a similarity of awkward titles: *Rogers-isms: The Cowboy Philosopher On The Peace Conference*, and *Rogers-isms: The Cowboy Philosopher On Prohibition*. But then a mystery developed. On a contract calling for a series of six such booklets, only two were ever printed. Yet the most respected and selective *Who's Who in America*, in several biannual editions, mentions the existence of a third book in this series, *What People Laugh At*. Was there ever such a manuscript? Where did that information come from, which appeared in a most checked and edited and rechecked publication?

The legal and physical battle for or against the enforcement of the Eighteenth Amendment to the Constitution, better known as Prohibition, caused much controversy in the land and gave Will endless material for his humor. Since he grew up in an area where illegal stills were used, whether alcoholic beverages were legal or not, the topic was familiar to him. He rarely drank, though there was liquor at his home for visitors all during Prohibition. Guests usually brought a bottle of illegal spirits as a "hostess gift." Rogers never took a position for or against Prohibition. It was his belief that drinking, or abstention, was a strictly private decision. He had no illusion about the amendment's lack of effectiveness and made light of polls:

The South is dry and will vote dry. That is, everybody that is sober enough to stagger to the polls will.

Even America's elected officials were not safe from his humor on that subject. Will knew exactly where to place the blame for the nonenforceable law:

Bill, Mary, and Jim Rogers.

Look at Congress—it votes dry and drinks wet.

Will left New York on June 5, for what he would later call "The Celluloid Coast" and "Divorce Divide." Hollywood was already gaining the enviable appellation of being the motion picture capital of the world, while simultaneously acquiring the unenviable reputation for being the center of short-lived marriages. Will would quip:

. . . you know, when you was [going to get] married you had to give three days' notice. You used to have to in this state, to give the intention of marrying. Well, they did away with that now. That was longer than most of the marriages in California was lasting. So they did away with that. So now you don't have to file any intention of marrying at all. In fact, you don't have to give your right name according to this new law. You just pay a small amusement tax is all.

Will was now just a few months short of his fortieth birthday. Men in most professions were at the peak of their careers, yet here was Will Rogers, just starting out on a brand new endeavor about which he had only an ill-defined idea: "I thought pictures were made up of just three people: Mary Pickford, Charlie

The Rogers family on Long Island, New York, around 1916 or 1917. Jimmy is in the front seat with his father; Mary and Bill are in the back seat with their mother.

Chaplin and Douglas Fairbanks." How was he to know that it was going to become the most important success of his life?

He went house hunting and rented a spacious two-story mansion on Van Ness Avenue. Having arranged everything necessary for the family's comfort, Will reported to the Goldwyn studios weeks ahead of the stipulated date, inadvertently upsetting production plans. But, as so often happened in Will Rogers's life, this setback turned to his advantage. He met with Clarence G. Badger, a director who understood him.

Page 71, "Leaving Rogers, Arkansas . . . ," *Will Rogers*, by Betty Rogers, © 1941.

Page 71, "It was nice then . . . ," ibid.

Page 72, "Will quietly hustled . . . ," ibid.

Page 72, "Years later . . . ," Weekly Article #563, October 8, 1933.

Page 75, "Tell me, Mrs. Rogers . . . ," *Will Rogers*, by Betty Rogers, © 1941.

Page 75, "Billy wants a boy . . . ," Betty Rogers's letter to C. V. Rogers, August 21, 1911.

Page 77, "It was the following . . . ," *Will Rogers*, by Betty Rogers, © 1941.

Page 83, "Daddy decided . . . ," Sterlings' interview with Dorothy Stone Collins, May 25, 1970.

Page 85, "Will rented a house . . . ," ibid.

Page 85, "It was that accident . . . ," ibid.

Page 87, ". . . my first car . . . ," Weekly Article #157, December 13, 1925.

Page 88, "Will Rogers, cowboy . . . ," *New York Herald*, July 23, 1915.

Page 88, ". . . they turned the lights out . . . ," Sterlings' interview with Dorothy Stone Collins, May 25, 1970.

Page 94, "I was called on . . . ," Weekly Article #8, February 4, 1923.

Page 95, "The question . . . ," *The Extemporaneous Line*.

Page 95, "Rex was responsible . . . ," Weekly Article #522, December 25, 1932.

Page 96, "I remember that first day . . . ," *T. G. P.* Article, 1933.

Page 96, "I went to the barber . . . ," Weekly Article #662, August 25, 1935 (posthumously published).

Page 97, "It was made . . . ," ibid.

Page 97, "The Motion Picture News . . . ," *Motion Picture News*, May 10, 1918.

Page 97, "But as there seemed . . . ," *New York Times*, October 13, 1918.

Page 97, "The *New York Times* . . . ," *New York Times*, June 8, 1919.

Page 99, "The South is dry . . . ," Daily Telegram #66, October 26, 1926.

Page 100, "Look at Congress . . . ," *Rogers-isms: The Cowboy Philosopher on Prohibition*, © 1919,

Page 100, "Will left New York . . . ," broadcast, January 28, 1934.

Page 100, ". . . you know, when you . . . ," Good Gulf broadcast, May 19, 1935.

Page 100, "Men in most . . . ," *Motion Picture Classic*, November 1918.

A publicity still for Goldwyn's silent film *Jubilo*, 1919.

"Galloping Pictures"

"Old Hollywood is just like a desert water hole in Africa. Hang around long enough and every kind of animal in the world will drift in for refreshments."

Preparing for Will Rogers's arrival, the Goldwyn Studio brain trust had held a conference. It was agreed that while he had a brilliant mind, was a very funny humorist, and was famous in certain areas of the United States, his forté was cerebral jocularity rather than physical—that is to say, a visual one. It was obvious that his major appeal lay in the one talent which films were not yet able to present—his verbal patter. What then to do with the star of one medium that Hollywood could not yet exploit? For that matter, why did Sam Goldwyn ever sign Will Rogers in the first place? What was one to do with him? Of course, it could be argued that *Laughing Bill Hyde* had been a successful experiment, and that it had shown that Will could do more than just hold his own against other actors, but that could have been a onetime fluke. In any case, now that he was under contract, it was decided that Will would not be presented on film as being a run-of-the-mill comic. That would be left to the way silent humor was usually depicted on the screen—by slapstick, pratfalls, ineptness, and pie-in-the-face. The humor Will would be expected to provide would be restricted to the development of the plot, and to those panels that, in silent films, served as either conversation or thought. Those could—and would—be mostly written by Rogers. And so Will was ascribed the character of a wise, kindly, lovable man not always treated fairly by fate, though he did receive justice or its bountiful rewards by the end of the last reel. In other words, Hollywood realized that it was best to present the man he was, the real Will Rogers. It was not only typecasting but, as some wise observer noted, it presented Will Rogers to the viewing public as the one American believed by other Americans to be the representation of them all.

Will Rogers on film was probably best described by a *New York Times* review:

Rogers is becoming for many one of the established screen characters. His personality is a substantial thing, apparently, that can be photographed—at any rate. It emerges from his figure on the screen—and, contrary to rather the positive expectation of some, he has distinct pantomimic ability. His smile, his homeliness, his awkward manner, his odd gestures are, of course, part of his make-up, but if they were

The Rogers home in
Beverly Hills. It was
the first home Will
and Betty owned.

*an end in themselves they would soon become tiresome. Their charm is in the fact
that they serve to cover thoughts and feelings; they are expressive. In other words,
Rogers acts. He usually impersonates the same character—it may be himself—but
he makes it live and have meaning. It is genuine.*

The first film planned in California for the new Goldwyn star was to be *Almost
a Husband*, based on the story *"Old Ebenezer"* by Opie Read. Will's co-star was
Peggy Wood, the singer and actress. As Sam Goldwyn had drawn up the production schedule, the director of Rogers's first film was to be Victor Schertzinger. But
since Will appeared three weeks ahead of schedule and his contract period was
to start as of the day he walked on the set, there was an immediate problem.
Schertzinger was in the middle of an important feature and would not be available for several weeks. Sam Goldwyn had to act fast. He switched the directorial
duties for *Almost a Husband* to Clarence G. Badger. Clarence could not have been
happier. He had come to believe that he was condemned for eternity to grinding
out meaningless comedies. He did not know Will personally but had seen him on
stage numerous times, and when he heard that Rogers had been signed by the
studio "would gladly have given my eye teeth to be his director."

The plot of *Almost a Husband* was improbable, yet uncomplicated: Sam Lyman
(Will) takes a job as a schoolteacher in a small town in the South. During a forfeit
parlor game at a social gathering, the penalty for Sam and Eva (Peggy Wood), the
banker's daughter, is to go through a mock marriage ceremony, performed by the
first man to enter the house. This turns out to be a newly ordained minister, and
the ceremony is perfectly legal. Zeb Sawyer, who has been pursuing Eva without
her encouragement, demands that Eva divorce Sam at once. But Eva, to avoid the

Jimmy, Bill, and Mary in a horse-drawn cart with Betty on the Goldwyn studios lot.

unwanted suitor forced on her for financial reasons by her father, asks Sam not to release her. Zeb now sets night riders on Sam and decides to ruin Eva's father, banker McElwyn, by starting a run on his bank. Sam, having just sold a novel and thus having cash on hand, and by a ruse of pretending to bring new money into the bank, saves McElwyn, and then musters enough courage to propose to Eva, who he had secretly loved.

Will enjoyed his work with director Clarence G. Badger, and told Sam Goldwyn that he would like this harmonious collaboration to continue. Ordinarily actors, even ascending stars, did not yet request directors, but Goldwyn saw to it that throughout the rest of Will's contract, Badger was his director.

Whatever it was that had prompted Sam Goldfish to sign Will Rogers was proven as shrewd recognition of movie potential with the reviews of *Almost a Husband*. The *Motion Picture News* of October 25, 1919, wrote: "The inimitable Will Rogers . . . has the gift of perfect composure, which, with his seeming indifference, gives the impression of simplicity and spontaneity, the two highest attributes of an actor's art."

Building on the critical success of his first film under the Goldwyn banner, *Jubilo* went into production. This was based on a very popular *Saturday Evening Post* story by Ben Ames Williams. It tells of a good-natured hobo, who's named Jubilo by his fellow hoboes for his cheery habit of singing the old spiritual of that same name. Jubilo witnesses a train robbery. Fearing distressing involvement with the law if he were to come forward and testify, he moves on. In his wandering he comes to a ranch where he asks for food. He is taken in, fed, and treated kindly by the owner and his daughter. Asked to help out, he breaks his hobo habit and for the first time performs manual labor. While helping the rancher out of his difficulties, and repaying him for his kindness, he falls in love with the daughter and asks her to marry him.

Throughout his film career, Will Rogers liked the idea of playing hoboes— indeed he played several. He would even play Jubilo again in a sound film. Will

Lunch break for the cast and crew of *Jubilo*, 1919.

was happy working on this story until word came from the front office that Goldwyn was going to rename the film. Rogers, who had grown up singing spirituals and like many Americans loved the song "Jubilo," was upset about the proposal of a name change. He sent Goldwyn, who happened to be in New York, a telegram.

Samuel Goldwyn
469 Fifth Avenue
New York City, NY   *October 17, 1919.*

Thought I was to be a comedian but when you suggest changing the title of Jubilo you are funnier than I ever was. I dont see how Lorimer of the Saturday Evening Post ever let it be published under that title. That song is better known through the South by older people than Geraldine Farrar's husband. we have used it all through business in the picture but of course we can change that to "Everybody Shimmy Now." suppose if you had produced "The Miracle Man" you would have called it "A Queer Old Guy." but if you really want a title for the second picture I would suggest "Jubilo." also the following:

A Poor But Honest Tramp
He Lies But He Dont Mean It
A Farmer's Virtuous Daughter
The Great Train Robbery Mystery
A Spotted Horse But He Is Only Painted
A Hungry Tramp's Revenge
The Vagabond With A Heart As Big As His Appetite
He Loses In The First Reel But Wins In The Last
The Old Man Left But The Tramp Protected Her
What would you have called "The Birth Of A Nation"?

Will Rogers.

Will's mockery and ultimate logic were not lost on Goldwyn, and the film was released under its original title. There was no further discussion on this, though a minor problem did arise the following year. The year 1920 was a presidential election year. The Republican National Convention was set for early June in Chicago; the Democratic counterpart was scheduled to open June 28, in San Francisco. Will Rogers had committed himself to cover both for the Newspaper Enterprise Association (NEA). As he was in the midst of shooting *Honest Hutch* on location near San Francisco, Will had been confident that the schedule could be worked around him while he was briefly away, if not in Chicago, then surely in nearby San Francisco. The decree from the front office, however, was a firm rejection of his request. Perhaps this was just a quid pro quo repayment for the embarrassment caused when Will publicly forced Goldwyn to back down and keep *Jubilo* as the name for Will's film. Possibly, the decision was really based on economic or logistic necessities. Whatever the real reason, Will was prevented from attending either national political convention.

Betty with five-year-old Mary.

Not being able to observe the conventions in person, Will arranged with the NEA that he would furnish at least ten gags daily. The column, titled *Will Rogers Says*, introduced Will as "Unbranded Famous Oklahoma Cowboy Wit and Goldwyn Motion Picture Star." Will admitted immediately that he was not attending the Chicago convention; he professed that in order to obtain correct inside information, he had gone instead directly to the powerful Senator Boies Penrose of Pennsylvania, generally considered one of the "king makers" in the Republican party. Familiarizing himself with the previous day's major news stories or events at the convention, as gleaned from newspaper reports, he would then pretend to ask Senator Penrose leading questions and elicit his own humorous answers. What he was doing now was almost the same routine he had followed when preparing for his nightly Ziegfeld shows. He would read the papers, pick his topics and then think up his jokes; however, unlike his Ziegfeld shows, where he would add his personal touch and Oklahoma twang, he would now simply telegraph his gags into NEA's editorial offices.

He frequently "tested" his gags on whoever was near at hand when he finished his list. If his fellow actors or the technicians or grips laughed and understood them, all was well. If they did not, he would make up new gags. These are some of the quips he eventually sent on:

The only way to keep a Governor from becoming a Senator is to sidetrack him off into the Presidency.
   "But," I asked him, "isn't the Presidency higher than Senator?"

*He said, "Why, no; the
Senate can make a sucker out
of the President—and generally does."*

Grandma Blake
reading to the
children.

*I asked Pen: "How does it
come the New York delegates
are practically uninstructed."*

Boies remarked to me: "You can't instruct a New Yorker, he knows it all."

*Mexico don't know how to get rid of [Pancho] Villa. Loan him to us for a Vice-
President. That would get both nations rid of him.*

California appeared to have been a fortunate choice as the new home base of
the Rogers family. Will was to be busy making films for Goldwyn, Betty had four
children to raise in the land of three-quarters sunshine and one-quarter rainy season, and the children had the whole outdoors for their playground. There were
swimming pools and riding rings; it was a paradise. It all was just too perfect to
last. It didn't.

In mid-June 1920, while Will was still on location near San Francisco, shooting *Honest Hutch,* his three sons developed sore throats—or at least what was
thought to be just sore throats. Quite late their illness was correctly diagnosed as
diphtheria. Will was immediately notified and drove all night, racing 600 miles
south over country roads, to his dangerously ill children. When he arrived at his
home at 4 A.M., the youngest, twenty-three-month-old Freddy, had died.

Though the Democratic National Convention was not to open until June 28,
Will's first column had to be filed that day. In an incredible act of concentration
and stoicism Will found the inner strength to sit down at his typewriter and compose his jokes for NEA. He had signed a contract and he was obligated; he had to
deliver. His emotional state can easily be discerned when the original columns he
typed that day are examined. Will had developed a unique typing style—usually
all capitals, and when his "hunt-and-peck" system hit a wrong key, Will would
not correct it. His unorthodox spelling and his bizarre punctuation were even

worse than his carefree grammar and syntax. Unlike the usual practice of typing only on one side of the paper, now Will would type on both sides. On that day he would begin some sheets on one end of the paper and type toward the middle; then, for whatever reason, he would take the sheet from the typewriter, reverse it and type from the opposite end toward the middle.

Will Rogers acting for his family in their home theater.

Courtesy of the Will Rogers Memorial Commission

Young Will Jr. and Jimmy recovered, while Fred Stone Rogers's death became a topic that was from then on carefully avoided. The little boy's existence was almost denied. In the two million words Will Rogers would write in his lifetime, little Freddy is referred to just twice, but neither time by name. In the weekly article of May 11, 1924, Will had been writing humorously about the shooting of cattle as the accepted "medical" treatment for hoof-and-mouth disease, a serious plague affecting cloven-hoofed animals. Obviously still in deep sorrow and anger over the fact that anti-diphtheria serum had not been readily available for his sons when Freddy's life could have been saved, he lashed out—though never alluding to his own emotional involvement:

The three children (left to right: Jim, Mary, Will Jr.) on stage performing for their parents.

Courtesy of the Will Rogers Memorial Commission

If your hog has the cholera the whole state knows it and everybody is assisting in stamping it out. You can have 5 children down with the infantile paralysis, more deadly 10 times over than any foot and mouth disease, and see how many doctors they send out from Washington to help you. . .

How many children die every day from some contagious disease, that would be living if we exercised the same vigilance over a child that we do over a cow?

The other time little Freddy is referred to is in an illusory letter to Will's friend, the famous Western artist Charles M. Russell, who had just recently died. Will, in a most revealing display of love and tenderness, asks Russell, who now resides "up there," to deliver messages to his father, mother, and sisters and

. . . when you see a cute looking little rascal running around there kiss him for me. Well cant write you any more Charley dam paper's all wet, It must be raining in this old bunk house.

Will called their Beverly Hills home "The House That Jokes Built." The riding ring is in the foreground.

There are no baby photographs of little Fred Stone Rogers, and there are no open reminders anywhere in the Rogers home. If there ever was a drawer somewhere in which a grieving mother had kept little Freddy's clothes, or first shoes, it is not known. There are no mementos in the ranch house in Pacific Palisades, California, which has been kept to this day as if the family had just left a few minutes ago and would return momentarily. His name appears nowhere, not even on his last resting place, which is in the family crypt on the grounds of the Will Rogers Memorial and Birth Place, in Claremore, Oklahoma. Without details, a massive granite block simply bears the name "Rogers." Though there are no visible reminders of Freddy, there is no doubt that either Betty or Will ever failed to think of the little child they lost.

Providing humorous panels for Goldwyn films did not seem enough exercise for Will's wit. In one of its headlines *Variety*—metaphorically speaking—reported: "Will Rogers Talks for Gaumont." The publication explained further that "the Gaumont people are to add a monologue feature to their News and Graphic releases. Will Rogers is to do the talking for them on matters topical. In this they are following the Aaron Hoffman idea of the *Topplitsky Says* series." In an earlier letter dated February 18, 1920, the details state that each week, for a salary of $750, Will would furnish fifteen original gags and 100 feet of film to the Consolidated Film Company in San Francisco.

What all that meant was simply that under the title of *The Illiterate Digest*, Will just provided the same type of humorous comments he had used on the Ziegfeld stage. Only now there were filmstrips shown in motion picture houses, silent of course, and the remarks had to be read while photos of Will accompanied the words. He was prominently identified as a Goldwyn star, which gave free publicity to his studio. Here are just some of those remarks:

- Prohibition has done one thing; it has drove the price of whisky up.
- Headline in paper says: THIEVES GET $2000 WORTH OF LIQUOR—must have taken two bottles.
- Everybody is trying to solve the traffic problem. If the prices of automobiles keep on going up that will solve the traffic problem itself.
- At the Convention Ohio claims that they are due a president as they havent had one since Taft, but look at the United States, it hasn't had one since Lincoln.
- Headline says: Bandits from other cities are coming to L.A. The landlords here are going to have competition.
- Rich New York divorcee sues for more alimony, claims she cant support their child on 50 thousand a year. Somebody's feeding that kid meat.
- Be a good joke on Ireland if England said: We give you freedom just like America, including prohibition.

The strip, though popular, did not run too long. There were two reasons for its demise, and both are explained by an exchange of letters. The first letter was from a Mr. William Beverly Winslow, a New York lawyer who represented the Funk & Wagnalls Company, publishers of *The Literary Digest*. In his letter Mr. Winslow stated that his client had requested him to write to Rogers "in regard to

Betty, Mary, Jimmy, and Bill. Horseback riding was a common activity at the Beverly Hills home.

your use of the phrase *The Illiterate Digest,* as a title to a moving picture subject gotten up by you, the consequences of which may have escaped your consideration."

Mr. Winslow then proceeded to point out that his client had for the past two years presented a filmstrip *Topics of the Day,* selected from the press of the world by *The Literary Digest.* He went on to make his case by cordially enumerating facts which were to prove that by Will's use of the words *Illiterate Digest,* the prestige of his client's *Literary Digest* was "being lowered."

The second letter was the response, in which Will Rogers used the most effective weapon—humor—to disarm Mr. Winslow, and through him, Mr. Winslow's client:

> *Los Angeles, Cal.*
> *Nov. 15, 1920.*
>
> *Mr. Wm. Beverly Winslow*
>
> *Dear Sir,*
>
> *Your letter in regard to my competition with the Literary Digest received and I never felt as swelled up in my life. And I am glad you wrote directly to me instead of communicating with my Lawyers, As I have not yet reached that stage of prominence where I was committing unlawful acts and requiring a Lawyer. Now if the Literary Digest feels that the competition is too keen for them—to show you my good sportsmanship I will withdraw, In fact I had already quit as the gentlemen who put it out were behind in their payments and my humor kinder waned, in fact after a few weeks of no payments I couldent think of a single joke. And now I want to inform you truly that this is the first that I knew my Title of the Illiterate Digest was an infringement on yours as they mean the direct opposite. If a magazine was published called Yes and another Bird put one out called No I suppose he would be infringing. But you are a Lawyer and its your business to change the meaning of words, so I lose before I start.*
>
> *Now I have not written for these people in months and they havent put any gags out unless it is some of the old ones still playing. If they are using gags that I wrote on topical things 6 month ago then I must admit that they would be in competition with the ones the Literary Digest Screen uses now. I will gladly furnish you*

Mary, Jim, and Bill. Will is in the background, preparing to mount his horse.

with their address, in case you want to enter suit, And as I have no Lawyer you can take my case too and whatever we get out of them we will split at the usual Lawyer rates of 80-20, the client of course getting the 20,

Now you inform your Editors at once that their most dangerous rival has withdrawn, and that they can go ahead and resume publication, But you inform Your clients that if they ever take up Rope Throwing or chewing gum that I will consider it a direct infringement of my rights and will protect it with one of the best Kosher Lawyers in Oklahoma.

Your letter to me telling me I was in competition with the Digest would be just like Harding writing to Cox and telling him he took some of his votes,

So long Beverly if you ever come to California, come out to Beverly where I live and see me

Illiterately yours

WILL ROGERS.

Will never again heard from Funk & Wagnalls, and he wrote off his own letter as a misspent effort on someone without a sense of humor.

I was sore at myself for writing it. About 6 months later I came back to join the Follies and who should come and call on me but the nicest old Gentleman I had ever met, especially in the law profession. He was the one I had written the letter to, and he had had Photographic Copies made of my letter and had given them around to all his lawyer friends.

> *So it is to him and his sense of humor, that I dedicate this Volume of deep thought. I might also state that the Literary Digest was broad-minded enough to realize that there was room for both, and I want to thank them for allowing me to announce my Illiteracy publicly.*

This exchange of letters would serve Will Rogers some years later as "Two Letters and a Dedication" for one of his books, called *The Illiterate Digest.* It contained about thirty weekly articles and illustrations. Even though this book featured the identical syndicated newspaper articles that had only recently appeared in hundreds of newspapers in the United States and Canada, it sold extremely well in both countries.

Sam Goldwyn had picked up the option to extend Will Rogers's contract into the second year. The films were artistically praised both for Will Rogers's performances and their production values. Some received high praises, such as *Doubling for Romeo,* which was on the *Photoplay* list of Best Pictures of 1922, and named number eight of the Year's Best Films by *The Reel Journal,* both prestigious publications. But all that praise did not convince Will. In an interview he explained his view of himself:

> *I'm not an actor. I'm a rope thrower. I can't act. I can't be nothing but myself. And I don't aim for an argument with a picture taker, but I can't see any sense in an awkward maverick like me tryin' to look sweet and pretty before a camera.*

The Goldwyn company was getting deeper into serious financial trouble now. Financial records, if they are to be believed, show that Goldwyn lost less than $41,000 on the twelve films Will Rogers made for him under the contract. This would average about $3,400 per film. Will's salary during those two years of the contract was $273,000, or less than $23,000 per film. The motion picture industry is famous for its creative bookkeeping. To claim a loss of just $41,000 over a two-year period on twelve projects, on which the star received more than a quarter-million dollars, would not pass an Internal Revenue audit unchallenged. There was obvious gross mismanagement, what with hundreds of actors, technicians, writers, editors, suppliers, and relatives. It would not be long before Sam Goldwyn's studio would lose its identity and become part of Metro-Goldwyn-Mayer, with Sam Goldwyn being forced out of the new company to become an independent producer.

At the expiration of his contract, Will Rogers, too, was out, no new contract having been offered. Will went back to New York City, where a number of offers awaited him. And

Will and Betty taking a swim at their Beverly Hills home.

then, of course, there was an idea that Will had fostered for some time—that he would produce his own "galloping pictures."

Will had coined that phrase because when those early films were shown in motion picture houses, there was an unevenness of the flow from one frame to the next. Since cameras were activated by a cameraman turning a crank by hand, the quality of evenness depended on the steadiness of the operator. Every one of them surely tried to keep an absolutely even speed, but human muscles are subject to a number of influences, and the slightest variation in speed would project itself on the screen in magnification. Watching early films, this jerking—or as Will said, galloping—action of frames is obvious.

Will giving Mary a ride on his back in the pool.

The *New York Times* of July 10, 1921, announced that Will Rogers would head his own company, producing two-reel comedies. The article also mentioned Clarence G. Badger in connection with this project. As Will had been most comfortable with this director at the Goldwyn studio, it made sense that he would want him for his own films. Apparently Clarence had been approached and was willing to come to work with the new company—if and when it was formed. But first, there were an exasperating number of legal and business routines to be observed, licenses and insurance coverage to be obtained, staff to be hired, and a dozen or two other details which had not been expected but kept cropping up.

While the envisioned Rogers film enterprise was slowly shaping up back home in Los Angeles, there was the matter of earning an income. Will found that quite easy. He appeared for the Shubert organization. There was the Crescent Theatre in Brooklyn and then at the Winter Garden Theatre in Manhattan, where Will appeared nightly. Then Flo Ziegfeld wanted Will for performances at the Midnight Frolic, which now started at 11:00 P.M. As the times of Will's appearances at the various places did not conflict, he could work for the Shuberts and Flo on the same evenings. Will, being by himself, now stayed at the famous Astor Hotel right on Times

Square. His commute to either the Winter Garden or Ziegfeld's New Amsterdam Theatre was just a matter of a few blocks in either direction.

Betty and the children stayed in California. As it was thought that Will's junket into New York would only last until all formalities for the film company were completed, it made little sense to uproot an entire household. Who could have foreseen that this trip would extend into many months?

In December 1921, Rogers made his shuttle arrangements more difficult by tightening his schedule. He took on personal appearances, each to last only a few minutes, at various Loew's Theatres around town, while spending twenty minutes at the Midnight Frolic. An evening's timetable looked like this: His first show was at Loew's Metropolitan in Brooklyn at 8:00 P.M.; next he was booked at Greely Square in Manhattan at 8:30; then at American and Roof at 9:00; and Loew's State at 9:30. Then it was off to the Frolic at

Jim and Mary playing in the sand at the Beverly Hills home.

Jim and Mary on the swimming pool slide.

11:00. Other weeks the theatres where he was to appear would change, but not the time schedule. It became quite challenging not to be late. Of course, at all these places Will could use the same material, but it had to be fresh daily. The Loew's chain paid Will $1,500 a week, while Ziegfeld paid $1,000. The total was less than Goldwyn had paid, but then there was a difference between the return that a motion picture could earn with thousands of performances and that of a live show, which was gone when the theater emptied.

On Monday, January 9, 1922, Will Rogers joined the touring *Ziegfeld Follies* in Philadelphia. There was now a brand-new business understanding between the two men. It was an agreement rarely, if ever, heard in those days. Will Rogers, now a movie star, would be paid a minimum guar-

Will and Mary playing in the family sandbox.

antee of $500 plus 10 percent of the gross. That first week in Philadelphia, for example, Will's percentage was $1,450, while the second week was an even better $1,876.80. The following month, when the Follies played Washington, D.C., Will's share for the week ending February 11, 1922, rose to $2,519.30. For the rest of the tour, Will's percentage share was always close to $2,000 per week.

Returning to New York, Will was still busy in Ziegfeld's shows, with audiences standing four deep in the back of the theater. He spent the daylight hours making an independently produced film, *The Headless Horseman (The Legend of Sleepy Hollow)*, in which Will portrayed Ichabod Crane. Because location shots were conveniently scheduled for nearby Sleepy Hollow, New York, and Hackensack, New Jersey, Will could easily be back for evening performances.

Carl Stearns Clancy, the film's producer, who paid almost $20,000 for Will's services, told of a whimsical episode that had not been planned. It seems that in the sequence in which the conceited Bram Bones intends to intimidate the already fainthearted schoolmaster Crane by having his friends ride by his home at night, pretending to be members of the Headless Horseman's brotherhood, one of the stunt men failed to show up. Will Rogers offered to fill in. Changing his clothes, he joined the extras and together they all thundered several times past the camera, until the director felt he had enough variations and angles to cover the ride.

When the scene was edited, the director intercut a sequence showing Ichabod Crane's reaction to the night riders. Will's Crane, on hearing the sound of the "ghostly" hoof beats—provided partly by himself as one of the riders—is shown taking a flying leap into his bed, pulling the covers over his head. When Will saw the edited sequence later, so Clancy recalled, he was highly amused at the fact that here he was, shown both scaring and being scared. After all, as Will Rogers

Will Rogers and
Snowy Baker teach-
ing rope tricks to
Will Jr. and Jim.

Will as chef at an
outdoor grill.

said about motion pictures on another occasion, "It's the grandest show business I know . . . where an actor can act and at the same time sit down in front and clap for himself."

When all the legalities had been properly observed, and the Rogers film company was ready for operation, Will returned to California. It had taken so much longer than he had thought:

Well, folks, I am writing my little Swan Song to New York. I am like Merton of the movies; I am going out into the broad spaces. I have been for 52 weeks, one solid year telling my mangy little jokes to Broadway. I only came into New York expecting to stay three or four months. They have been mighty good to me here . . .

Will Rogers was now going to learn that there was more to the motion picture production business than just telling a good story on celluloid. No matter how well you may tell that story, if nobody gets to see it, you might as well have saved money and effort. Will's first project was a simple story to record for all time his dexterity with the lasso. The cast for *The Ropin' Fool* included beautiful Irene Rich, who appeared in so many of Will Rogers's films as his wife that Will—who loved puns—dubbed her his "reel wife." Also in the cast was Guinn Williams, whom Will had taken under his wing. Though a grown man, he appeared to Will like a "big boy," and as he was often a visitor at the Rogers home, Will simply called him "Big Boy." That name was shortened to just "Big," and to the Rogers children he was "Uncle Big." The name "Big Boy" appeared so apt that it became generally adopted, and for the rest of his career—which was extensive—his film credits would list him as Guinn (Big Boy) Williams.

Will and the children playing on the swings at their Beverly Hills home.

Will with Jim and Mary.

For his spectacular lasso demonstration in *The Ropin' Fool,* Will used his rider from the old vaudeville days, Buck McKee. To make the catches show up better, they chose a little black pony named Dopey. ("We called him Dopey, but we meant no disrespect to him.")

Will used white shoe polish to make the rope distinct as it would swirl around the little black horse. To show the intricacies of a simple rope swishing at great speed through the air, Will used—what was then—a new procedure called "slow motion." It is still exciting to watch Will perform with seeming ease those catches that made him so famous in vaudeville. *The Ropin' Fool* is still available today, and is probably the most popular Will Rogers legacy.

Two more projects were filmed. *Fruits of Faith* and *One Day in 365* (working titles were *Home Folks* and *No Story At All).* The former, a short, was a stirring tale of faith that was so powerful it overshadowed most feature films that followed it on the same program. The latter never reached completion. By this time most of the family's assets had been liquefied to meet rapidly mounting expenses, but still, debts were piling up. Will had produced two quality short films, but had no means for profitable distribution. Large production companies were not about to allow an upstart to profit from their investments and outlets. This was still the time when the major producers had their own motion picture theaters. Years later the courts would break up these restrictive ownerships.

Bankruptcy was never an option for Will. His innate character and upbringing would not allow him to cause others to lose money on him. He arranged with his creditors that he would go back to New York City, where he would earn enough to pay off every dollar of his indebtedness. New York City had always been good to him.

With Betty, he decided that the family should stay in California, while he would go back to Broadway. The Rogers family was through with producing films. From now on, if someone wanted Will in motion pictures, they would have to come to him. The Good Lord obviously did have it in mind for Will Rogers to be a star, but not a producer as well.

And so it was back to The Great White Way. The year 1922 was another election year, and Congressman Ogden Mills from New York City's Upper East Side silk-stocking district was running for reelection. Theodore Roosevelt Jr. asked Will if he would consider coming to Town Hall to address a fundraising gathering for a family friend. Will wanted to refuse. He had always tried to appear unaligned and absolutely neutral as far as either political party was concerned, and this speech could be misunderstood. But Will replied that he would come to Town Hall, and excused his seeming Republican partisanship by declaring that "A Roosevelt hint is the same as one of my wife's commands."

Will had never met the candidate and he made no secret of it:

> *I have spoken in all kinds of joints, from one of Mrs. Vanderbilt's parties on Fifth Avenue to Sing Sing in Ossining, but this is my first crack at a political speech and I hope it flops. I don't want to go over and then have to go into politics, because up to now I have always tried to live honest.*
>
> *A great many think I was sent here by Mr. Mills' opponent, but this is not the case. I don't know his opponent. But he must be a 'scoundrel.' From what I read of politics, every opponent is. . . .*
>
> *Mr. Mills is quite a novelty. He is one of the few men that didn't go into politics through necessity. He was wealthy when he started. Not as wealthy as he is now but he had some money, and he went into politics to protect it.*
>
> *I don't know the man, that is why they have asked me to come here and speak, because I was perhaps better qualified to say something nice than some one who did know him.*

Will spoke substantially more, but that was his style and when it was all over, Will could say with absolute assurance: "The poor fellow, he don't know it yet whether I am for him or against him." Whichever Will was, Mr. Mills did win the election and was returned to Congress. Ten years later he became U.S. Secretary of the Treasury.

When *The Headless Horseman* opened at the Capitol Theatre in New York City on November 5, 1922, Will was busy at the Harris Theatre on West 42nd Street donating his time at a benefit for Hebrew orphans. Completing his performance, he had to rush up the street to the New Amsterdam Theatre, where the Follies had already begun. During all this time, just around the corner on Times Square, *The Headless Horseman* was playing to a sold-out house.

The Mills speech had unexpected consequences: Will Rogers was flooded with requests to address every benevolent organization and—as he said—every group of manufacturers of goods that the American people could very well get along without.

Unlike other public speakers, Will did not have a pat speech that he would deliver at every opportunity. Instead he would give considerable thought and time to make each speech individual to suit the occasion. His fee was $1,000 per speech, and organizations and conventions lined up to have him be their guest speaker. After all, they did not want him to enlighten them. They had those dull, motivational shop talks all day long. The high point of any convention is the

A Goldwyn Pictures publicity insert card sold with Neilson's chocolate bars.

festive banquet. They all had come to New York City to have some fun, to be entertained, to enjoy themselves. What a thrill it would be to return home—wherever that was—and be able to claim: "We had Will Rogers entertain us! No! Not at the theater. He came to our dinner. I was as close to him as I am to you right now!" Several of these speeches were recorded by the Victor Talking Machine company on 78 rpm recordings and are now collector's items.

Will's speech to the Bankers' Association had their attention immediately:

> *Loan Sharks and Interest Hounds! I have addressed every form of organized graft in the United States—excepting Congress. So it is naturally a pleasure for me to appear before the biggest.*
>
> *You are without a doubt the most disgustingly rich audience I ever talked to, with the possible exception of the Bootleggers Union No. 1, combined with the enforcement officers.*
>
> *Now I understand you hold this convention every year to announce what the annual gyp will be. I have often wondered where the depositors hold their conven-tion. . . . I see where your convention was opened by a prayer and you had to send outside your ranks to get somebody that could pray. You should have had one cred-itor here, he would have shown how to pray.*

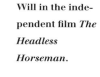

Will in the inde-pendent film *The Headless Horseman.*

Lois Meredith and Will in *The Headless Horseman.*

A poster for *The Headless Horseman,* 1922.

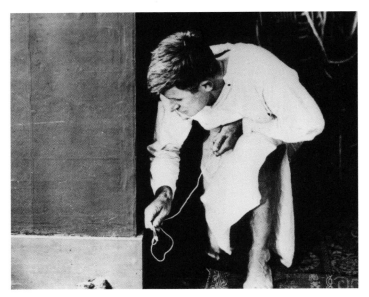

A still of Will from
The Ropin' Fool.

I noticed that in the prayer the clergyman announced to the Almighty that the bankers were here. Well, it wasn't exactly an announcement, it was more in the nature of a warning. He dident tell the devil, he figured the devil knew where you were all the time. . . .

Will you please tell me what you do with all the vice-presidents a bank has? I guess that's to get you more discouraged before you can see the president. Why, the United States is the biggest business institution in the world and they only have one vice-president, and nobody has ever found anything for him to do. . . .

You have a wonderful organization. I understand you have ten thousand here and with what you have in various Federal prisons that brings your membership up to around thirty thousand. So, good-bye paupers, you are the finest bunch of Shylocks that ever foreclosed a mortgage on a widow's home.

The week before Christmas Will added another accomplishment to his already multifaceted career. His first "Weekly Article" appeared in syndication by the McNaught Syndicate. It would be the official beginning of his highly successful writing career. He had previously written two columns—one called *The Worst Story I Heard Today*, the other based on a fictitious discussion of the recent news between a cowboy named Powder River Powell and Soapy, the local barber, during the cowboy's weekly clean-up visits—but they used artificial formats, which, while humorous, hid Will's greatest asset: his humanness. In the new column, Will Rogers talked to his reader, one-to-one, telling you what he had done since you had read him last, a week ago. This weekly article became a favorite tradition and created an audience that wanted to meet him. In the larger cities as well as in the smaller towns, these weekly articles were eagerly read, for they not only entertained but also brought the news into focus, explained it, endorsed it or criticized it. Men and women who had never seen him in a film wanted to know what this man—who spoke directly to them, who was one of them, who did not pretend to be smarter than them, and who did not talk down to them—looked like. Charles Wagner, a packager of lecturers, saw the possibilities in a tour. It certainly would be worth a short tryout.

In the meantime, the exceptional demand for Will Rogers's appearance at meetings, conventions, and fundraisers continued unabated. It became so important to conventioneers to be addressed by him that at times Will would have to speak at several festivities a night. As for speeches at banquets, Will's record stood at twelve separate appearances in eighteen consecutive days. There were conventions of the Varnish Salesmen, the Building Superintendents, Furrier Trades People, Retail Milliners, United Corset Manufacturers, the Produce and Flour

Club, the American Committee for Devastated France, National Hosiery and Underwear Manufacturers, the Detective Force of New York, the National Association of Manufacturers—there seemed to be no end of organizations, all coming to New York to meet, all wanting to be addressed by Will Rogers. The harder Will worked, the more people wanted to see and hear him. It may sound like he was joking, but there may have been more than just a dab of truth when he wrote:

> *I have spoken at so many Banquets during the year that when I get home I will feel disappointed if my wife or one of the children don't get up at dinner and say, "We have with us this evening a man who, I am sure, needs no introduction."*

Not all of the speeches were recorded; unfortunately, the one Will delivered at a banquet given at the Astor Hotel on Times Square, New York, for his old side-kick Tom Mix was not. The atmosphere was festive, the crowd distinguished, the food delectable, and Rogers was in great form, and yet that dinner is only memorable for what Mix said about the food afterwards: "I et for two hours and didn't recognize a thing I et except an olive."

Of course, Will's eight weekly appearances in the Follies continued to be sold out. A *New York Times* report on March 5, 1923, pointed out that the *Ziegfeld Follies* had just completed its tenth capacity month in succession. But changes were afoot:

> *As soon as he finishes his present engagement with* The Follies *Will Rogers will go to the coast to make his announced series of 13 2-reel comedies under the management of Hal Roach, . . . For distribution by Pathe Exchanges.*

Lunch break for Will, son Jimmy, and Guinn "Big Boy" Williams (right, holding a bottle of milk).

Courtesy of the Academy of Motion Picture Arts and Sciences

The follow-up item printed by the *New York Times* on Tuesday, May 20, reported that Eddie Cantor, who had left the *Follies* a few years earlier, would now return in triumph on June 4, replacing Will Rogers.

On Monday, June 11, 1923, Will Rogers was busy in Hollywood, beginning an exhausting shooting schedule for the Hal Roach Studio. For the next eleven months, almost daily, including some Sundays, Will was before the cameras making two-reel silent comedies. There were no interruptions; the moment one film was concluded, the next one was ready to be started. With such conveyer-belt-like schedules, it was not unexpected that there were frequent retakes, interrupting the continuity of the next production. Day in and day out, it was the same routine. The money was good, but Will was not happy. Without sound he was now doing the type of physical humor Hal Roach was famous for, but which was alien to Will: "All I ever do on the Roach lot is run around barns and lose my pants," he complained to Rob Wagner, a friend of his who was also a director.

Wagner received a telephone call from Warren Doane, Hal Roach's studio manager: "Will isn't satisfied with the stuff he's doing here, and he has asked us to let you direct him in a picture. Have you any ideas?"

Will Rogers in his production of *Fruits of Faith*, 1922, which co-starred Irene Rich and little Jimmy Rogers.

Rob Wagner had: "Only this, Metro-Goldwyn-Mayer played Will as the character actor, which he isn't, and you have been playing him as a red-nosed comic, which is profane. How would it do to get on the screen what the *Follies* are paying him three thousand dollars a week for? If we could get Will Rogers up there, we'd have something."

The answer from the front office was a go-ahead, and the result was a parody of a then very popular dramatic feature film, *The Covered Wagon*. Will wrote the parody and connecting panels, while Rob was the director of the only Hal Roach–produced Rogers film that deserves to be remembered, *Two Wagons, Both Covered*.

The *Los Angeles Times* film critic, not usually given to undeserved praise, wrote in his review:

Incidentally, it's really too bad that the public won't see this picture at its full length. When I saw it (at the preview) it was 2,600 feet, but the demands of exhibitors, I was told, would necessitate shortening it to 2,000 feet. Which is a pity, for it was a gem as it stood.

This two-reeler not only drew critical praise, but was immensely popular with exhibitors and the public. The Hal Roach Studio front office ascribed its success to a lucky happenstance and returned Will Rogers to more shameful buffoonery.

Will became resigned to work out his obligation: "I'll walk through this stuff until my contract's ended. Then back to the *Follies*."

Ziegfeld had been after Rogers with telegrams, asking him to return. Surely a *New York Times* announcement made in May had something to do with it. The paper revealed that this year's edition of the Ziegfeld Follies was leaving the New Amsterdam Theatre "prematurely" on its annual cross country tour, because it was losing money. Just the year before, starring Will Rogers, the Follies had played continually to capacity houses. Now, after Will had been gone for a year, it had a losing season.

Will's contract with the Hal Roach Studio ended on May, 12, 1924. Roach tried hard to persuade Rogers to re-sign for another year, but placing the children into the hands of a competent household staff, Will and Betty left Hollywood the following day for the East. They stopped off briefly in Oklahoma, visiting the family. Will had lost his pants for the last time; it was back to the *Follies*.

As rehearsals for the new *Follies* would not begin in Atlantic City until mid-June, Will Rogers undertook to write five articles for the McNaught Newspaper Syndicate, covering the Republican National Convention in Cleveland. William Jennings Bryan, who had been three times the losing Democratic nominee for the presidency, was to be one of the fellow reporters. Rogers and Bryan arrived at the same time in the press section in the Convention Hall:

One of Will's earliest columns.

As we entered the hall everybody stood up. Both of us looked at each other rather embarrassed, as we didn't know which one the demonstration was meant for. But we were soon set at ease on the subject, when we found out that they were rising to sing one of our national anthems, which, by the way, the Republicans don't know any better than the plain people.

Bryan and I had no sooner got in the hall than they commenced to pray. The preacher started reading his prayer, which was new to me. Where I come from if a

Me with your Pop, and my polo instructor My Best Will Rogers

Will and Hal Roach
with polo ponies,
circa 1922.

man can't think of anything to pray about offhand, why, there is no need of him for praying. If they couldn't find a Republican that knew how to pray they should have called in a Democrat. They are all praying this year.

The prayer was very long, but, the parson may have known his audience and their needs better than me.

Then Mr. Bryan turned to me and said: "You write a humorous column, don't you?"

I looked around to see if anybody was listening and then I said: "Yes, Sir."

He said: "Well, I write a serious article and if I think of anything of a comical or funny nature, I will give it to you."

I thanked him and told him: "If I happen to think of anything of a serious nature, I will give it to you."

When he said he wrote seriously and I said I wrote humorously, I thought afterwards we both may be wrong.

The 1924 Democratic National Convention opened in New York City on the same day as the *Ziegfeld Follies*. Will Rogers had written five articles covering the Republican Convention and was now retained to cover the Democratic one also. As he had done for the convention in Cleveland, Will set a flat fee for this reportage. He would never do that again. What neither he nor anyone else could have foretold was the lengthy infighting. It took 102 ballots to finally settle on a candidate, John W. Davis. Will was obligated to write eighteen articles. As a lark he signed one of those articles with his eldest son's name, having Will Jr. claim that his father had aged so much since the beginning of the convention that the job had been handed to the next generation.

On one ballot, the Arizona delegation voted two half votes for Will Rogers for president. It was not the first time that Rogers's name was mentioned for a high office, and it would not be the last.

In August, Will returned to one of his great distractions—polo. He had been playing the game for years and was an acknowledged star with a respectable handicap. Polo seemed to have been invented for a man like Will Rogers. It combined all the outdoor activities Will loved. The only way it could have been improved would have been for someone to come up with an idea to involve a lasso.

Now in August, the middle of the *Ziegfeld Follies'* New York season, international polo matches were being played on Long Island. Will just had to see the world's foremost players fighting for the championship. The unfortunate part was that these games were played on Wednesday and Saturday afternoons, the very days on which Broadway shows have their matinee performances. Will had been taking several of those key afternoons off to attend crucial matches. Reports of Will's truancy had reached Florenz Ziegfeld Jr. Something would have to be done.

Matinee patrons had a right to see the identical show with the identical cast that the evening crowd saw. Ziegfeld wrote a letter:

F. ZIEGFELD, JR.
NEW AMSTERDAM THEATRE
NEW YORK

August 22, 1924

My dear Bill:

I tried everywhere to get you on the phone today before leaving for Easthampton, but it was impossible to find you.

Gene Buck tells me he had a long talk with you and we are to see the new skit Tuesday at 3 P.M.

Gene also told me you insisted on being away three matinees during the Polo Games—that your heart and soul are set on seeing these games. You know Bill, there isn't anything in the world I would not do for you, but you must realize we have an enormous organization, enormous expenses, and with the productions necessary now with The Follies it takes a year to get our production back. To give matinees without you in them would be absolutely impossible.

There is only one thing to do. Of course it is going to entail a great loss, because unquestionably our matinees will be greatly hurt. There is only one solution—give the matinee on Friday instead of Saturday, and on Monday instead of Wednesday. Mr. Holzman will see you about this, and I think we can get a good story through the dramatic column so we will be able to have them, owing to your desire to see the Games I agreed to this so you know in what high esteem I hold you.

What the result will be Bill we will only have to wait to determine, but I want to please you in every way I possibly can. I would like to talk with you, so if you can call me at 115 M Easthampton when you get this I will be glad to talk with you.

Very sincerely yours,

[signed] Flo
Mr. Will Rogers
Ziegfeld Follies
New York City

This was a most important letter, in which America's foremost show producer offered to change a long-established tradition in the theater, just to accommodate his star. But the letter meant little to Will Rogers. At the right hand bottom corner, he scribbled "over" within parenthesis, ran his pencil several times across the typed message and used the clear back of the paper to begin chapter 2 of his autobiography.

From all records it appears that despite the Ziegfeld concession, Will never took another matinee afternoon off, nor were the matinee days altered. Perhaps the important games had already been played, or the championship had been decided. In any case, it is incredible that such a change of matinees was actually

Will with Robert Wagner, the director of *Two Wagons*.

considered and offered, and certainly indicates the measure of Will Rogers's importance.

This was the time when the rotogravure section of the Sunday *New York Times* edition would feature what seemed like "Society Pages," a quasi-pictorial account of what "society" was doing with, or against, each other. One of the young men currently most frequently featured was an English visitor, the Prince of Wales. Whether the prince was mingling with the so-called beautiful people or playing polo, no issue of the section seemed complete without him. When local papers from coast to coast printed pictures of the Prince of Wales falling off his horse while playing polo, and made snide remarks about the frequency of these unscheduled dismounts, Will was the quick defender:

> *I ain't going to tell any jokes about this English prince falling off his horse. I fall just as much, of course my falls don't attract as much attention, but they hurt just as much.*
>
> *I never saw a picture of him falling unless the horse was falling too. Can't see any humor in that. What are you going to do when your horse falls? Go down with him or stay up in the air until he comes back up under you?*

The New York establishment entertained the prince, who liked to dance. He was a much vied for guest at society balls and banquets. Of course, the prince, being single, was the voraciously pursued prime subject of a number of society ladies and of many determined, socially ambitious mothers of unmarried daughters as well. It was at one of these gala occasions that the after-dinner speaker, Will Rogers, met the prince. Improbably, these two men formed a strange fellowship. Though everything in their backgrounds had been so different, they shared their love of horses, both played polo well, and both had an independence of thought. There was just one more point that may have been responsible for this sort of bond between the two men—neither wanted, or needed, anything from the other. Will would joke about the prince, but he would also defend him.

When both men were to attend a polo game at the John Shaffer Phipps estate, on Long Island, New York, the prince invited Will to share his limousine for the trip. Two days later Will was invited as a guest to a party at the exclusive Piping Rock Club. The prince personally requested that Will be invited.

The press reported that at an auction of seven of the prince's polo ponies, Will Rogers bought Jacinto, a chestnut gelding, for $2,100 and presented it to Patricia, the daughter of Florenz Ziegfeld and Billie Burke. Will had the last word on that deal with the prince:

It was reported in the press that I purchased one of his ponies for $2100. Now that was a mistake. I bought one but it was for Mr. Flo Ziegfeld's little daughter, and it was him that paid for it. I have some alleged polo ponies of my own; in fact I think I have the best string of $40 polo ponies in the world, so you would hardly get me giving $2100 for some old pony just because he belonged to the Prince. I wouldn't give $2100 for the Crown, much less a horse. But anyway he was a very nice, gentle, real kid's pony, and little Patricia Burke Ziegfeld was tickled to death with him.

She had him following her all around, even into the house, and that made a big hit with Mr. Ziegfeld, so he told me, "What do you know about that pony? Why, Patricia brought him right into the house." I told him, "why, the barns that pony has been used to while he belonged to the Prince of Wales, you were lucky to get him to go into your house. The pony must have thought he was slumming." That's the reason I did not get one. I knew I could not support one in the manner in which it had been accustomed.

There were other signs of Will's growing prominence. While his image had been used in connection with publicizing the vaudeville shows of years past, as well as the motion pictures and Ziegfeld productions, he had stayed away from the purely commercial exploitation of his popularity:

Now, in my more or less checkered career before the more or less checkered public, I have been asked to publicly endorse everything from chewing gum, face beautifiers, patent cocktail shakers, ma junk sets, even corsets, cigarettes and chewing tobacco, all of which I didn't use or know anything about. But I always refused.

I saw the English Derby one time, I think it was 1906 and a horse named Spearmint (I think it was) won it, but I wasent chewing much gum then and dident bet on him.

Years later, looking back, Will mentioned some of his commercial endorsements. By that time he was Hollywood's number-one box office attraction. His broadcasts had been sponsored by national products, and he mentioned Ford cars on many an occasion at no charge, yet he was driving a Buick. It seems that Henry Ford did send Will the first Model T car to roll off his assembly line—as a gift.

But time and circumstances changed his needs, and he was trying to raise money any way he could, as long as it was moral and legal. The American Tobacco Company came with an offer. Would Rogers write ten advertisements for their cigarette tobacco Bull Durham? The honorarium would be $2,500. Will did not smoke, but he did have huge debts in California. He accepted the offer on condition that he could state that he, himself, did not use tobacco in any form. The company took a chance on trying out such a strange advertising method, and agreed. The gamble of having the spokesman announce that he did not use the product while asking others to buy it paid off handsomely. People read the lengthy, humorous endorsement which featured Will's picture and the company's logo, and felt that if Will Rogers endorsed a

A publicity insert card of Will sold with Nestle's chocolates.

On the Roach lot, 1923. Director Robert Wagner is in the back seat. The driver is Hal Roach, sitting next to Will.

product, it had to be good. When a noted piano company asked Will to be their spokesman in an advertising campaign, Will agreed under similar conditions. He claimed that while he did not play the piano, this particular brand was the best he had ever leaned against.

Before the first Bull Durham advertisement even appeared, the company, having seen the first few outlines, negotiated for a new total of twenty-six advertisements, offering to pay $500 each, starting as of January 1, 1925. At later times, Will would also be asked to endorse chewing gum and other items.

As the year 1924 came to an end, Will celebrated his forty-fifth birthday. He had made great inroads on the debts he had incurred with his motion picture production venture. His activities included daily performances for *The Ziegfeld Follies,* frequently preceded and/or followed by addresses to conventions or banquets. He also had to supply copy for corporate advertising and for a regular weekly column of some 1,500 words. His tax return for 1924 showed a gross income of $157,428, that he had a wife and three children, and that he also supported two nephews.

Page 103, "Will Rogers on film . . . ," *New York Times,* July 26, 1920.

Page 104, "He did not know . . . ," biographical account of C. Badger; *Will Rogers in Hollywood,* by Bryan B. and Frances N. Sterling, © 1984.

Page 105, "Zeb now sets . . . ," night riders—masked riders at night (for example Ku Klux Klan) intending to frighten those targeted.

Page 105, "Sam, having just sold . . . ," only trims and clips are extant.

Page 106, "That song is better . . . ," Geraldine Farrar—famous operatic soprano, married Lou

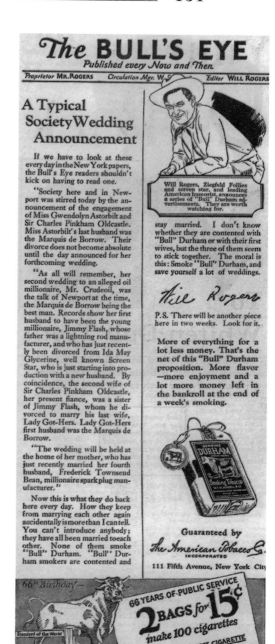

An original Bull Durham Tobacco advertisement.

Will and Will Jr. returning from their European tour aboard the SS *Olympic*, 1925.

Courtesy of the Will Rogers Memorial Commission

Just Blathering

"I am notoriously long winded. I think that's where
people get the idea that I ought to be in politics. But when
I get started I do like to blather away."

In mid-December 1924, W. C. Fields and Eddie Cantor suddenly became temporary members of the cast of *The Ziegfeld Follies,* replacing Will Rogers when word
had come that Maud, one of Will's sisters, was seriously ill. Taking the fastest train
west created a problem. Being an express train, it would only stop at major cities.
The small town of Chelsea, Oklahoma, Maud's home, was not one of them. Will
had to stay aboard the fast train while it sped past Chelsea; it stopped only when
it reached Tulsa, Oklahoma, some 40 miles beyond his intended goal. There was
no scheduled local train that could take him back to Chelsea. Will had to buy 175
tickets before the St. Louis & San Francisco Railroad would furnish him with a
special engine and coach for the unscheduled solo trip back up the line.

Maud began to recover. Two days after Will left her to return to New York
City, two brand new Buick sedans were delivered to Chelsea, one for sister Maud,
the other for sister Sallie—presents from their kid brother, Willie.

The Jewish Theatrical Guild of America planned its First Annual Dinner to
honor Eddie Cantor, one of its most famous members. Will Rogers was invited to
be one of the speakers. After all, Will and Eddie had been friends for a long time.
On the evening of Sunday, February 1, 1925, Will stepped to the rostrum. To
everyone's surprise, Will began a ten-minute speech in Yiddish. True, his Yiddish
had a distinct Western inflection, but it was Yiddish. It was the first time that anyone had ever heard Will Rogers utter a word in that language publicly, and he
was the hit of the evening. After he had finished his monologue, Will repeated
the speech in English for those who did not understand it the first time. Of
course, his English, too, had a distinct Western inflection.

What nobody knew was that Will had first written the speech in English, then
had hired a rabbinical student to translate it into Yiddish. Next, the speech had to
be typed phonetically, so that Will could learn to pronounce the words. After that,
Will had the student come for four weeks to supervise Will's study and reading of
the speech. All that for a ten-minute speech to show his friendship for Eddie.

In March, Will went to Washington, D.C., in Bernard M. Baruch's private railroad car. Both men had been invited by the Gridiron Club for their annual spoof

Will and the three children on horseback.

of the president and his cabinet, at the New Willard Hotel. Among the guests was a man who was then much in the news—Brigadier General William (Billy) Lendrum Mitchell.

> *After the dinner I met him for the first time, and he asked me if I wouldn't like to go and see Washington with him the next morning and that he would call at the Hotel for me. So I foolishly told him yes.*
>
> *Well, the next morning he came and got me and we drove across the river to an aviation field. I thought naturally that he was going to show me the field, but instead of pointing out any places of interest, an assistant handed me a straight jacket, a kind of a one piece suicide suit and a kind of a Derby hat with a brim turned down over your ears. It slowly began to dawn on me that at last there was going to be some flying done in the Army, and that I was supposed to be one of the participants. . . .*
>
> *Well, there was so many standing around that there was no way to back out. Right at that moment I thought the fellows who were trying to get this Mitchell out of the air service were right, and I wished they had got him out sooner. He said, "Do you use cotton in your ears?" He seemed to think that I was an old experienced aviator. I says: "No I only use cotton in my ears when I visit the Senate*

Gallery." I couldn't imagine what the cotton was for unless it was to keep the dirt out of your ears in case of a fall. . . .

A man buckles you in so that you won't change your mind after you leave the ground. Mitchell says, "I will point out the places of interest to you." I didn't see him point nor I didn't see what he pointed at. I have always heard when you are up on anything high, don't look down; look up. So all I saw was the sky. The trip from a sightseeing point of view was a total loss to me, outside of seeing the sky at short range.

Washington's home at Mount Vernon might have been Bryan's in Miami for all I know. We flew around Washington Monument and if the thing had had handles on it he would have lost a passenger.

Here I was a thousand of feet up in the air when you can't even get me to ride a tall horse. I had always figured that if the Lord had intended a man to do any flying he would have sprouted something out of his back besides just shoulder blades. He asked me if I saw the Mayflower, the President's private tug. How was I going to see it unless it was flying over us? I didn't come any nearer seeing it than I'll ever come to riding on it. When we landed and got out and walked away I was tickled to death. I thought the drama was all over. But it wasn't.

The most impressive part of the whole thing was in his next few words. He says: "You have been with me on the last flight I will ever make as Brigadier General. Tonight at 12 o'clock I am to be demoted to a Colonel and sent to a far away Post where, instead of having the entire Air Force at my command, there will be seven Planes." Well, I got a real thrill out of that. To think that I had accompanied such a man on such a memorable flight.

On May 11, 1925, Will was addressing church leaders at a luncheon in the McAlpin Hotel on Herald Square in the heart of New York City. He had received word that his sister Maud's condition was worsening. Instead of a witty talk, he told the assemblage about the sister who had been his part-time mother. Tears were streaming down his cheeks while he told of the good deeds she had performed. Will was somewhat heartened when the ministers and laymen present prayed for Maud.

Four days later, on Friday, May 15, 1925, Mrs. Maud Ethel Rogers Lane died at 4:45 A.M. at her home in Chelsea, Oklahoma. Will left New York as soon as the news reached him. While he had been prepared for her death, having only recently visited with her and seen her decline, the finality of the news seemed difficult to bear. For publication on May 24, 1925, he had to write his usual weekly article:

A few days ago I was asked by one of the big Ministers of New York City to come to a Luncheon and speak to over 300 Ministers and prominent Laymen. . . .

I told him I didn't know what to talk about . . . But, anyway, I went and never in my life did I face an audience with as little preparation. Well, I floundered around from one subject to another. The Minister in introducing me had said that I had been raised a Methodist and I had. So when I got off on that I just couldn't help but speak of a thing which I didn't want to speak of. I knew what would happen if I did.

Out of a large family of which I am the youngest, I have two Sisters living. And I couldn't speak of any Church without bringing in the work that those two Sisters have done, in the little town in which they both live. It's Chelsea, Oklahoma, which means nothing in your life, but it has meant a lot to people who have lived in association with them.

They started in this little Western Town some 35 years ago. They helped build the Methodist Church, the first church there. They have helped every Church, they have helped every movement that they knew was for the best upbuilding of their community. They have each raised a large family of Boys and Girls who are today a credit to their community. They have carried on the same as thousands of Women have carried on in every small and Big Town in the World. They don't think they are doing anything out of the ordinary. They don't want credit. They do good simply because they don't know any other thing to do.

The reason I spoke of this personal thing is because I couldn't help it. My Wife was waiting at the train right then for me to see her off to the sickbed of one of these sisters. I didn't tell this to the Ministers because they are my sisters but because none of them who has given his entire life and time to God could have given any more than they have. They have given their all.

The roping ring in Beverly Hills. Will is in the back in the center.

Mary Rogers on a polo-training horse at the Pacific Palisades ranch.

Will on Bootlegger, his favorite polo pony.

Now when I had finished my little talk to rush to the train to see my wife off, I had something happen that had never happened before and I have spoken at a great many affairs. The entire 300 stood up and offered a silent Prayer for my poor afflicted Sister. That was days ago.

Today, as I write this, I am not in the Follies, the carefree Comedian who jokes about everything. I am out in Oklahoma, among my People, my Cherokee people, who don't expect a laugh for everything I say.

That Silent Prayer that those 300 Ministers uttered didn't save my sister. She has passed away. But she had lived such a life that it was a privilege to pass away. Death didn't scare her. It was only an episode in her life. If you live right, death is a Joke to you as far as fear is concerned.

And on the day that I am supposed to write a so called Humorous Article I am Back home. Back home, at the funeral of my Sister. I can't be funny. I don't want to be funny. Even Ziegfeld don't want me to be funny. I told him I wanted to go. He said: "I would hate you if you didn't." I told W. C. Fields, the principal comedian of the show. He said: "Go on, I will do something to fill in." Brandon Tynan, my friend of years said: "Go home where you want to be and where you ought to be."

After all, there is nothing in the world like home. You can roam all over the World, but after all, it's what the people at home think of you that really counts. I have just today witnessed a Funeral that for real sorrow and real affection I don't think will ever be surpassed anywhere. They came in every mode of conveyance, on foot, in Buggies, Horseback, Wagons, Cars, and Trains, and there wasn't a Soul that come that she hadn't helped or favored at one time or another.

Mary Rogers and Sarah, the family's pet calf.

Now, we are in the South, of the South, and according to Northern standards we don't rate the Negro any too high. Well, I wish you could have seen the Negroes at her home on the day of the Funeral. Before her death, she said: "They are my folks, they have helped me for years, they are all my friends. When I am gone I don't want you Children at my Funeral to show any preference." That's the real South's real feelings for its real friends. Death knows no Denomination. Death draws no color line. Some uninformed Newspapers printed: "Mrs. C. L. Lane sister of the famous Comedian, Will Rogers." They were greatly misinformed. It's the other way around. I am the brother of Mrs. C. L. Lane, "The friend of Humanity." And I want to tell you that as I saw all these people who were there to pay tribute to her memory, it was the proudest moment of my life that I was her brother. And all the honors that I could ever in my wildest dreams hope to reach, would never equal the honor paid on a little western Prairie hilltop, among her people, to Maud Lane. If they will love me like that at the finish, my life will not have been in vain.

Of the eight children Clem and Mary Rogers had given life, only two were now left, the second eldest and the youngest. When Willie's mother had died some thirty-five years earlier, his older sisters Sallie and Maud had tried to fill the void left for the ten-year-old. In the years since, Will had tried to divide his love and time evenly between his two remaining siblings. Whenever he visited Chelsea, he would stay first with one, then with the other, so that neither would ever feel that there was a preference in his heart—for there was none. Now that only the two of them were left, the bond with Sallie would become even closer. Will would never miss an opportunity to come and spend a few days, or even a few hours, with her. He would constantly urge her to come to his California home. One of Sallie's children, Pauline Elizabeth (called Paula), had been stricken with infantile paralysis, and when she required a series of operations, Will paid for them and then saw that little Paula had a first-rate education, culminating with a master's degree in English from the University of Missouri.

Will was a family-oriented man. All relatives, whether his own or Betty's, were welcome at his home. He was generous with his money, helping close relatives, friends, and just people in need. When he appeared in the Broadway production of *Three Cheers,* beggars were assured of a nightly dollar bill. When word spread of the largess—in the 1920s a dollar bought a lot of food, or drinks—beggars from all over town crowded the stage exit waiting for Will to emerge. Will, who wore no makeup, usually was the first to leave, but the crowds remained, hoping that other stars would be equally generous. Fellow actors often had to call police to clear a way for them to get to their cars. When Will and a movie company filmed in a railway yard with real hoboes at Barstow, California, Will gave them all his money and then had to borrow enough from fellow actors to get home on.

Back in New York, Will received a letter from Charles L. Wagner, confirming arrangements for a two-month concert tour beginning October 1, 1925, and ending November 30. The flat fee would be $60,000. If this tour proved successful and an extension was indicated, Wagner would have the option to continue the tour until December 16, for an additional fee of $22,500. The October beginning of the tour was Rogers's idea, so that he could stay with the Ziegfeld show until its New York City summer run was terminated.

In Bartlesville, Oklahoma, a movement took form to run Will Rogers for governor of Oklahoma. The *Inola News* fully endorsed the action, claiming: "Will Rogers couldn't possibly make a worse joke of Oklahoma politics than we have enjoyed for years, so let's go!" Will totally rejected any personal involvement in politics. He was convinced that his place was on the sidelines, as an observer and reporter. The next day, after Will had declined Oklahoma's honor, the Kiwanis Club of Rogers, Arkansas, suggested publicly that Will become a candidate for the highest office in that state. This, too, Rogers declined to follow up.

In the middle of August 1925, Will Rogers broadcast one of the strangest speeches ever heard. He had committed himself to address the Second Annual Radio Industry Banquet at New York's Commodore Hotel, a talk which—as they

Family relaxing with Sarah, the calf who thought she was a member of the family.

then said—was to be "radiated" by twelve stations. Will didn't realize that in his contract with Charles L. Wagner, he was specifically prohibited from broadcasting prior to the start of the lecture tour. When he was made aware that he would be violating his contract, Will faced the dilemma of having to breach either his contract or his commitment to deliver the speech. He sat at the head table and pondered over a solution until the final minute. When he was introduced he stepped to the microphone, and for the next fifteen minutes he was sparkling. His topic was a most humorous excuse, explaining why he would be unable to deliver a speech that evening.

On the first day of October 1925, in the company of the DeReske Singers, Will Rogers opened his lecture tour and wrote about it in his weekly article:

> *When you read these immaculate English lines, I may have met some of you personally. I break out into what is advertised as an alleged "Lecture Tour," on the night of October first, at Elmira, New York. If I survive I proceed. If not, they should at least announce to the world what happened to me.*
>
> *We can't find out what to call it. It's not exactly a lecture but by the time you read this it will perhaps have been named. I think we will get a title for it from the comment the two fellows will exchange on leaving the Elmira Opera House. It's a kinder get together tour to meet my readers, and I want to meet them personally in my dressing room, each one of them. Business concerns go over the country every once in awhile to meet what they call their "men in the field." Now that is the prime object of my pilgrimage. My readers are the "men in the field" and we want to get together on what is the best way to remedy the running of National affairs during the coming year. I am making what the politician calls a swing around the Circuit. But I am not like the Politician who wants to "meet the Voter." I want to meet the Taxpayer, and that is very seldom the voter.*
>
> *Now I haven't got much of what you might call a Show with me. There is just a Male Quartet and myself. When my talk on the affairs of our Nation and the world in common (and it is) gets dull why the Quartet will sing. That gets your mind off me, and when they have sorter got you soothed back to sensibility I break out again and give you (if the audience stays) the real inside dope on our hired help in Washington. I know more scandal than a White House Cook.*

Mary Rogers.

It may have been envisioned as an experiment by an experienced booking entrepreneur, but it proved to be a most successful undertaking that would not only last through the anticipated extension of six weeks, but for another couple

Betty, Will, Jim, and Mary in Beverly Hills.

of years. The original thought had been that one single man, speaking for, say, ninety minutes, could not possibly hold the attention of an audience. There just had to be a change of pace, say, a quartet that would sing familiar songs. (Will liked the quartet, though he was not exactly impressed with their selection of music, but he had not been consulted.) And so it had been structured. The quartet would open the show, then introduce Will Rogers, who would speak about local concerns and national goings-on. Then there would be an intermission followed by a repeat of the first half, only this time Will would speak on world events. All this was in the most entertaining, humorous terms for which Will had become justly famous. Usually, when the allotted time for the evening performance had been reached and Will had finished his prepared part, applause would repeatedly call him back onstage. Finally, perhaps tired, he would sit down on whatever chair or stool was handy, and continue to ad-lib. If no chair was available he would simply sit down on the edge of the stage, with his feet dangling into the orchestra pit, and continue as if that were the most normal way for the show to go on. If there was no hurry to catch a certain train for the next engagement on the following day, some monologues lasted as long as three hours.

Since the show was booked to perform every day in a different town, travel arrangements and reservations had to be made well in advance. If the distance to the next engagement was great, traveling was usually done during the night, with the group leaving a town right after the evening performance. If the next city could easily be reached within a few hours, Will and the quartet would stay overnight and leave early the following morning. Frequently there was some festivity or official welcome planned to receive Will Rogers to a city. There might be

Betty Rogers and
her children.

the presentation of a key to a city, or some scroll; there might be a tour of the
town, with a stop at a school, a hospital or some other structure deserving civic
pride, like a dam, a power plant, or a new city hall. In Elmira, for example, officials took Will in tow and had him visit the Elmira Reformatory, where he was
also asked to speak.

As soon as he could disentangle himself from the proud city fathers, Will
would usually call at the town's newspaper office, where he could find out local
conditions, problems, and events, which he could then mention humorously that
evening in his monologue. Those local references were really the only new material every night. The rest of the monologue was almost as his vaudeville presenta-
tions had been. The same topics and the same jokes could be used every night,

because not only were the audiences different, but the towns were, too. Of course, Will had become a master of improvisation. He could take an unexpected event and make it into something funny. Will always maintained that his "fresh-laid jokes" were the most successful ones. [Once, during the Great War, at the height of Germany's unrestricted U-boat attacks on Allied shipping, a number of reporters surrounded Will at a railroad station. "What," one of them asked, "do you think the Allies should do about these U-boat attacks?"

Will had not thought that the subject was one to joke about, but the reporters looked at him expectantly. He had to say something. "I have a solution to stop those submarines," he said, having read that they had difficulty operating properly in warm waters. "Yes, just heat the Atlantic Ocean to the boiling point and as the water bubbles and forces those tin cans up, we just shoot 'em down." There was some scattered laughter, but the reporters were not satisfied. "How are you going to heat the Atlantic to the boiling point, Mr. Rogers?" they asked. Will smiled. "Don't bother me with details; I'm a policy MAKER!"]

Will and the quartet soon established a routine. They adjusted their personal lives so they would leave together, have their meals on time, check into a hotel and find out when to check out, and how to get to the railroad depot together. All went uneventfully until Ft. Worth, Texas. They missed connections, by fifteen minutes, with the last train of the day for Wichita, Kansas, where they were booked the following evening. Waiting until the next scheduled train in the morning would not get them to the theater in time. "Will plunked down $1,100 for an engine and a day coach and traversed his home state in regal splendor."

Playing in the Washington, D.C., area in December, Will took the opportunity to drop into the improvised courtroom at the old Census Bureau offices, to witness the court-martial of Brigadier General Billy Mitchell. When Major General Robert Lee Howze, the presiding officer, noticed Will Rogers enter, he stopped proceedings, stood up, and asked Will to come to the front. The court then took a short recess to officially receive him. Will was then invited to take a seat among the attorneys and the trial resumed.

On April 2, 1926, Rogers and the DeReske Singers were preparing for their show in Goldsboro, North Carolina, when Will received a telegram. It was from Florenz Ziegfeld trying to persuade Will to return to the *Follies*, as—so Mr. Ziegfeld admitted—the show was losing money. But Will had a contract for his speaking engagements; he was not the man to break it. And even though the lecture tour was to close shortly for the summer, he replied that his plans for the next few months were set. He was taking his eldest son to Europe, where he was later to be joined by Betty and the other two children.

The lecture tour closed its highly successful season in Philadelphia on April 20, 1926. (Increased by his earnings from the tour, Will's gross income for 1925 was $225,467.18.) Will went on to Washington to obtain a passport and letters of introduction from Vice President Charles G. Dawes and the famed banker Dr. A. H. Giannini. Rogers sailed aboard the steamship *Leviathan* with his son Will Jr. on May 1. Five days later the ship docked at Southampton. London was in the grip of a general strike, which seemed to be carried on in a most civilized manner. Will and his son visited the House of Commons and looked in on the House of Lords. They had dinner with Lady Astor, one of the famed American-born Langhorne sisters and the first woman to sit in England's Parliament. Describing the viscountess, a fourteen-year-old Will Jr. wrote in his diary: ". . . she is just like mother in a lot of ways. . . ."

The Prince of Wales's equerry called Will Rogers to arrange for a visit to St. James's Palace, the prince's official residence. Will spent more than an hour with the prince, and the two men discussed general matters. In one article in his series of reports of the trip for the *Saturday Evening Post*, published under the title "Letters of a Self-Made Diplomat to his President," Will repeated some of the conversation. One sentence in the article covering that visit proved Rogers to be a most astute analyst of his fellow man. Making a reference to the fact that President Coolidge had come from the vice presidency upon President Harding's death, Will correctly formed an opinion of David, Prince of Wales, the Crown Prince of England who almost became King Edward VIII:

> *"But just between you and I, Calvin, he don't care any more about being King than you would about going back to Vice President again."*

Will made application for a visa to the Soviet Union, then arranged to visit the Continent. Young Bill was all for flying across the Channel, while Will Sr. was a little worried about flying over water. Not wishing to seem apprehensive in front of his son, he finally agreed. They packed and then left for the airport.

> *We drove out to the edge of London, and when you drive out to the edge of London why, you have drove out to the edge of something. It begin to look from the Taximeter like London didn't have any edges. Between the constant checking of the Taximeter and the thought of that Airship over that Channel, why I was what you might call a mildly nervous man. Oh boy! It was a drizzling rain and a High wind. It seemed like the old U.S. Senate when they get started on Prohibition.*
>
> *There was eight or ten big planes out there and some smaller ones. . . Finally, a man that spoke what he thought was English said to me, "Do you want to go in a small plane or a big one?" Bill said a small one. I said a big one. I asked how many would be in the small plane and he said three. Bill asked if the small plane wasn't faster. He said, "Oh Yes."*
>
> *Well that didn't particularly appeal to me. I got to thinking and I couldn't think of a single thing that I was in a hurry to get to Paris for. So then I got Bill off to one side and I explained to him what a wonderful thing it would be to go home and tell about this big plane. Oh this Giant Aeroplane that he flew the Channel in. That if he told that just three of us flew over that would be no novelty, but if he could tell them a whole gang flew over, why that would be different. I was sparring to try and get some company, in fact as much company as possible, on there with me. I had read somewhere that there is supposed to be "safety in numbers."*
>
> *. . . Well, if you ever saw a beautiful country in the world to look at it's England from the air. You would just start to try to enjoy a wonderful old Castle and fields down below when something or somebody would take what air there was under us out and it would settle straight down like an elevator. Your stomach tried to change places with your head. Then we would find some nice concreted air roads and be sailing along fine. Then it would just remind you of surface roads over home. You would come to a place where somebody wouldn't vote road bonds and you would hit another bunch of ruts. The old stomache would commence to*

Will Rogers's first plane ride, in 1915.

sorter want to get up through your throat again. I looked back in the seat behind me, and poor little William had located a kind of a lunch basket effect that seems to be standard equipment on one of these cross-channel planes. He wasn't just examining it; he was seeing if it was practical. A Japanese across the 12-inch passageway looked like he would like to commit Hiri Kari. You know there is nothing in the world as sick looking as a seasick person. I think people look more natural when they are dead.

In Paris, father and son behaved like proper tourists and visited Notre Dame Cathedral, the Eiffel Tower, the Louvre, and watched a parade of American soldiers dressed in Revolutionary War uniforms. Will Rogers made arrangements once more to go into filmmaking. It supposedly started out as being just home movies, a record made of his and his family's trip through Europe. He did, however, have the highly professional Carl Stearns Clancy as producer and director, and John LaMond as cameraman. Later, back in the United States, Will would edit the footage into twelve "travelogues," add his own titles as narration, and turn them over to Pathé Ind. for distribution. Pathé was a most active film producer and distributor of news reports and shorts to motion picture houses.

I don't know exactly what they are—they ain't exactly travelogues; they ain't comedies 'cause comedies are gags that the people are used to laughing at. The plots are a little too clean for drama.

Will with William S.
Hart and the
DeReske Singers.

Well, to be honest, they are just about nine hundred feet of celluloid and take up about the same amount of time that a couple of close-ups in a love picture would take up. They ain't good and they ain't bad, they just take up fifteen minutes of a class of people that time don't mean a thing in the world to. The Saturday Evening Post *has already payed for the trip, talking about all over the country has made me more than I ever could have made in pictures, even if I had been a real star; the book of the trip has brought enough to pay for another trip. The Vitaphone staggered me to tell about it before their double-barrel contraption, and this is just another by-product; I wanted the reels to keep for myself to show at home in my old days, and I just had them make another print.*

In fact, there is the radio, that's another by-product I just thought of, that has paid me for them too. I was raised on a ranch, but I never knew there were so many ways to skin a calf. I like to forget Bull Durham paying me to tell about the same trip. . . .

Restless when not involved in stimulating work, Will decided suddenly that he and his son should look in on the League of Nations Preliminary Disarmament Commission session. Will's arrival "attracted more attention than many of the Delegates."

Will looked and listened, and listened, and listened some more, but then he diplomatically reported in his *Saturday Evening Post* article "A Letter from a Self-Made Diplomat to his Constituents" about his report to President Coolidge:

I told him that I had attended the first week of the preliminary Disarmament Conference in Geneva, that they had held the conference to see if they could hold a conference if they decided to hold a conference."

Teenager Will Jr., who had suffered right alongside his dad, was far less diplomatic in what he wrote about it into his diary, but he was just as accurate: "it was just talking about nothing."

America's Greatest Humorist

WILL ROGERS

THE PRINCE OF ENTERTAINERS AND ENTERTAINER OF "THE PRINCE"

25¢

Management,
Charles L. Wagner,

The front of a pamphlet for Will Rogers's lecture tour.

The next stop was Rome, where father and son were received in an audience with Pope Pius XI. Young Bill recorded the event by describing how they had been briefed on protocol, that when the Pope came into the room they all kneeled, that His Holiness extended his hand, which they all kissed, then the Pope placed his hand on Bill's head and asked "How many years?" to which Will started to reply thinking that the question had been how many children. But young Bill answered immediately "fourteen," and the Pope moved on.

Benito Mussolini, Italy's dictator, also responded positively to Rogers's request for an interview. Will recounted the meeting in length in his *Letters of a Self-Made Diplomat to his President:*

ROME, June 1, '26. [This is Rome, Italy, not Georgia.]
THE PRESIDENT OF THEM UNITED STATES,

My Dear Mr. President:

Well, I come clear to Italy, as you know, Boss, just to see Mussolini . . . He is the busiest man in the world today and I dident know if I would be able to see him personally and privately or not. . . . after all it has to be arranged through our ambassador, Mr. Fletcher. . . . Well, this Fletcher is a real go-get-'em Kid. . . .

Well, he got busy right away, and he arranged a date for me for Friday at twelve o'clock. Now that was about 6 days away . . . Well, the more I was there in Italy, and the more I would hear about him, and the more I would see what he had done, why, the bigger he got to me. As the date grew nearer, I commenced getting kinder scared.

Well, the day arrived and I said to myself, I am going in a-grinning, even if they decide to revive the old Roman Coliseum, and put me in there and give me just three jumps in front of a Lion.

I was accompanied by Mr. Warren Robbins, the next in charge under Mr. Fletcher at the Embassy. He was my Host and Interpreter. Right on the dot, at twelve o'clock somebody said something to Robbins in Italian, and I was headed for the most talked of, the most discussed . . . the man that I had never even in any

One of Will's telegrams from Russia.

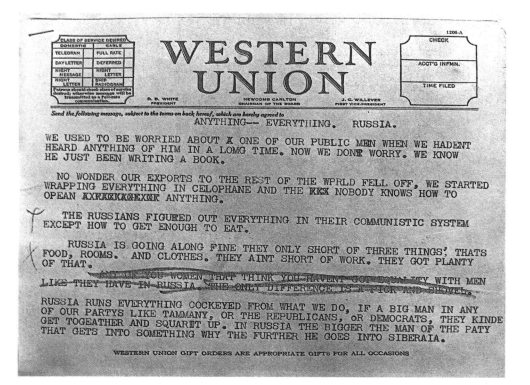

WESTERN UNION

ANYTHING— EVERYTHING. RUSSIA.

WE USED TO BE WORRIED ABOUT ONE OF OUR PUBLIC MEN WHEN WE HADENT HEARD ANYTHING OF HIM IN A LOMG TIME. NOW WE DONT WORRY. WE KNOW HE JUST BEEN WRITING A BOOK.

NO WONDER OUR EXPORTS TO THE REST OF THE WPRLD FELL OFF, WE STARTED WRAPPING EVERYTHING IN CELOPHANE AND THE NOBODY KNOWS HOW TO OPEAN ANYTHING.

THE RUSSIANS FIGURED OUT EVERYTHING IN THEIR COMMUNISTIC SYSTEM EXCEPT HOW TO GET ENOUGH TO EAT.

RUSSIA IS GOING ALONG FINE THEY ONLY SHORT OF THREE THINGS, THATS FOOD, ROOMS. AND CLOTHES. THEY AINT SHORT OF WORK. THEY GOT PLANTY OF THAT.

RUSSIA RUNS EVERYTHING COCKEYED FROM WHAT WE DO, IF A BIG MAN IN ANY OF OUR PARTYS LIKE TAMMANY, OR THE REPUBLICANS, oR DEMOCRATS, THEY KINDE GET TOGEATHER AND SQUARIT UP. IN RUSSIA THE BIGGER THE MAN OF THE PATY THAT GETS INTO SOMETHING WHY THE FURTHER HE GOES INTO SIBERAIA.

WESTERN UNION GIFT ORDERS ARE APPROPRIATE GIFTS FOR ALL OCCASIONS of his pictures seen smiling. This man, with all this on his mind, I was going in to see if I could get a laugh out of him, or find out what kind of a Duck he was. . .

So I says, "Come on, Claremore, lets see what Rome has got. I am going to treat this fellow like he was nobody but Hiram Johnson. Get your Lions ready for a foot race, in case I displease.

Well, I come in a-grinning. I thought he has got to be a pretty tough Guy if he don't grin with you. Well, he did, and he got up and come out and met us at about the 4th green, shook hands smiling, and asked in English, "Interview?"

I said, "No Interview." Well, that certainly did make the hit with him; he was standing facing me, and he put both hands on my shoulders and said, "Hurray, Bravo, No Interview."

I said to him . . . from all the pictures and all we know about you, you are looking like Napoleon, and I came to see is Mussolini a Regular Guy. Well, he got that in English, and it seemed to please him, and he seemed to start right in to prove to me that he was one.

He asked me if I spoke French. That was his first comedy line. Can you imagine me speaking French? I bet, though, I could start in and learn it as quick as I could English, at that. . . .

I told him I had just been in Geneva, and attended the Preliminary Dissarmament Conference, and what did he think about

The leading cast of the British film *Tip Toes*. From left: Nelson Keyes, Dorothy Gish, and Will Rogers.

Dissarmament? He again laughed, and winked at me as good as to say, "Why do you want to make me laugh." Then he replied, "No dissarmament; we dissarm when England dissarm on sea; when France in Air and land. So you see we never have to dissarm." Say there is the smartest thing I have heard in Europe, said in a few words. He then pulled another very funny line about this meeting which was on in Geneva, and which was just what they were doing. He said "They appoint committee; committee appoint committee; this committee appoint committee to appoint another committee, round and round, like dog biting at own tail." He said a saucer full right there. . .

I thanked him and told him there was only one other question that I wanted to ask him; that I knew lots of Italians over home, and that when I got back I wanted to have some message for them—what could I tell them?

Well, he laughed and put his hands on both my shoulders and said in English, "You tell 'em Mussolini, R-e-g-u-l-a-r G-u-y. Is that right Englais." He said, "Mussolini no Napoleon, want fight, always look mad; Mussolini, laugh, gay,

The ground-breaking ceremony for the new Ziegfeld Theatre. From left: Will, Billie Burke, Patricia Ziegfeld, and Florenz Ziegfeld Jr.

like good time same as everybody else, maby more so"—and he winked. "You tell that about Mussolini." Those are the very words he said to me to tell you.

While still in Rome, Will was notified that his application for a Russian visa had been approved and could be secured at the Soviet Embassy in London. He and Will Jr. returned to England via Spain. There he had meetings with King Alfonso and Primo de Rivera, that country's dictator.

While Will's influence and prestige were steadily increasing in America, it seems remarkable that his importance was already recognized abroad. For surely, without that cognizance in foreign leadership circles, Will Rogers, a private citizen, would never have been received by His Holiness, the Pope; by King Alfonso of Spain; or by the Prince of Wales, Mussolini, Emon de Valera, or Primo de Rivera. And especially as a newspaperman, he would never have been so easily granted an entry permit into the Soviet Union.

Once having the visa secured, Will prepared to fly to Moscow. He made arrangements for his son's care. Next he rid himself of all items that dictatorship could misinterpret. He even discarded addresses people had given him, books, newspapers, notes he had made for articles. He reduced the amount of clothing he carried to two pairs of socks, an extra set of underwear, and just one suit, lest his surplus be misinterpreted as a sign of flaunting capitalism. He was not about to give any cause as a foreign reporter to be accused of fostering anti-Soviet inclination: "I had seen pictures of long trains wending their way along the Trans-Siberian Railway hauling heavy loads of human freight, when nobody had a return ticket but the conductor. So if I thought of an alleged wise crack, it was immediately stifled before reaching even the thorax."

Will Rogers's 1926 visit to the Soviet Union is well documented in his articles and in the collection of those articles into the booklet titled *There's Not a Bathing Suit in Russia & Other Bare Facts.* It is amazing that on his very short visit into a land where he did not know the language, Will could come away with so much information and insight, substantiated and true. Some of his pearls of observation made part of America squirm with concern, while the other part chuckled:

The Russians figured out everything in their Communistic system, except how to get enough to eat.

Communism to me is one third practice and two thirds explanation.

Siberia is still working. It's just as cold on you to be sent there under the Soviets as it was under the Czar.

The only way you can tell a member of the Party from an ordinary Russian is that the Soviet man will be in a car.

I am the only person that ever wrote on Russia that admits he don't know a thing about it. On the other hand, I know just as much about Russia as anybody that ever wrote about it.

The Communism that they started out with in Russia, you know, the idea that the fellow that was managing the bank was to get no more than the man that swept it out, that talked well to a crowd, but they got no more of that than we have.

Everybody gets what he can get, and where he can get it, and it takes about two to watch one, and four to watch those two.

They have a great many schools in Russia, which seem intended not so much to eliminate illiteracy as they are to teach propaganda.
   Political propaganda starts with their A B C's.

They informed me: 'We are a very serious people, we do not go in for fun and laughter. In running a large country like this, we have no time for appearing frivolous. We are sober."

I wanted to tell them that what they needed in their government was more of a sense of humor and less of a sense of revenge.

It was the *New York Times* which informed its readers on July 15 that, according to a report from London, "Will Rogers, the famous American Cowboy Comedian, signed a contract today with British National Pictures to appear in a film entitled 'Tip-Toes' . . . Rogers just arrived here [in London] from Moscow." It must have seemed strange to the American theatergoers that in an age of only silent films, anyone would want to film a Broadway musical for which George Gershwin had written the music. Starring with Will would be Dorothy Gish and a British comic, Nelson (Bunch) Keyes.

Will was back again at the Ranelagh Club, this time to play polo as an honored guest. It was barely two decades since he had performed there before King Edward VII. Will had traveled many miles since then.

And lest this vacation to Europe become too leisurely, Will offered to help an old friend, Charles B. Cochran. Considered by many to be the British Florenz Ziegfeld Jr., Cochran realized that the current edition of his Revue at the London Pavilion seemed lackluster. It desperately needed the injection of star-quality adrenaline; would Will try to provide the essential life-saving stimulant?

Will had been on London's stage before, but that was in the days when he had his roping act, with Buck McKee riding Teddy across the stage, and when his chatter was coincidental. Now the rope would be gone, and all he would have on stage with him would be his sparkling mind, his unconventional sense of humor, and his obvious compassion for his fellow human being. Would that be enough for the British public? Both Will Rogers and Charles B. Cochran were willing to take a chance.

Of all the British newspapers, the foremost in importance is the *Times of London*. Its opinion was sought and respected. After viewing the cowboy from Oologah on his opening night at the Pavilion Theatre on London's Piccadilly Circus, the paper's theater critic wrote:

> *Mr. Will Rogers, the American comedian and film actor, appeared on Friday night in Cochran's Revue at the London* Pavilion. *He is presenting each night for a season of at least six weeks the "turn" that has earned him such popularity in America. He walks on the stage in an ordinary shabby suit—and just talks. At*
> the first performance on Monday night, he talked a little too much, but that mistake can soon be rectified. At the beginning Mr. Rogers seemed a little timid. He need not have been. Humour of the kind in which he delights, is international and, in a very few days he will be attracting all London to the Pavilion.

And James Agate, Britain's foremost critic, did not spare compliments, either. Reviewing the addition to the Cochran Revue in the following Sunday's *Times*, he wrote of Will Rogers:

> *A superior power had seen fit to fling into the world, for once, a truly fine specimen—fine in body, fine in soul, fine in intellect.*

The *Times* reviewer was right. Will Rogers did attracted crowds to the Pavilion, and played to capacity houses every night. Among the important visitors who came to see him were the Prince of Wales, the Duke of York, the Duke of Connaught, Princess Marie Louise, and Princess Helena Victoria. There had been no contract between Will and Cochran; the matter of payment had never been discussed. Charles Cochran recalled Will's modesty in their deal over salary:

> *When he appeared for me at the Pavilion, he refused to name his price, saying: "Pay me what I am worth." I sent him a check for $1,000 at the end of the week, and he sent it back with the remark, "I'm not worth it."*

Cochran then sent his theater manager with a blank, signed check, asking Rogers to fill in any amount he thought proper. Will tore up the check.

Before leaving the United States, Will had spoken with Adolph S. Ochs, publisher of the *New York Times*. The publisher made an offhanded remark, suggesting to Rogers that if he saw anything in Europe that he thought the *Times* could use, he should wire it, and the paper would pay for the transmission. On Thursday, July 29, 1926, Will sent a cablegram to the *New York Times*.

> *Nancy Astor, which is the nom de plume of Lady Astor, is arriving on your side about now. She is the best friend America has here. Please ask my friend, Jimmy Walker, to have New York take good care of her. She is the only one over here that don't throw rocks at American tourists.*
>
> *Yours respectfully, Will Rogers.*

The *Times* editor thought the telegram important and placed it on the top of the first page of the second section. It would be the honored place for the next 2,816 daily telegrams Will would send.

It is almost impossible to overstate the impact and significance of Will Rogers's daily columns. In an age when news coverage was almost entirely through newspapers—radio was still the new kid on the block—Will's observations not only highlighted the latest national and international developments, but readers received his impartial commentary and understanding. In the years that followed, it was this column of rarely more than 300 words that was first read by almost forty million Americans, including the president of the United States. It was this deceptively short column that would make Will Rogers one of the most talked about and important voices in the country.

Will was still appearing for Charles Cochran when, at the beginning of August, Betty Rogers arrived with Mary, then thirteen years old, and Jimmy, age eleven. The family was reunited with Will and eldest son Bill in London. For Will there were the daylight hours at the film studio and the matinees and evening performances at the Pavilion. Betty took her offspring to learn English history firsthand. There was the obligatory viewing of the "changing of the king's guard" at Buckingham Palace; the Tower of London; the Old Curiosity Shop; and dinner at Ye Olde Cheshire Cheese, which had been the favorite tavern of Charles Dickens and Doctor Johnson. One Sunday, Will having no commitments, the whole family took a trip to Hampton Court, built in 1515, the onetime residence of Cardinal Wolsey. As Mary wrote in her diary, the family almost got lost in the intricate maze in the palace garden.

A special act of generosity by Will Rogers endeared him to his new British fans. It was the kind of comfort Rogers would have provided without a moment's hesitation in his native country, but the fact that an American, a foreigner, should help the Irish, especially the very poor, touched both the Irish and the British. It was a tragedy in which forty-seven men, women, and children burned to death in a ghastly fire in Dromcolliher, a village in County Limerick, about 36 miles southwest of Limerick city, on the border of County Cork. It started at a "Cinematograph Entertainment," a motion picture showing—a rare treat for everyone.

> Since there is no public hall in the village, the films were shown in a large loft over a garage—the upstairs portion of a wooden building [which] had one door, reached by an ordinary ladder from the floor of the garage.
>
> About 200 people, including many women and children, were packed into this room. The program had just started when a film burst into flames. As the projecting machine was placed near the doorway, escape from the room would have been difficult. Only those near the door had a chance in the panic to get away in safety. Many women and children were trampled under foot and it was not long before the ladder, which formed the only means of egress, collapsed, leaving the people trapped within the loft. The room by this time was a mass of flames. . . .
>
> The fire is believed to have been caused by the carelessness of a cigarette smoker or by the presence of a lighted candle near the operating box.

"Mayor" Rogers poses for a publicity shot with the Beverly Hills Fire Department.

The very next day, William T. Cosgrave, president of the Irish Freestate, opened a fund for the relief of Dromcolliher. Will not only contributed substantially to the fund, but also performed a benefit performance:

> *Mr. Will Rogers, the American comedian, has come to Dublin specially to appear this evening at a concert which has been organized at short notice on behalf of the fund.*

There were no fanfares for Will Rogers, just a handful of lines in the newspaper, hidden away on an inside page. But he had not gone to Dublin for publicity. This was the right, the decent thing to do—and Will did it.

In mid-August Will broadcast from England for the highest fee ever paid "to a radio talker in this country—the check going to a hospital charity at Rogers's request." But Will was not through yet. He was already making a film, appearing nightly at the Pavilion Theatre, still writing his weekly columns, writing feature-length articles for the *Saturday Evening Post* , and then he took on—for a period of three weeks—nightly appearances at the Prince's Supper Club.

It was only when school for the youngsters and contractual commitments for Will called that the Rogers family returned home aboard the *Leviathan*. While aboard they learned of the devastation caused by a hurricane that had hit Florida. While in mid-Atlantic, Will arranged for a benefit performance for relief of the hurricane victims. One of the passengers aboard was the recent U.S. secretary of state, Charles Evans Hughes. Will wrote a script in which he gave the distinguished future chief justice of the Supreme Court all the humorous lines, while he kept the "straight" lines for himself. The show was an artistic and financial success and raised $30,000 in the first-class section. It was repeated twice more in additional classes. The total raised was $48,600. Will was pleased with the amount raised, but commented: "We raised that from a crowd coming home—imagine how much we could have raised if we had got a hold of 'em going out."

(Will's generosity was becoming very well known. Earlier in the year, his tour had been booked into New York City's Carnegie Hall for a one-night stand. The next day, Monday, April 12, Will sent a check for $2,500 to the United Jewish Campaign of New York. Interviewed about this eminently generous amount while rushing to catch a train leaving for Philadelphia, Will Rogers bared a hitherto unknown side of his personal credo. He said:

I make it a rule to play every Sunday night for charity. . . ."

When Rogers landed back in New York on September 27, Adolph Ochs wanted him to continue his daily squibs from wherever he was, but no finances were discussed beyond that the *Times* would cover the transmission charges. In fact, several days later, when the *Boston Globe* wanted to run the telegram as well, the *Times* insisted that it had exclusive rights. When the McNaught Syndicate took over, exclusivity stopped, though it was always the *Times's* editorial offices that would receive the telegram and then forward it to subscribers.

Planning to see George H. Lorimer of the *Saturday Evening Post* in Philadelphia, Will inquired of the White House whether he could come to see the president. A return telegram not only invited Will, but offered an invitation to stay the night at the White House, and if notified of the time of arrival, a White House limousine would be waiting for him.

Rogers was so surprised at the invitation that he sent a return telegram to check that this was not someone's hoax.

Everett Sanders. White House. Washington. D.C.

> *If that gentleman is not kidding me that is the greatest honor that ever fell my way and I not only appreciate it but I am going to take you up on it, I have to stop off tomorrow, (Thursday) and see Mr. Lorimer in Philadelphia. Then I am coming on down there in the afternoon, Just think the only non office seeker that ever slept in the White House. I have an awful lot to report.*
>
> *I will be there one night if I have to put a cot in the Blue Room. If he will run again I will carry the solid south for him. I will wire from Philadelphia. If this is*

The Rogers family at Will's installation as "mayor" of Beverly Hills.

Three great stars: Douglas Fairbanks, "Mayor" Rogers, and Tom Mix.

not on the level you better stop me in Philadelphia. Just think it will be the first meal I ever had on the Government, and its just my luck to be on a diet now. Its Mrs. Coolidge I want to meet.

Regards till somebody wakes me up.

W. R.

It was not a prank, and Rogers spent about twenty-four hours with the Coolidges. He came away surprised to have discovered that "dour Cal" was a well-informed, amiable, very human man with a dry sense of humor. He found Grace Coolidge a warm, charming woman, very much like Lady Astor. While he would joke about both of them in the future, his fondness for both showed at all times.

Will took a plane back to New York City. Since his flights into and out of Russia, Will had become converted to travel by plane. Henceforth he would take a plane whenever there was one available. He obtained a special pass, signed by Eugene Vidal, head of the Aviation Section of the U.S. Department of Commerce, which allowed him to be a passenger on mail flights, provided he wore a parachute and that his weight did not add excess to the permissible legal cargo total.

It was back to the routine of the lecture tour with the DeReske Singers. All was just as it had been during the last season, only now Will would add his experiences of the past summer, his stay in England, his flight into Russia, his observations on the Preliminary Disarmament Conference. He brought to his listeners a feeling of a firsthand report. He had verbally delivered a similar report to Franklin D. Roosevelt—then a New York lawyer, between government positions—which FDR described as being more humorous and more accurate than any he had received before.

On December 8, Will and the quartet were to appear at New York City's Carnegie Hall for the benefit of the City's Committee of the State Charities Aid Association. Will paid $500 for a seat in the balcony for Betty, while he helped judge a Charleston contest. It was mentioned in the local newspapers that the crowd refused to leave until after eleven o'clock. The following afternoon, Will was the master of ceremonies at the cornerstone-laying for the new Ziegfeld Theatre, at Sixth Avenue and 54th Street. Present were Betty; Florenz Ziegfeld Jr.; his wife, Billie Burke; and their daughter, Patricia, who recalled:

Will Rogers was there, and he saw that I was not very charmed with the whole procedure. It was cold, and there wasn't much going on, so he said: "Here, Patricia, have a piece of gum." So I was chewing the gum merrily, and my mother

Will Rogers inspects the police force as "mayor" of Beverly Hills.

The Rogerses' beachfront property.

caught me. "What are you doing with that gum in your mouth?" I thought that it would be perfectly all right if I said that Mr. Rogers had given it to me. But it wasn't. She said, "Spit it out!" But I tucked it up on the roof of my mouth, because it was sort of a sacred piece of gum, because Will Rogers had given it to me.

On December 21, 1926, when Rogers interrupted his lecture tour to return home for Christmas, a new job awaited him. During his absence he had been "elected" mayor of Beverly Hills, and a large crowd came to greet him at the Santa Fe Railroad station. The mayor's position was, of course, mostly ceremonial, as the city of Beverly Hills was administered by a board of trustees.

From the station a lengthy parade, including forty Rolls-Royce cars, led him to Beverly Hills. Here Will took the oath of office while the Los Angeles Fire Department band played "The Old Gray Mare." Then world-famous film star Douglas Fairbanks, as chairman of the reception committee, took the podium and "demanded" that the new executive provide for the poor of Beverly Hills and spearhead a movement for private swimming pools, bridle paths, and golf courses, to be cared for out of public funds.

Replying, Will addressed the crowd: "It don't speak well for your town when this many of you haven't got anything to do but come to meet me." He also said that his first official act would be to enlarge the suburban jail, and that he would be the only mayor who is purposely funny. "I'm for the common people and as Beverly Hills has no common people, I'll be sure to make good." But he was proud to have been chosen by his friends and neighbors, and signed his daily columns as "Mayor Rogers." He summed up Beverly Hills: "My constituents, I don't claim that they are all good, but the most of them is at least slick." Will's "reign" is riddled with beneficial acts, paid for by His Honor out of his own pocket; among his gifts was a gymnasium that Rogers built for the local police department, and a handball court.

Almost a year later, the California legislature decreed that in any town of the sixth class governed by a board of trustees, the chairman of the board of trustees had to be known as the mayor. Will was out of office, but as usual, he had the last word:

There is only one thing that makes me sore about the whole thing and that is this. This new law applied to cities of the sixth class only. My Lord, if I had known that I was ruling in a city of the sixth class, I would never have taken the thing in the first place. Mayor of a sixth-class city—why, I will be years living that down.

Will Rogers ended 1926 by purchasing, on December 31, 418.69 feet of Santa Monica beach for $357,000 from R.C. Gillis, payable with 6 percent interest over the next five years. In the following two years he would add even more beach to his holdings, and in one case even a lighthouse. It was Will's maxim: "I had been putting what little money I had in Ocean Frontage, for the sole reason that there was only so much of it and no more, and that they wasent making any more."

Page 134, "After the dinner . . . ," Weekly Article #126, May 10, 1925.

Page 137, "And on the day . . . ," Weekly Article #128, May 24, 1925.

Page 138, "One of Sallie's . . . ," Paula McSpadden Love became the first curator of the Will Rogers Memorial; her husband, Robert W. Love, was the manager.

Page 140, "Now I haven't got . . . ," Weekly Article #147, October 4, 1925.

Page 143, "Will plunked down . . . ," *Claremore Weekly Progress*, November 26, 1925.

Page 144, "But just between you . . . ," "Letters of a Self-Made Diplomat to his President", London, May 20, 1926.

Page 145, ". . . sorter want to get up . . . ," Weekly Article #184, June 20, 1926.

Page 145, "I don't know exactly . . . ," advertisment for Bull Durham, signed "Mayor Rogers".

Page 146, "Will's arrival . . . ," *Tulsa Daily World*, May 18, 1926.

Page 146, "I told him that I . . . ," "A Letter from a Self-Made Diplomat to his Constituents".

Page 149, "So I says . . . ," Hiram Johnson—Republican senator from California.

Page 150, "So if I thought . . . ," *There's Not a Bathing Suit in Russia*, by Will Rogers, © 1927.

Page 152, "Mr. Will Rogers, the American . . . ," *Times of London*, July 21, 1926.

Page 152, "A superior power . . . ," *Times of London*, July 25, 1926.

Page 152, "Among the important . . . ," *Variety*, October 27, 1926.

Page 152, "When he appeared . . . ," *New York Tribune*, August 17, 1935.

Page 152, "Please ask my friend . . . ," James J. (Jimmy) Walker—mayor of New York City 1925–1932.

Page 153, "In the years that followed . . . ," interview by Sterlings with James A. Farley, President F. D. Roosevelt's postmaster general.

Page 153, "The fire is believed . . . ," *Times of London*, September 7, 1926.

Page 154, "Mr. Will Rogers, the American . . . ," *Times of London*, September 9, 1926.

Page 154, "In mid-August . . . ," *New York Times*, August 18, 1926.

Page 155, "I make it a rule . . . ," *New York Times*, April 13, 1926.

Page 157, "Will Rogers was there . . . ," Sterlings' interview with Patricia Ziegfeld Stephenson, January 4, 1971.

Page 158, "I'm for the common . . . ," *New York Times*, December 22, 1926.

Page 158, "He summed up . . . ," Weekly Article #236, June 19, 1927.

Page 159, "There is only one . . . ," Weekly Article #244, August 28, 1927.

Page 159, "It was Will's maxim: . . . ," Weekly Article #381, April 13, 1930.

Will Rogers delivers his radio program.

"Squawkies" and "Whistlies"

*"I hold only two distinctions in the movies,
being the ugliest man in 'em and still having
the same wife I started out with."*

1927 started in a strange way for Will. Because of inclement weather he was forced to take the train, instead of a plane, east. He never had difficulties going into a deep, thoroughly refreshing sleep anyplace:

> *Will Rogers . . . breezed into Detroit today along with a snow storm . . . [he] failed to respond to the Pullman porter's summons . . . when he wakened, his car was in the yards about five miles from the nearest taxi cab.*

The booked lecture tour had taken on a new format. The quartet was no longer part of it. Will had chosen instead his nephew Bruce Quisenberry, Betty's sister's son. He became the factotum, in charge of everything from making sure that travel arrangements had been properly made to going out and buying new clothing while Will soaked in the hotel's bathtub. Being booked to perform every night in a different town, the two men never stayed long enough in one locality to send out laundry and expect it to come back in time. Will had long ago solved the problem by simply buying new shirts, underwear, and socks, and leaving the used items behind. As for pajamas, so one of the DeReszke singers revealed, Will would only wear the trousers. After taking the pins out of a new set on the train, he would just toss the new jacket out the window. This gave rise to the thought that from coast to coast there had to be an uninterrupted trail of brand new pajama tops cluttering up the railroad's right-of-way, giving silent testimony to the fact that Will Rogers had come this way.

The spring thaw of 1927 brought on some of the worst flooding ever seen along the Mississippi River. Thousands were forced from their homes and had to flee for their lives. Houses were swept away; men, women, children, and beasts drowned. It was more devastating than anyone could recall. The various aid organizations were extended beyond their capacity to help. Will wanted to assist, too. He successfully persuaded Florenz Ziegfeld to let him use the brand-new theater on New York's West Side on a Sunday evening, when it would be dark. He then asked the world-famous tenor John McCormick to join him, and together they

Mary Rogers and her polo pony, Ann Pennington, circa 1927.

staged a benefit concert for the Mississippi River flood victims. Will flew from Beckley, West Virginia, to New York just for the concert, and the two men raised $15,000 that evening.

The following Sunday found Will back in New York, having flown in from Vermont, where he had been performing. The National Vaudeville Artists Benefit Fund was collecting money for the sanitarium at Saranac Lake, in upstate New York, by simultaneously presenting four shows at four different theaters in New York City—the Hippodrome, the Metropolitan Opera House, the New Amsterdam, and the Century. Will Rogers appeared at all four theaters, which together raised $110,000 on that single Sunday evening. This sanitarium, which provided free health care to any show business related patient, would be renamed after Will's death. It became the Will Rogers Sanitarium at Saranac Lake. For decades contributions would be solicited in theaters and motion picture houses to maintain it. When the sanitarium became dated and awkward to reach after local train service ceased, the facility was closed. A vastly expanded and modern clinic and rehabilitation center was set up in White Plains, New York. It still performs its charitable work for current and former show business personnel, in the spirit of the man whose name it still bears.

Looking at his schedule and daily journal, which document his professional commitments and his charitable pursuits, it is easy to accept Will's account that by May 23, 1927—only the 143rd day of the year—he had not only given 188 performances, but had "shown" in every state of the Union.

Early in June Will returned to his home in Beverly Hills, complaining of a stomach pain. The following week, he had what was called an attack of nervous indigestion. X-ray pictures were taken. When they were read—and when Will developed jaundice—Drs. E. C. Moore and P. G. White advocated immediate admission to the California Lutheran Hospital. The following day Will was operated on for the removal of gallstones.

In two articles in the *Saturday Evening Post,* entitled "A Hole in One," Will described what led up to the operation and his part in furnishing the body. The articles were later combined and published as a best-selling hardcover book with the title *Ether and Me.*

While the articles were funny, Will's condition was far from it. Bill, the eldest son, remembered only too well how his mother called the children together and

they all prayed for their father's recovery. Telegrams and letters arrived from a concerned citizenry, including the president of the United States. There were almost hourly bulletins broadcast on Will's condition.

On the day following the operation, the hospital announced: "Will Rogers spent a fairly good night." It may have seemed "fairly good" to the hospital, but there were long stretches when it seemed doubtful that Will would even pull through. Round-the-clock nursing was necessary for the next three weeks. During his stay in the hospital, Will Rogers learned that he had been elected a life member by the American Red Cross. After Will Rogers returned home, weeks of bed rest were part of post-operative care.

Despite his operation and the slow recovery that followed, Will had not missed a single deadline on either his daily or his weekly columns. Now rapidly becoming bored by the inactivity forced upon him, Will thought up a contest. He offered $500 to the first Ford car that would make it nonstop from Claremore to his home in Beverly Hills. It was a challenge that sounded whimsical. That is, it was a funny thought until 4 A.M. Wednesday morning, July 13, 1927, when Mr. and Mrs. J. Collins of Tulsa aroused the Rogers family to claim the $500 first prize. It was reported that Mrs. Rogers "not too enthusiastically" rubbed her eyes and received her husband's invited guests. Half an hour later, Mr. Trobert Kloehr and Mr. Ross Hutchins, both of Claremore, arrived and claimed second prize—though none had been offered.

Around noon a third motorist arrived and was handed a check. By this time, Will had safely removed himself to the cabin in the hills of Pacific Palisades, where no car would find him. There is no official record of just how many ambitious drivers were tempted to enter this contest. But then again, this was the era of marathon dances and similar pointless contests. After all, even Charles Lindbergh's heroic solo flight across the Atlantic was really in pursuit of a $25,000 prize.

Will had a more meritorious idea, which did not work as well as he hoped. By now firmly convinced that air travel was the best way to get from here to there, he heard from pilots that it was frequently difficult to determine from the air if they had reached the town they were seeking. They thought that there should be some identification on at least one rooftop in each town. Will sought help from his readers. It worked in some instances, but not enough. So he gave the valid idea some incentive. On May 1, in his daily column, he offered to pay for the paint it would cost to print the name of any town on the largest roof available. Well, the bills just rushed in by the bag:

Charles Lindbergh and Will Rogers.

Courtesy of the Will Rogers Memorial Commission

Now I sure did mean well, but I just gnawed off more than I could chew. Pontiac, Michigan, sent me a bill for 98 dollars. I thought somebody was going into the paint business up there. . . .

The Kansas Chamber of Commerce advised me that as the State was at that time having a "Paint and clean up week" and that would I just mind including enough to paint and clean up Kansas. Now can you imagine me cleaning up Kansas? Can you imagine anybody cleaning up Kansas? Even Carry Nation couldent do it. . . .

Will Rogers amended his offer from supplying the paint to paying only for the brush. The rush of letters asking for money abated almost immediately to a trickle.

Will's next film project was to star in the film based on Charles Hale Hoyt's popular old stage play, *A Texas Steer*. It was an independent production by First National Pictures, Inc. As some scenes were to be shot in Washington, D.C., and Will was still recuperating from his recent operation, he decided to take the train as a more appropriate and sedate form of travel. Before leaving California he wired President Coolidge for permission to use parts of the White House and grounds for the film, and to the producers' surprise, permission was granted.

Stopping off briefly in Kansas City's Union Station, Will Rogers was inaugurated as the first president of the Amalgamated Association of Defunct City Fathers. As the deposed mayor of Beverly Hills he qualified for membership. Another honor, somewhat more distinguished-sounding, was to follow when he reached Washington. In its auditorium, the National Press Club presented him with a parchment scroll appointing him "Congressman-at-Large for the U.S. of A." Rogers, in his acceptance speech, feigned shame that this unfortunate thing had happened to him. "My folks always raised me right and warned me about being a congressman. I guess I am one of the few persons for whom they ever got a gang together, to humiliate me publicly." But he signed some of his daily and weekly articles as "Congressman at Large."

The hub of the farce *A Texas Steer*, simply put, is the Eagle Rock Dam Bill—the dam was to be near Red Dog, deep in the heart of Texas—and the graft that is expected to flow most liberally from it. As Will wrote:

Just finished taking scenes here in Washington for a movie of the old stage play, Hoyt's A Texas Steer. It was the story of a man elected to Washington on bought votes. We are bringing it up to date by not changing it at all. In the stage version he didn't know what to do when he got in Congress. That part is allowed to remain as it was. He used to play poker more than legislate. That's left in. There was a little drinking among the members at that time. For correct detail in our modern version that has been allowed to remain in.

> *Yours for government buy the people,*
> > *Congressman at Large,*
> > > *Rogers.*

A slight embarrassment occurred when one of the limousine chauffeurs had to be hired to double for Will in a scene in which he was supposed to ride a

**Thirteen-year-old
Jimmy trick-riding
on his horse Billy,
1928.**

horse—hell for leather—down Pennsylvania Avenue. But the doctors' strictest order had been that Will was not to ride for at least a year. Now newspapers were reporting all over the country that cowboy Will Rogers had to hire a double to do his riding for him.

While the National Press Club ceremony was, of course, a jest, year's end found Will on an actual diplomatic mission. Relations between the United States and Mexico had never mended since the days of President Wilson and the exchange of reproving diplomatic notes. There were many prior problems. The major contention, however, was still the American armed pursuit of Francisco (Pancho) Villa, the Mexican revolutionist, onto Mexican soil. Villa, infuriated with Washington's recognition of his opponent, had crossed the border and attacked a U.S. military post. He was then chased by a U.S. army detail, under the command of General Pershing, back across the border, which was, of course, an invasion of an autonomous and friendly neighboring country. That had been the cause of the friction between President Wilson and the Mexican government. And though all this had happened ten years earlier, the ill will had persisted.

Will, being a civilian who had no personal political interests or ambitions, was unofficially asked to come to Mexico to see whether he could use his talent for building familiarity to soften America's image with the government south of the border. The thought was primarily advanced by Dwight W. Morrow, President Coolidge's former schoolmate at Amherst, and now ambassador to Mexico. He thought that bringing two famous men to meet with President Calles and his ministers would indicate interest in America's neighbor to the south. Ambassador Morrow also invited Charles A. Lindbergh, the current hero of America and the world.

Rogers was the first to arrive, as Lindbergh was to attempt a nonstop flight from Washington, D.C., to Mexico City. While Lindy was waiting for the right weather conditions, Rogers, by just being his usual self, became the center of Mexico's attention and proved an excellent delegate for his country. He joshed and joked, played polo on President Calles's team, went on sightseeing trips with him, inspected irrigation projects and agricultural schools, impressed him by performing rope tricks and then watched him perform in the bullring; the two men had developed a relationship before Lindbergh arrived a week later.

Ambassador Morrow's plan to improve the relationship and ties between the two countries at the top level succeeded beyond expectations, and there was even an unforeseen consequence: Charles Lindbergh met Morrow's daughter Anne Spencer; they fell in love and were married in June 1929.

The year 1928 began with one of Will Rogers's rare slips. Dodge Brothers' automobiles had planned to start the new year with an innovation in radio programs, impressing its listeners with the advancing technology. It was to be a coast-to-coast presentation, featuring major stars performing from studios in different parts of the country: Will Rogers, the master of ceremonies, was to broadcast from Los Angeles (in fact his home in Beverly Hills), Paul Whiteman and his orchestra would be heard from New York, Al Jolson from New Orleans, and Fred Stone and daughter Dorothy from Chicago. Dozens of technicians had rehearsed the switching of "feeds" for days, so that listeners would not even be aware of the difficulties in having the program originate from four different locations, yet sound as if they all were in the same studio. Everything worked perfectly and the program went off without a mishap. The problem arose from something Will Rogers did. Few people outside his circle of friends knew of Will's talent for imitation. Hearing a voice just once was enough for him to be able to copy it so accurately that even the subject's mother would have had difficulty differentiating between the original and Will's imitation. Welcoming the listeners and introducing the show, Will made a few humorous remarks then said:

Will prepares for his air mail flight, 1928.

Courtesy of the Will Rogers Memorial Commission

Now folks, Dodge Brothers have arranged a real surprise for you. That on account of its nature they naturally couldn't advertise it, because he thinks autos have contributed to the success of the prosperity. Get ready for a real surprise. It's Mr. Coolidge, who wants to take this opportunity to deliver a short message to America. ALL RIGHT MR. PRESIDENT:

Ladies and Gentlemen, it's the duty of the President to deliver a message to the people on the condition of the country. I am proud to report that the condition of the country as a whole is prosperous. I don't mean that the whole country is prosperous, but as a whole it's prosperous. That is, it's prosperous for a whole. A whole

*is not supposed to be prosperous, and this country is certainly in a hole. There is
not a whole lot of doubt about that.*

*Everybody that I come in contact with is doing well, Hoover, Dawes, Lowden,
Curtis, Al Smith and McAdoo are all doing well, but not as well as they would like
to be doing this time next year. Mellon has saved some money, for himself, and gave
a fair share of it to the Treasury. He is the only Treasurer that has saved faster
than Congress could divide it up. Congress is here now to split up what he has
saved. It would have been cheaper to send each Congressman and Senator his pro
rata share, and saved the whole expense and reason for holding this Congress.*

There were mixed reactions to Will's imitation of the president. Some wondered whether this was indeed Coolidge, while others were convinced that it was.
Will was surprised. He felt that he would have insulted his listeners' intelligence if
he had announced that this had not been President Coolidge. Surely the man in
the White House would not have spoken such gibberish; how could anyone even
think that Silent Cal would utter such nonsense?

Arriving back in Washington, Will dashed off an apology to the president and
then he explained publicly:

*I found on my arrival in Washington that some people had censored me severely
for leaving the impression the other night that Mr. Coolidge was on the radio. Well,
the idea that any one could imagine it was him uttering the nonsense that I was
uttering! It struck me that it would be an insult to any one's sense of humor to
announce that it was not him.*

*So I wrote Mr. Coolidge a note explaining, and received a two-page letter
within thirty minutes from him, written all in his own longhand, saying that
he had been told of it, but knew that anything I did was done in good-natured
amusement, and to not give it a moment's worry. He also thanked me for my kind
reference to him on various occasions of which he had heard.*

*I knew my man before I joked
about him. It's as I have often said:
You can always joke good-naturedly a
big man, but be sure he is a big man
before you joke about him.*

Will had returned to Washington,
as he had been asked to appear before
the House Flood Control Committee.
Having traveled up and down the
Mississippi River in 1927 on his fund-
raising tour for the flood victims, the
House sought Rogers's opinion and
observations. Will came away expecting little help from the government
for past and future victims:

*You hear a good deal about what
Congress is going to do for the*

Will Rogers,
Dorothy Stone, and
Andy Tombes per-
form a scene from
Three Cheers for the
injured Fred Stone
(seated, right) and
his wife, Allene.

Mississippi Valley. I don't want to discourage the Valley but I would advise them to put more confidence in a boat builder. I got more faith in high ground than any Senator I ever saw.

When you talk about poor people that have been hit with this flood, look at the thousands and thousands of Negroes that never did have much, but now it's all washed away. You don't want to forget that water is just as high up on them as it is if they were white. The Lord so constituted everybody, that no matter was color you are, you require the same amount of nourishment.

The return to his travels as monologist began on January 25. This time it would be a twelve-week tour, again without the quartet, and again with Bruce Quisenberry. Will had a lot of new material and had had weeks to develop it. And then there was something new. *Life* magazine, then devoted to humor, announced that Will Rogers would run for the presidency. Most assumed that this was going to be some of Will Rogers's typical humor, while others began to think of it as a viable suggestion.

As 1928 was, of course, a presidential election year, Will again undertook to cover and report on both national conventions. This writing assignment would be in addition to his regular daily telegrams and his weekly articles. In June, flying via Western Air Express to the Republican National Convention in Kansas City, his plane was just landing at Las Vegas, Nevada, when it flipped over and slid to a halt on its top. Will was shaken and dazed when released from the wreckage, but recovered quickly.

Another plane had to be sent to continue the journey. A few hours later he boarded the substitute plane to continue on to the convention. The schedule called for refueling and a mail pickup in Cherokee, Wyoming. This was one of those small country airports, with just a plain grass area as its landing strip. The only piece of equipment denoting this to be an airport was a tall pole with a wind sock indicating the wind direction. Gaining speed for the takeoff there, one of the plane's wheels hit a gopher hole, cracked a strut, and flipped over. Again, Will was miraculously unhurt, but once more he had to wait several hours before another plane could be dispatched to take him the rest of the way.

Will, who now had become the country's major advocate for aviation, downplayed both as "incidents," rather than "accidents." His only complaint was that somewhere in those two "incidents" he had lost his overcoat. But the day was not over yet. Arriving over Kansas City in terrible weather, the plane had to set down on a miry field with the water and mud splashing way up to the windows. There had been an official reception planned, but the welcoming committee was delayed by weather and traffic. Will left the airport on his own before any designated greeters arrived.

This convention was expected to be a quiet, dull affair. William Allan White, famous owner and editor of the Emporia *Gazette*, was quoted as describing it the "dreariest public occasion since the burial of William McKinley." But in spite of the fact that there was little life at the convention when everyone knew that Hoover would be the nominee, there was quite some animation—albeit from a bottle—in an illegal lounge in the press quarters. It must be remembered that this was still the period of Prohibition, with the law imposing abstinence on all those who wished to observe it. The press corps, in general, was not among the volun-

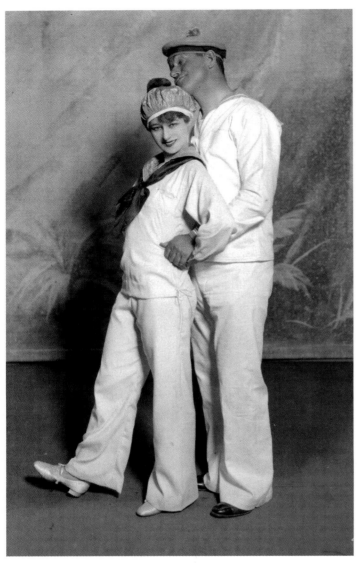

Will with Dorothy
Stone in *Three
Cheers.*

teers. The occasion became, as such strictly private defiances of the law sometimes will, ever more stimulating. It erupted when H. L. Mencken, the number one curmudgeon of his age, pointed his finger at Will Rogers, who had just entered, and yelled: "There is the most influential editorial writer in America!"

"Look at the man," he shouted. "He alters foreign policies. He makes and unmakes candidates. He destroys public figures. By deriding Congress and undermining its prestige, he has virtually reduced us to a monarchy. Millions of American free men read his words daily, and those who are unable to read, listen to him over the radio. . . . I consider him the most dangerous writer alive today."

"Come on now, Henry, you know that nobody with any sense ever took any of my gags seriously," remonstrated Rogers.

"Certainly not," Mencken countered. "They are taken seriously by nobody except half-wits, in other words by approximately 85 per cent of the voting population."

Despite Mencken's seemingly insulting outburst and his uncivil tone, these two men were friends and remained so. In fact, when *Life* magazine finally unveiled its mock campaign for Will Rogers as the presidential candidate of the Bunkless Party, Mencken was one of the earliest public supporters. When it sponsored Will Rogers's "Bunkless Party" campaign, it knew that he would point out the inanities of the promises the various candidates made. Will Rogers's campaign promises immediately exposed the other parties' follies. His Bunkless Party guaranteed "whatever the others don't, we promise." Its stand on Prohibition showed up the other parties' straddling of the issue: "We promise," announced Will, "wine for the rich, beer for the poor, and moonshine for the prohibitionists." But the main campaign promise was Will's vow "that if elected, I will resign."

On election day, *Life* magazine proudly announced that Will Rogers had been overwhelmingly elected by the large, silent majority. Will, as promised, kept his campaign promise and resigned. But between "nomination" and "resignation" a surprisingly large number of America's newspapers—though knowing that this was a strictly humorous series—seriously editorialized on the feasibility of a real

Rogers campaign. It was felt that most assuredly, he had the background, the depth of understanding, the political acumen, the character to be a winning candidate. But Will would not even consider it.

With Herbert Hoover nominated, Will left Kansas City for Salt Lake City, aboard an airmail plane with two hundred and six dollars' worth of airmail stamps pasted on him. He had to get home and make preparations for the Democratic Convention and the beginning of the fall part of his lecture tour.

Because of Will's enthusiasm for aviation his best friend, Fred Stone, had been taking flying lessons. Not just satisfied with hiring a pilot, he wanted to be able to operate a plane himself. Stone, being a well coordinated, athletic man, proved an excellent student and had advanced to soloing in a short time. But something went wrong. It was never determined whether it was machine or man, but five days after Will left on his lecture tour, Fred Stone lay in a Groton, Connecticut, hospital, having been seriously injured in a plane crash. So serious was the physical damage to both his legs that for days doctors felt that amputation was the only way to save his life. When Will rushed to his friend's bedside and saw the dancer's crushed body and heard the news about Fred's legs, he burst into tears and had to brace himself against the wall to keep from collapsing.

A publicity photo for Fox Studios. This is one of the few pictures in which Will's hair is combed back.

Courtesy of the Will Rogers Memorial Commission

Will tried to cheer his friend, and visited with him for several days, but his own commitments had to be addressed. Fred, a professional trouper, was fully aware of that.

The Democratic National Convention of 1928 was held in Houston, Texas. The same crowd that had reported the Republican Convention met again here in Houston, and the good-natured bantering continued. It was said of Will Rogers that he made as much news as he reported. It was Will Durant, the philosopher and writer, who stated: "There is Will Rogers, the most sensible man on the floor, laughing at everybody, and yet seeing the human worth in all. . . ."

Probably the most accurate description of Will Rogers's contribution to the quadrennial display of public tomfoolery covering up private dealings was stated by a reporter for the *Review* of Decatur, Illinois:

> *[Will Rogers] a national institution . . . poked fun at both the Republican and Democratic conventions, but no dispatches from the conventions have been read with more interest than those sent by Rogers . . . His jibes and jolts are taken as humor, but they have a way of staying with you.*

One of the great demonstrations of altruistic friendship in show business was made by Will Rogers. Fred Stone and his daughter Dorothy were to have started rehearsing the new musical *Three Cheers* at the New Amsterdam Theatre on Monday, August 27. But Stone now lay encased in a plaster cast, confined to a specially equipped bed at the Lawrence and Memorial Association Hospital in New London, Connecticut. Fred would not be able to fulfill his contract to sing and dance—if indeed he would ever walk again. It was then that Will Rogers canceled his lecture tour, offered to reimburse every theater owner the amount they expected to gain from his appearance, and stepped into his friend's show. Charles Dillingham, the producer, could not have hoped for a better solution to his problem. He had invested much in the show at this point, and many jobs depended on it. If there was anyone who could make a Broadway audience forget the artistry of a performer like Fred Stone, it was Will Rogers. It was true that while the two men had little in common as far as their talents were concerned, each was at the top of his fame and could equally attract a crowd. In fact, as he had shown all over the country, Will Rogers alone could draw a full house, hold it easily for three hours, and still have the audience clamor for more.

Right from the beginning of rehearsals, it became obvious that this rendition of *Three Cheers* was going to be a quite different show than had been written. Dorothy Stone, its female star, recalled the days.

All through rehearsals, Will was reading from the script. At the dress rehearsal in Springfield, Massachusetts . . . he was still reading this thing. So I looked for Mr. Dillingham—I called him "Uncle Charley" because I had known him ever since I had been a tiny child—and I said, "Uncle Charley, I think we ought to postpone the opening, because Will doesn't know his part."

And Uncle Charley said, "Dorothy, I have news for you. Will is never going to know that part, because he is not going to do it."

I said, "You mean he is going to leave?"

And Dillingham said, "No, he's not going to leave, but he's got something up his sleeve, and I'd like to know what it is. And we are going to open because I want to know what this guy is going to do. Just remember this, this is going to be a type of show you have never seen in your life!"

So that night in Springfield, we were all standing in the wings, waiting for Will to make his entrance. The audience gave him an ovation that you've never heard. Then this is how he started his first scene—he walked down to the audience, took the script out of his pocket, and said: "Now here it says that Fred is to do a flip-flop, a back somersault, a stiff fall, and an eccentric dance to open the show. Now I'm not going to do that! I'm going to talk about Hoover!" And he threw the script into the orchestra pit. Well, the audience just shrieked, they just shrieked. But I just stood there. My father's method had always been that every bit of business, every line, was rehearsed to the nth degree. And I thought, "Oh my God! What's going to happen?"

Well, Will proceeded to do a marvelous monologue about Hoover. And I stood in the wings and wondered when I'd go on. When, just as I was wondering whether I should change clothes, or go on, or stay there, or what, Will turned and saw me in the wings. He said, "Dorothy, honey, come here! Come on stage and meet your Daddy's friends." I came on, and he put his arm around me, and he talked to

Rehearsal for *They Had to See Paris*. From left: director Frank Borzge, Will, Fifi D'Orsay, and music director Con Conrad, 1929.

me for a while; I know we didn't do our scene at all. I don't know what we did. Will just talked to me, and he finally said, "Now you run and change your clothes for that number you're going to do with the leading man." The audience didn't even know there was a leading man, because I hadn't met him yet on stage. . . .

So I went off, and changed my clothes—and—the whole show was musical numbers and nobody knew why they were there, because there was no book that led up to them. All of a sudden, two perfect strangers, that hadn't met, would come out and do a love song. But the audience adored it. It was brilliant, it was topical—and it was what they wanted. It wasn't Three Cheers; it was a one-man show.

[The next night] was all together different—the whole show was just cut to musical numbers, and Will. And that's how we opened in New York, and they just loved it. [As for other shows] They had the same format, the musical numbers came in about the same place, and we had a line of Tiller Girls, but Will was different every night.

Even though it was an unusual musical show, receipts never fell below a most respectable $42,000 per week, and tickets were hard to get. Will did wonder about the especially high prices of theater tickets for New Year's Eve:

The cast and crew of *They Had to See Paris*, with Will Rogers in the center. Will's right hand rests on Marguerite Churchill; his left hand rests on director Frank Borzage.

Our musical shows are getting $11 a seat. That's box office prices and one patron was able to get one at that price at the box office—[not from a speculator]—and dropped dead with amazement before he could get to it. It would take Coolidge, Al Smith and Hoover playing the Three Musketeers in Yiddish to be worth $11.

Three Cheers closed its run in New York City and opened the following Monday, April 22, in Boston. That first week, so it was reported, the box office of the Colonial Theatre took in a most impressive $56,000. The successful tour continued until it permanently closed in Pittsburgh.

We opened in October 1928, and Will was in it until June 1, 1929, because he had a motion picture commitment. He had to leave the show, and you just couldn't put anyone else in, and you couldn't go back to the old book. So we closed.

On March 22, 1929, while the New York Stock market was chalking up new highs every day, Will and Fox Film Corporation's vice president W. R. Sheehan had signed a letter of agreement which called for Will to star in four films in a sixteen-month period beginning June 1, 1929. Will was to assist in creating and writing original matter, such as dialogue of dramatic and comedy lines; assist in the selection and construction of stories and continuity thereof, and the selection

of cast; edit, criticize, revise, adapt, compose and create scenarios and titles, and write the text thereof. The full payment for these four films was to be $600,000.

Fox Film Corporation risked a huge sum on a new venture. While Will Rogers had already appeared in numerous films, even the generous contract with Goldwyn had only paid a grand total of $286,000 for a total of twelve films. Of course, Goldwyn's contract was signed in 1919 while Fox came along ten years later, when it seemed that money could be made selecting any company just by sticking a pin into a list of traded stocks and then asking your broker to buy it in the morning and sell it in the afternoon. This was part of the Roaring Twenties and the house of stock certificates was still standing, though there were some indications that its foundation was none too solid.

The film industry, too, could be viewed with suspicion. The new films, though revolutionary because they reproduced sounds, were far from satisfactory. In 1927 the first full-length motion picture with sound was released. It was also the end of numerous careers of favorites, because too many times the voices of stars once only seen were now heard, and those voices just did not fit the images so carefully nurtured. The public would not accept a "vision of ultimate perfection" with a broad regional inflection, or worse yet, an unintelligible foreign accent. Will diagnosed it accurately when he wrote:

Everybody that can't sing has a double that can, and everybody that can't talk is going right on proving it . . . everything is 'Ennunciation.' I was on the stage 23 years and never heard the word or knew what it was.

It can be said that the first all-sound motion picture, *The Jazz Singer,* starring Al Jolson, had its technical shortcomings. Yet it was a major breakthrough, and as such was the forerunner of many advances expected to come. But the next developments were painfully slow to materialize. And even when they became available, the cost of replacing existing projection equipment in smaller, neighborhood motion picture houses was expensive. Even with the latest devices, there were major problems with lining up film and sound, with recording and reproducing sound correctly and faithfully. Voices were distorted and many natural sounds did not record well. And even if the sounds recorded all right, sound equipment would not reproduce them correctly. There were a lot of unwanted and unexpected squeaks and creaks, resulting in films that Rogers dubbed "squawks":

> *I went to see one of the new "Squawkies" the other night. It was billed as, "Metro Goldwyn's first sound picture," and the only sound in it was Monte Blue whistling.*
>
> *It never reproduced a word he said, or any of the others, but it did whistle when he did. It dident even whistle the same tune he whistled, but it did whistle when he did. Well, that wasent bad, for he had done his whistling in the south seas, and this whistling was done in the Studio, so you couldent expect them to remember what he had whistled three months before. But that's what they was selling as a sound picture was Monte's whistling.*
>
> *Now I like Monte, he is a dandy actor, but I don't like to be hornswoggled into going in to just hear him whistle. For he is not what I would call an A-No. 1 good whistler. I paid to see a "Talkie" and all I got was a "Whistlie".*

While the advent of sound in motion pictures meant the death knell to many a great career, it was precisely what Will Rogers's talents needed. His writing ability had taken him to the top of that medium. He was the most widely read and quoted columnist with a daily and a weekly column, and his books sold well. He was the most widely recognizable person in the United States, since his photograph and articles about him constantly appeared in newspapers and magazines. His lectures

The house and grounds in Beverly Hills.

were sold out; he was one of the highest paid after-dinner speakers and was always in demand. He gave freely of his time and effort to every deserving charity, and his promised appearance assured a successful campaign. Advertisers even paid him to declare that while he did not use their product, he thought highly of it. His wit, his philosophy, his conscience, his innate honesty and sincerity had made Will Rogers into a national icon. And there was more to come. He was yet to make a film in which his viewer could hear him speak. America of the 1920s and early 1930s adored Will Rogers, trusted him, and never worried where he came from, or where he would ever go. He was theirs and as long as he was there, some things were still right with the world.

When Will arrived at Glendale airport after closing *Three Cheers,* Betty was there to greet him. But there, also, was a delegation from Fox, consisting of management and a camera crew with reporters to record the arrival of their newest star—or what they hoped would be their star. While the Fox people wanted Will to come directly to the lot and begin work, Betty whisked her husband off to their home in Beverly Hills.

Will's first film for Fox was *They Had to See Paris,* co-starring Irene Rich as Will's socially ambitious wife. Will, as Pike Peters, a garage owner in Claremore, Oklahoma, becomes suddenly wealthy when an oil well on his property begins to produce at the rate of a thousand dollars a day. Mrs. Peters now wants to go to France to find a titled husband for their budding daughter, played by beautiful Marguerite Churchill. This film also introduced Canadian-born Fifi D'Orsay as the "Parisian Bombshell."

At the end of June 1929, the home at 925 N. Beverly Drive in deepest Beverly Hills was destined to undergo some relatively minor alterations. Mary was now sixteen, and it was agreed that she should have her own wing of the house with all the amenities a young lady should have. While the work was to be done, the family moved for the summer to their ranch in Pacific Palisades. Originally bought as a weekend retreat and quite rustic, it was far away from the city, out in the country along a two-lane dirt road which years later would be known as Sunset Boulevard. The house, no more than a large cabin, now became a grand toy where Will could practice his gift for development. This talent was given wide reign when contractors found the Beverly Hills house infested by termites. As more parts of the house were found to be affected and in need of replacement, Will and Betty became more certain that they would not rebuild on that site. Instead, the house in Beverly Hills was razed and the large corner lot sold. Pacific Palisades was to become the family's permanent home.

Family life on the Pacific Palisades ranch proved quite different than Beverly Hills had been. Here, away from the nearest neighbor, were interesting trails to ride; the acreage still undisturbed, was open for exploration. There was a small cabin a short distance away, hidden from the main building to increase the feeling of rustic simplicity. There was no swimming pool, but Will ordered a polo field, a riding ring, a polo practice cage, a barn which would house almost two dozen horses, and a tennis court for the children.

Will Rogers fled Los Angeles on September 17, 1929. It was a practice he followed on the openings of most of his films. He just did not like to be involved in all the hoopla of a Hollywood film premiere—especially for his own films—and he was obviously embarrassed by the attending pretense.

The stables at the
Pacific Palisades
home.

I was a sitting around home after finishing an "Audible," and as it was to appear with a sort of ballyhoo opening, why, I figured I better kinder take to the woods till the effects kinder blew over. I wanted 'em to kinder fumigate around before I appeared in person back home.

They was opening my first talking picture tonight in Los Angeles and charging those poor people five dollars, and I just couldn't stand by and be party to such brigandage. First-night audiences pay their money to look at each other, so if they get stuck tomorrow night, they can't blame me. It will be because they don't look good to each other.

This opening was an especially grand affair. It was held at Hollywood's Fox-Carthay Theatre on September 18, 1929, and the master of ceremonies was Jack Benny. Will need not have worried; the film played there for weeks. The naturalness of Will Rogers's acting style plus his sincerity immediately made him and his role delightful to watch and to hear. Even the usually critical and reserved *New York Times* had to admit: "Mr. Rogers is capital."

The film immediately received general public acceptance and wide recognition in the industry. The November 1929 issue of *Photoplay Magazine* named Will Rogers's the best performance of the month; *Film Daily*, one of the most prestigious motion picture related periodicals, indexed *They Had to See Paris* as number four on its Honor Roll of The Best Films of 1929, while the *Film Spectator* of January 4, 1930, placed it in sixth position and the January 5, 1930, issue of the *New York Times* voted the film as number seven of its top ten list. Fox knew immediately that it had struck pure gold when it had signed Will Rogers to four films. It also knew that to wait to tie him up would be folly.

But a calamity of hitherto unknown scope had befallen the world in the meantime. The stock market collapsed in October 1929, setting off the deepest economic depression in history, ultimately affecting the entire civilized world. Millions lost employment, while employers lost millions. Dreams were dashed, paper profits vanished, businesses tottered or went bankrupt. Despair became an uninvited guest in most homes, and even God seemed to have gone away with-out leaving man his prayed-for daily bread.

Much, too, changed in Will Rogers's life. While around him distress began to take over his country, he was about to become the foremost movie star of his era. Celebrating his fiftieth birthday on November 4, 1929, he had already reached the pinnacles in several professions, all of them without having to step on competi-tors, since he had created every peak for himself. There simply was no one like him, and never had been. And still there were more mountains to climb. Coming to Hollywood, he had entered a domain where youth and beauty were deemed essential requirements for stardom. Yet Will Rogers was not young, nor could it truth-fully be said that he was beautiful, though his inner radiance was obvi-ous. Now he was to com-pete in a business where he did not fit any estab-lished category. He was a "leading man," but cer-tainly not like a Clark

The Rogers family polo team.

Gable or a Tom Mix; still by 1932 he was number nine among the top ten box-office favorites. He barely trailed Clark Gable that year, and twelve months later, in 1933, he led all males in Hollywood. He would never be topped by another male for the rest of his life.

Ever restless, Will decided to look in on the Five Power Preliminary Naval Disarmament Conference held in London in January 1930. He sailed aboard the North German Lloyd liner *Bremen*. As his next film was to be *So This Is London*, this offered Will the opportunity to make certain observations firsthand that could be used in the production.

Will Rogers attended several meetings of the conference. The five powers were the United States, Great Britain, France, Italy, and Japan. The object eventu-ally was to arrive at some semblance of parity in their respective military ship-building programs. After observing the meetings, Will was doubtful of the efficacy of this type of conference:

The American delegation arrived this afternoon and went into conference at once at the American bar and sunk a fleet of schooners without warning.

They brought eighteen young typewriters with 'em. That's four and a half blondes to the delegate, and I can write in long-hand, left-handed everything that will be done here in the next month.

Well, the conference met today and appointed a commission to meet tomorrow and appoint a delegation who will eventually appoint a subcommittee to draw up ways and means of finding out what to start with first.

I met Admiral Takarabe, one of their [Japan's] principal delegates out at Ambassador Dawes's last night and on leaving I shook hands with him very warmly, and said: "Admiral, I am going right home to America and I want to say that I have shook hands with the winner."

Joe Robinson, [Senator from Arkansas] said to me: "Will, the whole thing is not different from old Arkansaw politics, only the food is a little fancier."

Will returned to the United States aboard the SS *Ile de France*. The crossing was a stormy one. The ship finally limped into the New York City harbor two days behind schedule, delayed by a freak Atlantic storm. Will made a stop at Washington to report to Vice President Curtis and a number of senators, then moved on to Claremore, Oklahoma. He stayed at the just-completed hotel named in his honor:

Will Rogers, a crack polo player, goes after the ball still high in the air at a game in Santa Monica.

Here I am sitting in the brand new, most up to date hotel in the Southwest, the Will Rogers Hotel in Claremore. It's six stories high.
I know now how proud Christopher Columbus must have felt when he heard they had named Columbus, Ohio, after him.

In March 1930, Will took on another new task. Having successfully tackled the newspaper and film markets, he now was prepared to enter the newest medium, radio, on a regular basis. While he had done the odd broadcast, doing a regular show would be quite different. True, radio was the newest kid on the block, but Will had no concerns about doing on the air what he had done right along in vaudeville and on the lecture circuit. On March 19, he signed a contract for a series of thirteen weekly broadcasts, sponsored by E. R. Squibb and Sons, to be carried by the Columbia Broadcasting System. Each talk was to last twelve to fifteen minutes for a total salary of $72,000. Some smart reporter figured that it would amount to almost $500 per minute. Will established an unusual

Will's desk in his study at the Pacific Palisades ranch.

format in that he chose single subjects for each broadcast. Subjects ranged from personalities in the news, including Charles Lindbergh, President Hoover, Vice President Curtis, and Alfred E. Smith, to topics such as the arms conference, Prohibition, Boston, and Chicago.

When the series concluded, E. R. Squibb and Sons published a pamphlet giving the text of all twelve broadcasts. There was a great demand for these booklets, and to this day a great market exists for original issues.

Will's next motion picture was *Lightnin'*, based on the book by Frank Bacon and the play by Winchell Smith and Frank Bacon. The action takes place in Nevada, at a hotel for divorcing wives who are fulfilling the mandatory six weeks' residency period. Divorces were easily granted in Nevada, the only requirement being that whichever party sought the divorce had to have been a bona fide resident of Nevada for a period of six weeks. Then it was a mere formality to have the marriage dissolved.

In the story of *Lightnin'* the hotel is—to complicate matters—astride the boundary line between California and Nevada. Guests had to keep out of the section of the hotel that extended into California, as the six-week-residency law clearly stipulated that should the divorce-seeking party leave the state of Nevada during that period—however briefly—a completely new residency of six weeks had to be established.

The film was the first big chance for a tall, handsome young actor named Joel McCrea:

I was cast as his [Will's] son in law, the juvenile lead. I met Will sitting in a buggy. The director, Henry King, asked me whether I had met Mr. Rogers, and when I said no, he introduced me. That was 1930, and it was the beginning of a friend-

The living room at the Pacific Palisades home. At the far right is the "Ziegfeld Window."

The fireplace in the main cabin of the Pacific Palisades home.

ship which you kind of felt the moment I got there.

Our first scene was on that buggy. Will was supposed to talk quite a bit, then I had a line, and then he talked on quite a bit longer. He improved it as he went along, and everybody got to laughing, but when the time came for me to talk, there was no cue. So the director said, "What's the matter, McCrea, isn't it your turn?" I said it was, but that I had not received my cue. So Will just said to me: "Joe,"— he always would call me "Joe"— "Joe, you ain't like these other actors; you're kinder like me. You ain't very good looking, and you ain't a very good actor. You're just a cowboy, and I'm going to help you. You see what I do, I change the dialogue. I write a good deal of it myself. Sometimes I improve it, sometimes I don't, but I go along with it. And when I think I have said enough, I'll stop, and then I'll poke you and then you talk. I'm not going to do it for the other actors, but I'll do it for you."

Lightnin', Will Rogers's third film for Fox, was previewed by the studio. By this time it had become quite obvious to the executives at Fox that Will Rogers was a powerful drawing card, and that the initial successes had not been a fluke. The important part was that he had originally been signed for only four pictures. He had to be tied to the Fox studio, and the sooner the better. A contract, almost a letter of understanding, was drawn up, stipulating that Will would make six additional films for the studio, now for a total salary of $1,125,000. Though Will Rogers did not know it, he had been hired to help keep Fox Film Corporation from financial failure.

In the early 1930s, almost half a century after the U.S. government had so generously decreed the arbitrary distribution of the Indian Territory in approximate 40-acre parcels, the bill for the folly came due. What had always been lush bluestem grazing land and open range had, with the stroke of a bureaucratic pen, been converted into lots barely big enough for fields. With the new railway and fields available, the farmers streamed into the prairie states and began to plow up the land.

What no one seemed to consider was that from the Gulf of Mexico in the south to the Great Lakes in the north, there is a wide swath across the country's midsection called "Tornado Alley." Storms, tornadoes, or just strong winds sweep across the flat, open prairie. Especially in early spring, when the freshly plowed and seeded fields are most vulnerable, that part of the country experiences its most devastating tornadoes, blowing away the valuable topsoil. In the early 1930s, the winds and drought would not let up, carrying so much soil from the states of Texas, Arkansas, Oklahoma, Colorado, and Kansas that it dimmed the sun. At high noon it was dark, with the steady winds forcing the fine soil through every crack, whether around windows, between logs, or under doors. There was no way for farmers to plant a crop, and certainly no chance of harvesting one. It was a disaster not only for the farmers and their families, but for all those in the

Will and Maureen O'Sullivan in *So This Is London.*

Union who depended on their crops. The area, now known as the Dust Bowl, starved both man and his animals.

In January 1931, Will flew to Washington, D.C., for a meeting with President Hoover. Having observed the enormous damage in the Dust Bowl and the human misery in numerous states, Will pointed out that the government should financially assist the Red Cross in its overwhelming humanitarian tasks. President Hoover, so Will reported, felt that it would set a damaging precedent for the government to assist private agencies. Will saw it differently:

> *Congress yesterday turned down the 15 million food bill, and passed 15 million "to improve entrances to national parks." You can get a road anywhere you want to out of the government, but you can't get a sandwich.*
>
> *They seem to think that's a bad precedent to appropriate money for food. They think it would encourage hunger.*

Being in Washington, Will met with Barton Payne, chairman of the American Red Cross, and some of his board of directors to see what he could do to help. What they discussed became the Will Rogers Drought Relief Tour. Will got private industry to supply a plane and fuel and the pilot, Captain Frank M. Hawks. Will offered his talent and countrywide recognition, and before long had transformed the experienced pilot into a veteran fellow performer. Their first stop was Arkansas, considered the worst-hit area in the land.

England, Arkansas, had made national headlines when a large group of hungry farmers and their families peacefully marched into town, demanding food from the local grocery store. This prompted Will to write:

> *We got a powerful government, brainy men, great organizations, many commissions, but it took a little band of five hundred simple country people (who had no idea they were doing anything historical) to come to a country town store and demand food for their wives and children, they hit the hearts of the American people, more than all your Senatorial pleas, and government investigations. Paul Revere just woke up Concord. These birds woke up America.*
>
> *I don't want to discourage Mr. Mellon and his carefully balanced budget, but you let this country get*

Will with Irene Rich, in a still from the movie *So This Is London*.

Courtesy of the Will Rogers Memorial Commission

THEY'RE still talking about "They Had To See Paris" and we know that "So This Is London" is a better role for that brilliant movietone star, Will Rogers. He's America's unofficial ambassador to the League of Nations, World Court —and the fun loving world.

The world's greatest humorist

George M. Cohan's international success **WILL ROGERS**

with **IRENE RICH**
FRANK ALBERTSON
Maureen O'Sullivan · Lumsden Hare
Bramwell Fletcher
Adaptation and Dialog by Owen Davis, Sr.
Directed by JOHN BLYSTONE

SO THIS IS LONDON

A poster for *So This Is London*, 1930.

hungry and they are going to eat, no matter what happens to budgets, income taxes or Wall Street values.

Washington mustn't forget who rules when it comes to a showdown.

As the *New York American* reported, "Will visited England, Arkansas, stopped at shacks of Negro tenant farmers, and . . . motored through barren acres of farm lands to the drought section of Pine Bluff." The next day Will performed in the Dallas-Fort Worth area "returning to his quarters at 3 o'clock, ordering a lunch of chili with a Bermuda onion sliced into it."

On Sunday Will made arrangements to appear in Austin, where he was "commissioned a Texas Ranger." On Monday, January 26, he gave a performance at a theater in downtown Austin, after speaking at a luncheon as guest of Governor Ross Sterling, collecting $2,500. He also addressed both houses of the legislature, then flew in a tri-motored plane to San Antonio for a night performance and a radio address.

Next it was off to San Angelo, Texas. "We got out at 7 A.M., drove 110 miles, put on a milkman's matinee at ten in Abilene, in Simmons University auditorium, then another 110-mile jump, by auto to Breckinridge, Texas." Their plane got stuck in mud and it was not until dark that they reached Dallas. The first week of their tour included thirteen cities and raised some $82,000 for drought and unemployment sufferers.

Will gives friendly advice to Joel McCrea in the film *Lightnin'*, 1930.

A Wills Cigarettes insert card promoting Joel McCrea and Will Rogers in *Lightnin'*.

The following week, Will opened the tour in his native state, in Oklahoma City. Will and Governor "Alfalfa" Bill Murray had their lunch at the governor's desk. Afterwards, Will addressed both houses in a joint session. The next day there was a performance at nearby Norman at 10 A.M. After that eye-opener at Norman—so the *Daily Oklahoman* reported—"Will cruised back to Oklahoma City for an extra battery for Frank Hawks's Hell Diver plane. He asked the mechanic at the Curtiss-Wright hangar where they went for chili and somebody said the Sunset Inn in Britton was the stuff. So we piled into Clarence Page's Ford and made for the Sunset Inn. . . . Will selected corned beef and cabbage and for dessert absorbed a full-grown bowl of chili."

Then they were off on a flight to Chickasha for a performance at 3:30 P.M.; then they flew to Ardmore for an 8:30 show. It was reported that Ardmore raised $4,000. Saturday, February 7, there was a show at the Coleman Theater in Miami, Oklahoma, at 10:30 A.M. Will was supposed to land at the Miami airport, but a low ceiling, fog, and poor visibility forced the plane down some five miles south of town. So here was America's premier entertainer, movie star, radio personality, and newspaper columnist, on a mission of mercy, just standing by the roadside, trying to thumb a ride into town. He finally made it. While Will entertained a large crowd, a young artist who was yet to become famous, Charles Banks Wilson, stood in the wings and made the sketches which later became a famous oil painting that now hangs on exhibit at the Will Rogers Memorial and Birth Place in Claremore, Oklahoma.

The tour continued through Tulsa, where donations totaled $20,000. In all, Will Rogers performed in twenty Oklahoma cities in seven days and collected more than $90,000. Then it was back to Arkansas. Rising at 5 A.M. at Fort Smith, Rogers motored to Russell and raised about $2,000 before breakfast. He postponed breakfast long enough to plant a Will Rogers tree on the campus of Arkansas Polytechnic College, where he spoke. Then he flew to Conway, where a thousand people met him at the airport, and raised $2,200. When someone invited him to stay for lunch, he replied that he didn't have time as he had to be in Hot Springs by 2:15 P.M. So the housewives got busy and prepared sandwiches, wrapped in a plain brown paper bag. Will ate them on the way to his next stop, where $2,500 was added to the relief fund. The day ended with three more shows in various locations in Little Rock. The following day, the last one on this tour, five performances were scheduled. When night fell, Rogers and Hawks were in Texarkana, having performed in fifty towns in just eighteen days, raising $225,000.

On the way back to Los Angeles, Rogers and Hawks stayed overnight in Albuquerque, since the weather report indicated a severe snowstorm ahead. As Will reported, "They gave us a dinner and we, just to keep our hand in, passed the hat there and collected a thousand dollars for their Red Cross fund."

The tour ended, and Will's daily squib of March 8, 1931, just speaks of a benefit polo game played by "youth" against "aged players." He makes light of the game, pointing out that the combined ages of the "youth" team was barely one hundred years, while the total years of the "aged players"—if you counted his own age as thirty-eight—would be just two hundred years. Yet he never tells his readers that he sustained a painful injury to his left wrist. Despite the injury, he finished the game. Two days later the wrist and hand were swollen so badly that X-ray pictures had to be taken. A fracture was detected and the wrist put in a cast, remaining painful for some time.

While his wrist was mending, Will pursued a new idea. Having decided that beachfront property he owned along the Pacific Coast highway might be an ideal location for a hot-dog stand and a gasoline service station, he applied for a building permit. To his surprise he found the local citizenry rising against it, filing protests. He immediately withdrew his application, and neither was built.

When news of a severe earthquake in Nicaragua became known, Will had a new mission. He obtained a certificate of health, sanity, and vaccination against smallpox from the City of Los Angeles Department of Health, and he was off to Managua. There the Marines' medical officer administered an additional shot against typhoid. After touring the sites of destruction caused by repeated shocks, Will entertained the American troops raising funds for the victims. He had a friendly meeting with Nicaragua's president, J. M. Moncada, and made a donation of $5,000 to the American Red Cross, stipulating that the money was to be spent in Nicaragua. After Will Rogers's death, Nicaragua issued a set of five postage stamps to honor the man who had come such a long way when help was needed.

Back in Los Angeles, Will sustained another injury while playing polo. His horse stumbled, throwing its rider, breaking a bone in Will's left ankle. Again, Will finished the game though in great pain. It had been barely a week since the cast had been removed from his wrist, and now his ankle had to be heavily bandaged. Sporting a "walking cast," he was able to walk without crutches or cane while filming *Business and Pleasure* with Jetta Goudal, Joel McCrea, and an actor who was to achieve fame as Frankenstein's monster, Boris Karloff.

While Will was still nursing his injured ankle, two Americans were on an adventure, testing both man and machine. Daredevil pilot Wiley Post and navigator Harold Gatty were on a round-the-world flight in a single-engine Lockheed Vega, named the *Winnie Mae*.

Aviation was still young, and Wiley Post was one of its earliest idols. He had been a stunt pilot, a parachute jumper, a winner of air races, and the hero of every boy who had his head in the clouds. And yet he had few of the visible attributes that usually make a winner. Wiley was only 5 foot 5 inches tall, was heavyset, and had only one eye. An accident in the Oklahoma oil fields had injured his left eye and when an infection threatened the right eye, doctors had no other means to save the healthy eye but to remove the infected one. With singular determination, Wiley taught himself to judge distances and heights accurately with just one eye. He re-obtained a pilot's license on the strength of his previous experience as a pilot and his safety record.

Post and Gatty completed their round-the-world flight in an astonishing eight days, fifteen hours, and fifty-one minutes. The two heroes received a ticker-tape parade up New York's Broadway and were honored at an official reception at City Hall before they began a triumphant tour of major cities across the United States. There were keys to cities, speeches, medals, and parades. When Post's home state of Oklahoma planned to honor the two men, Will flew to Tulsa to speak at the banquet feting them. It was the first time that Will Rogers and Wiley Post met. Will exhorted his friends in Claremore to prepare a level field that could serve as a landing place. Post and Gatty, with Will as their passenger, then flew the *Winnie Mae* from Tulsa to Claremore, where another reception awaited them.

A few weeks later, Post and Gatty and their wives were guests at the Rogers ranch. Away from the huge crowds, Will and the two men could sit at leisure, allowing the pilot and navigator to tell about their great flight and recount the hundreds of little details never known to the public until they appeared in the adventurers' book *Around the World in 8 Days*.

In the fall, Will was asked to participate in a special radio presentation on the topic of the President's Organization on Unemployment Relief. The broadcast would feature President Herbert C. Hoover. Will agreed at once, offering to do what he could to assist this effort.

Will felt strongly about the nation's unemployed. When Betty bought an early Christmas present, a tractor for the ranch, Will refused to use it. His explanation was simple. He pointed out that he wanted men to do the work because the tractor didn't have a family to support.

The special broadcast was scheduled for Sunday evening, October 18, 1931. Alone in the radio studio, without an audience, Will waited for his cue. Then he spoke, as he always did, without script or notes—just from the heart. He made some humorous introductory remarks, and then he came to the essence of the program:

> *The only problem that confronts this country today is at least 7,000,000 people are out of work. That's our only problem. There is no other one before us at all. It's to see that every man that wants to is able to work, is allowed to find a place to go to work, and also to arrange some way of getting more equal distribution of the wealth in the country.*
>
> *Now it's Prohibition, we hear a lot about that. Well, that's nothing to compare to your neighbor's children that are hungry. It's food, it ain't drink that we are*

Will on his benefit tour for Nicaraguan earthquake victims in 1931.

Courtesy of the Will Rogers Memorial Commission

worried about today. Here a few years ago we were so afraid that the poor people was liable to take a drink that now we've fixed it so that they can't even get something to eat.

So here we are in a country with more wheat and more corn and more money in the bank, more cotton, more everything in the world—there's not a product that you can name that we haven't got more of than any other country ever had on the face of the earth—and yet we've got people starving. We'll hold the distinction of

MANAGUA, NICARAGUA

FIRST DAY ISSUE
MARCH 31, 1939
Issued in commemoration
of **Will Rogers** for his
good will flight to Nica-
ragua in raising funds for
the relief of the Earth-
quake Sufferers of March
31, 1931.

On March 31, 1939,
Nicaragua issued
this five-stamp set
to honor Will
Rogers, who came
to the country's aid
after the 1931 earth-
quake.

being the only nation in the history of the world that ever went to the poor house in an automobile. . . .

These people that you are asked to aid, why they are not asking for charity, they are naturally asking for a job, but if you can't give them a job, why the next best thing you can do is to see that they have food and the necessities of life. You know, there's not a one of us that has anything [who can say] that these people that are without it now haven't contributed to what we've got. I don't suppose there is the most unemployed or the hungriest man in America that has not con- tributed in some way to the wealth of every millionaire in America. It was the big boys themselves who thought that this financial drunk we were going through was going to last forever. They over-merged and over-capitalized, and over-everything else. That's the fix that we're in now.

Now I think that every town and every city will raise this money. In fact, they can't afford not to. They've got the money because there's as much money in the country as there ever was. Only fewer people have it, but it's there. And I think the towns will all raise it because I've been on a good many charity affairs all over the country and I have yet to see a town or a city ever fail to raise the money when they knew the need was there, and they saw the necessity. Every one of them will come through. . . .

Now I want to thank Mr. Gifford, the head of this unemployment, thank Mr. Young, and I certainly want to thank Mr. Hoover for the privilege of being allowed to appear on the same program with him because I know that this subject is very dear to Mr. Hoover's heart and know that he would rather see the problem of unemployment solved than he would to see all the other problems he has before him combined. And if every town and every city will get out and raise their quota, what they need for this winter, why it will make him a very happy man, and hap-

*piness hasn't been a steady diet with our president. He's had a very tough, uphill
fight, and this will make him feel very good. He's a very human man.*

The response to this heartfelt speech was overwhelming. As Will wrote: "I
can't answer all the telegrams and letters, but I want to take this means of thank-
ing the most people that ever wired or wrote me on anything. . . ."

Will had made an arrangement with Fox Film Corporation concerning his
work schedule. Under his contract he was to appear in three or four films each
year, and rather than have these work periods scatter throughout the twelve
months, Will wanted to make all of them in a row—one right after the other—so
that he would have the rest of the year free for other projects. Having completed
his contractual obligations for 1931, and since the 1932 schedule allowed a hiatus
of several months, Will decided to take another look at the world. He would be
off to the Orient. There was a war going on, and Will felt that he had to write
about it firsthand. There was so much yet to see, and Will wanted to see it all.

Page 161, "Will Rogers . . . breezed . . . ," *Detroit Evening News,* January 13, 1927.

Page 165, "Now I sure did . . . ," Weekly Article #283, May 1, 1928.

Page 165, "I guess I am . . . ," advertisement for *A Texas Steer.*

Page 165, "Just finished taking . . . ," Daily Telegram #346, August 31, 1927.

Page 168, "It would have been cheaper . . . ," broadcast, January 4, 1928.

Page 168, "I knew my man . . . ," Daily Telegram #458, January 13, 1928.

Page 168, "You hear a good deal . . . ," Weekly Article #230, May 8, 1927.

Page 170, "Certainly not . . . ," *Convention Articles of Will Rogers,* Oklahoma State
      University, 1976.

Page 171, "It was Will Durant . . . ," *Richmond Times Dispatch,* June 28, 1928.

Page 171, "[Will Rogers] a national institution . . . ," *Review,* June 30, 1928.

Page 172, "Well, Will proceeded . . . ," Sterlings' interview with Dorothy Stone, May 25, 1970.

Page 174, "Our musical shows . . . ," Daily Telegram #758, December 31, 1928.

Page 174, "We opened in October 1928 . . . ," Sterlings' interview with Dorothy Stone,
      May 25, 1970.

Page 175, "Everybody that can't sing . . . ," Weekly Article #338, June 16, 1929.

Page 176, "I went to see . . . ," Weekly Article #297, September 2, 1928.

Page 178, "I was sitting around home . . . ," Weekly Article # 354, October 6, 1929.

Page 178, "They was opening . . . ," Daily Telegram #981, September 17, 1929.

Page 178, "Even the usually critical . . . ," *New York Times,* October 12, 1929.

Page 179, "The American delegation . . . ," Daily Telegram #1086, January 17, 1930.

Page 180, "Well, the conference met . . . ," Daily Telegram #1094, January 28, 1930.

Page 180, "Joe Robinson . . . ," Daily Telegram #1097, January 31, 1930.

Page 180, "Here I am sitting . . . ," Daily Telegram #1111, February 16, 1930.

Page 181, "I was cast . . . ," interview with Sterlings, May 24, 1970.

Page 184, "Congress yesterday . . . ," Daily Telegram #1398, January 15, 1931.

Page 184, "They seem to think . . . ," Daily Telegram #1391, January 7, 1931.

Page 184, "We got a powerful . . . ," Daily Telegram #1390, January 6, 1931.

Page 187, "On the way back . . . ," Daily Telegram #1424, February 15, 1931.

Page 187, "As Will reported . . . ," radio address, October 18, 1931.

Page 191, "As Will wrote . . . ," Daily Telegram #1637, October 21, 1931.

This photo, taken August 14, 1935, was one of the last photos taken of Will Rogers.

"I Never Have Been
to that Alaska"

"When Seward in '68 bought Alaska for $7,000,000
he even made up for what we had overpaid the
Indians for Manhattan Island."

On Thursday, November 19, 1931, Will left Los Angeles for the Orient. He realized that it meant he would be missing Christmas with the family, but his work schedule would not allow him such a trip at any other time in the foreseeable future.

There was something puzzling about Will's penchant for traveling. He was a devoted husband and father who loved his wife and children. He enjoyed his home and friends. There was never even a hint at a scandal, and yet, there was this drive in him to leave his comfortable home and peek over the horizon, to see what lay beyond. Will rationalized it as being part of his need for up-to-date information, so that he could be better-informed when he wrote and spoke on world affairs and conditions. He wondered about those editorial scribes in their "ivory towers" who solved all of the world's problems without ever having gone beyond the corner drugstore. He had circled the world, he had spoken with numerous world leaders, had visited foreign lands and seen their problems firsthand. And when he spoke about them, or the mines of Appalachia, or the barren prairie of Texas, or the flooded Mississippi basin, or the ethnic problems of the Balkans, or the railroad trains of Italy, or Communism as practiced in the Soviet Union, he knew more of their affairs than did almost any legislator in Washington. None of that could have been gleaned sitting comfortably in southern California, sipping orange juice.

And yet, such knowledge was acquired at a high price. Betty spent weeks alone, bearing the burdens of raising a family and managing a ranch with all its problems. The children missed their father. It was Mary who would say to Joel McCrea: "We resent you a little bit; you take so much of our father's time." There was a feeling among his children that not all the trips were as important as Dad would think them. But Will was the final authority. From our latter-day perspective, the war in the Orient—half a world away—could easily be called the beginning of World War II. But in 1931 it was merely the Sino-Japanese conflict.

(Japan, in retaliation for China's boycott of Japanese cotton goods, used an alleged explosion of a railway train as an excuse to occupy Manchuria, taking

Harbin and three eastern provinces. Japan, clearly flexing its military muscles, showed its intent on expanding control over much more of the Asian mainland and the East. China's president, Chiang Kai-shek, fighting a two-front war by facing both the Japanese and the Communists under Mao Tse-tung, could do little but slow Japan's progress. The Japanese, while still fighting the Chinese, would bomb Pearl Harbor in 1941, ally with Germany and Italy, and draw the United States into World War II. Japan's battle with the Chinese would last until the unconditional surrender of Japan in August 1945.)

Once aboard the SS *Empress of Russia*, Will discovered that his old friend Floyd Gibbons, the famous war correspondent, was a fellow passenger. Gibbons, too, was headed for the same Sino-Japanese conflict. As Will wrote: "If I had the world to pick from, there is no one I would rather go with. I met him in Warsaw, Poland in '26 when we were covering Pilsudski's revolution."

The trip from San Francisco took a northerly course and ran into a typhoon. Crossing the International Date Line, Will was definitely not happy: "Well, we lost a day, we gained a typhoon, we lost a life boat and I lost my whole internal possessions."

Will reported his own news to the country:

We had a Lifeboat washed off the top Deck. Now, those things are not just tacked up there . . . When that washed away, I said to myself, "The Old Senator has the right idea. Get your Foreign Relation news from a book"
One whole 24 hours we only made 50 miles, and most of that was up and down.

In Tokyo, Rogers and Gibbons lunched with Minister of War Manimi. Sitting cross-legged on the floor, they ate with chopsticks. Will joked that this mode of eating was a perfect way to start a diet, though he claimed that he finally became so proficient in the use of chopsticks that he could even catch flies with them.

Christmas Eve found Will in Shanghai. Though he visited the American Club, where he was instantly recognized, he felt lonely and vowed never again to be away from the family at Christmastime. Here, too, Will met with military leaders on both sides and came away with this summary:

The Japanese say they don't want China, and it's a cinch the Chinese don't want Japan. The Japanese say if the Chinese would get back twenty miles from Shanghai that they would quit fighting. The Chinese say if the Japanese would go back home, where they belong, they would quit fighting.

Will with Japanese actors in Tokyo.

So nobody really knows what they are fighting over. It's almost like a civilized European war in that respect.

By January 20 Will was in London to meet Betty, who was arriving aboard the liner *Bremen*. Together they flew to Paris, toured through Italy and Switzerland, and finally returned to the United States aboard the German Lloyd liner *Europa*. Will had gathered enough information to write several lengthy articles for the *Saturday Evening Post.* There was no doubt among those who knew him best that he was a shrewd observer and that his reports, be they to presidents, lawmakers, or his readers, were accurate, timely, and could be fully trusted. This was the easily overlooked but important and serious contribution of a man whom most judged merely by his bons mots. This under-

Will Rogers at a Sunday broadcast, 1933.

estimation was expressed by the famous writer Heywood Broun when he wrote, after Will had addressed the 1932 Democratic Convention: "I think it is a little ironical that the same convention which thinks that Will Rogers is a clown accepts Huey Long as a statesman."

Stopping in Washington, D.C., Will not only reported to President Hoover and Secretary of War Patrick J. Hurley, a fellow Oklahoman, but he also met with senators, congressmen, and House Speaker Garner. From Will's writings it is quite obvious that he was convinced of Japan's aggressive intentions not only on the Asian mainland, but in the entire Pacific area. In an article titled "Letter to the Philippines," he spelled it out for those who could not yet see it:

> *We will drag along with you folks on the pretext that we are protecting you and some day we will get in a war over you, and if we ever do, we will lose you before lunch. Japan can be in there and have a crop planted before we could get a fleet across that ocean. Any nation that thinks they can go six thousand miles away from home and fight a war, is crazy.*

Will would not live to see it, but the Japanese would attack and take the Philippines; the American garrison would be defeated and taken prisoner. But in 1931, few Americans paid much attention to either China or Japan. America was in the midst of the Depression, and personal survival was the major concern.

Before returning to California, Will and Betty paid a courtesy call on old friends, the family of former Ambassador Dwight Morrow. At their home in New Jersey, they saw Charles and Anne Lindbergh and played with their son, Charles Jr.:

Will Rogers turns his alarm clock over to Charles Winninger, who succeeded him. Will used the alarm clock to warn him when his allotted air time was up.

Had a fine day today over with the Morrow family in Jersey. The more difficulties pile up on us the more we realize what this country lost when we lost him [Ambassador Morrow].

The Lindbergh baby is the cutest thing you ever saw, walking, talking, and disgraced the Lindbergh name by crying to come away with Mrs. Rogers and I in the car.

Two weeks later, the Lindbergh baby was kidnapped and killed. Will recalled the last visit for his readers:

What a shock to everybody. But how much more of a one it is when you have seen the baby and seen the affection of the mother and father and the whole Morrow family for the cute little fellow.

Two weeks ago Sunday Mrs. Rogers and I spent the day with them. The whole family interest centered around him. He had his father's blonde curly hair, even more so than his dad's. It's almost golden and all in little curls. His face is more of his mother's. He has her eyes exactly.

His mother sat on the floor in the sun parlor among all of us and played blocks with him for an hour. His dad was pitching a soft sofa pillow at him as he was toddling around. The weight of it would knock him over. I asked Lindy if he was rehearsing him for forced landings.

After about the fourth time of being knocked over he did the cutest thing. He dropped of his own accord when he saw it coming. He was just stumbling and jabbering around like any kid 20 months old.

He crawled up in the back of the Morrow automobile that was going to take us home, and he howled like an Indian when they dragged him out.

I wish we had taken him home with us and kept him.

The abduction and the news of the death of the Lindbergh baby was the foremost subject in America. Because of Will's celebrity, the possibility of a kidnapping had concerned Will and Betty for a long time. It was for that very reason that Will refrained from writing much about his own inner circle, especially when the children were younger.

Late in February Will interviewed "Public Enemy No. 1," Al Capone. He spent two hours with the jailed gangster chief, who promised that if released in the care of a government agent, he would use his connections in the underworld to look for the kidnapped Lindbergh baby.

. . . but there was absolutely no way I could write it and not make a hero out of him . . . Everybody you talk to would rather hear about Capone than anybody you ever met. What's the matter with an age when our biggest gangster is our greatest national interest?

Mary Rogers (far right) with Lew Ayres (left) in the film *My Weakness.*

The Republican National Convention in mid-June was held in Chicago. It lacked the usual public excitement. The nomination promised little suspense, and the chances of President Hoover for reelection were certainly not promising in the midst of the deep Depression. Will, as usual, covered it for the McNaught Syndicate. When it was over—both President Hoover and Vice President Curtis were renominated—he summed up the Convention: "Well, the old Republican convention of 1932 went into either history or the ash can at three thirty this afternoon." It would either make history by having its nominees reelected, or it would be a complete waste.

The Democratic National Convention was held late in June, also in Chicago. This was a far more competitive assemblage, for the nominee was practically assured victory. Democratic hopefuls were Al Smith, the "Happy Warrior"; Governor Franklin D. Roosevelt of New York state; Nance Garner, the House Speaker from Texas; and a group of favorite sons. Will Rogers received twenty-two votes as his state's favorite son. At the time he was fast asleep in the press gallery, draped over another reporter's typewriter. When wakened and told of his "candidacy" he let out a laugh. The crowd cheered and asked for a speech, but Will declined. The biggest applause was reserved for him later, when he was literally dragged to the

Mary Rogers.

Will and Evelyn
Venable in *David
Harum*, 1934.

rostrum and asked to address the waiting delegates. He spoke for nearly twenty minutes, and had the crowd roaring with approval and laughter. Elmer Davis, the columnist, diagnosed the situation: "If some fellow'd got up and nominated Rogers right then, he'd have got two-thirds of the vote as quick as a secretary could have read the roll. . . ."

Rogers also got serious in his talk:

> *Now, you rascals, I want you to promise me one thing. No matter who is nominated, and of course some of you are going home disappointed that it was not your man, no matter who is nominated, don't go home and act like Democrats. Go home and act like he was the man you came to see nominated. Don't say he is the weakest man you could have nominated; don't say he can't win. You don't know what he can do, or how weak he is until next November. I don't see how he could ever be weak enough not to win. If he lives until November, he's in.*

Franklin D. Roosevelt was nominated and James Nance Garner became the vice-presidential candidate.

The trying times that would lead to Roosevelt's election had not been kind to Florenz Ziegfeld Jr. The Great Depression was not the moment to put on expensive Broadway musicals, which were risky in the best of times. Though Hollywood beckoned with the film production of some of Flo's Broadway musical successes, ill health plagued the man whose name had been synonymous with glamour and perfection. It seemed that most of his friends of the golden era had left him, but not Will Rogers. Still treating "Mr. Ziegfeld" with the same respect, Will remembered—as few did—that it had been this man who had started his career. True, they all had had talent, but talent without a stage to display it is talent undiscovered.

Early in 1932, when a dying Florenz Ziefeld Jr. could no longer conduct his Los Angeles radio interview show and had turned it over to his wife, Billie Burke, she asked Will Rogers to be her guest for a show. He immediately agreed. Introducing him, Miss Burke called Will "Ziegfeld's greatest star."

The two families had become close friends. When Ziegfeld's fortune had declined after the 1929 stock market crash and during the Depression that followed, he had gone to Hollywood to assist in the filming of a motion picture version of one of his Broadway productions. The Ziegfeld family stayed with Will and Betty Rogers. Patricia, though younger, fit in well with Bill, Mary, and Jim. Florenz Ziegfeld's failing health forced him to spend most waking hours in the Rogerses' ranch house. Though the house was high on a hill and the ocean could easily be seen from it, the living room had no window in the right direction. One day, while Will was at the studio working on a motion picture, Ziegfeld—still the great innovator—called in workmen and had a large picture window cut into the wall facing the ocean. When Will returned home that evening the window was installed, and all the debris had been removed. Everything looked as if it had been that way all along. To this day that window is referred to as the "Ziegfeld window."

When Florenz Ziegfeld Jr. died on July 22, 1932, it was Will Rogers who made all the final arrangements and, it is said, paid the bills. Of all the performers who reached stardom by appearing in the *Follies*, Will proved the one most infinitely grateful.

> *. . . I went with him on his Midnight Frolic Roof, in 1915. A many one of us got our start, our real start with him. Those were great old days those Follies days, packed houses, wonderful audiences, never bothered me as to what I was to do or say, never suggested or never cut out. And to think after 30 years of giving them the best in town he still has the best show in New York. That shows it wasent the performers that made Ziegfeld shows, (for hundreds have come and gone). It was just Ziegfeld. I think he holds the record for being Champion. He knew colors, and he knew beauty. He knew how to keep nudeness from being vulgar. His was a gift, and not an accomplishment.*

Will took charge of the funeral arrangements while Billie Burke and her daughter, Patricia, found seclusion in the Rogers home. It was a quiet, private funeral, marred solely by the minister's frequent reference to Flo as "Mr. Ziegfield," something the master showman had always detested. Will's column was his farewell:

> *Our world of "make believe" is sad. Scores of comedians are not funny, hundreds of "America's most beautiful girls" are not gay. Our benefactor has passed away.*
> *He picked us from all walks of life. He led us into what little fame we achieved. He remained our friend regardless of our usefulness to him as an entertainer. He brought beauty into the entertainment world. The profession of acting*

Will uses the movable outdoor grill he designed to entertain his sister Sallie and her husband, Tom McSpadden. Betty (right) works on embroidery.

must be necessary, for it exists in every race, and every language, and to have been the master amusement provider of your generation, surely a life's work was accomplished.

And he left something on earth that hundreds of us will treasure till our curtain falls, and that was a "badge," a badge of which we were proud, and never ashamed of, and wanted the world to read the lettering on it, "I worked for Ziegfeld."

So good-bye, Flo, save a spot for me, for you will put on a show up there some day that will knock their eyes out.

Yours, Will Rogers.

In September, Democratic presidential candidate Franklin D. Roosevelt came to Los Angeles on his campaign. Having been friends for a number of years, Will was asked to introduce Roosevelt to the crowd that had assembled in the Olympic Coliseum. Then, having several weeks before he was due to start his next scheduled film, Will was off again. This time it was a flight to South America. There was no pressing reason for it, beyond, perhaps, that Will had never been in most of the places on his schedule. It was a whirlwind tour, stopping at Mexico City, Managua, Panama City, Lima, Santiago, Buenos Aires, Montevideo, Porto Alegre, Santos, and Rio De Janeiro. He was back in New York before the end of the month. Asked whether he was rushing back so that he could vote, Will Rogers confessed that he never voted and that, in fact, he was not even registered.

In April 1933, Will began a series of weekly Sunday evening radio broadcasts. As usual, these shows were unrehearsed and no script or notes were used, though Will had mentally prepared for it. When the commitment was made, Will had stipulated that the $75,000 fee for this series of broadcasts was to be divided evenly between the Red Cross and the Salvation Army. The sponsor, Gulf Oil, apprehensive in case something were to be said that could cause a lawsuit, had sixteen-inch interim wax discs made during the broadcast. Those discs were stored against some future necessity. Over time some of these discs disappeared, while others were transcribed onto a more permanent medium. Today they are a record of what it was Will said, and how he said it.

The radio commentaries were a success right from the beginning. People who never had seen Will Rogers on a stage, or in a motion picture, or who had not read either his daily or weekly column, could now hear him on the air. It was as if he came to visit and talk to each and every radio listener personally. After hearing Will on the radio, an old classmate from the Kemper Military School days was heard to say: "Here is Will Rogers getting paid big money for saying the same things he used to get demerits for saying in the Mess Hall at Kemper."

Will's Sunday broadcasts had become so popular that his contract was renewed. The contract specifically stated that there was to be "no restriction or censorship upon his microphone." Will never abused that privilege, nor did he ever cause any problem for his sponsors or himself. There was only one minor difficulty. Since Will spoke without a timed script, he was cut off once by the expiration of his time. The following week he was back with an alarm clock, set to ring and alert him of the closing. The clock then became part of his regular shows.

In July came a note from the president, inviting Rogers to come to Washington and spend the night in the White House. This was the second time Will would sleep there, invited once by a Republican president—Coolidge—and once by a

Democrat—F. D. R. Invitations had continuously poured into the Rogers house-hold from many different organizations, requesting Will's presence at their functions. There were the motion pictures, the daily and weekly columns, and the broadcasts to think about; there was the family, and the numerous charitable performances he freely gave. Whenever there was a free hour, Will would be in the saddle in the roping ring, catching calves or goats. On Sundays he would still be the most competitive player on the polo field. But Betty noticed that her Will, who was now past fifty years of age, was beginning to slow down just perceptibly.

The children, too, had grown up. The years had quickly added up, and now that he was around the home a lot more because he was busy at the studio for months, the children had flown the nest and were away at college, or had begun to make lives of their own.

Will always maintained that Betty had raised four children to maturity, three by birth and one by marriage. They all developed differently. Will Jr., the eldest, was the studious type. He carefully read the *New York Times* daily whether he was in New York or in Tubac, Arizona. He read the latest books, followed show-business news, and saw as many plays as he could when he visited theater cities. He briefly pursued a show-business career, conducting the original morning show on television. He later appeared in motion pictures, playing his father in *The Will Rogers Story*, co-starring Jane Wyman as Betty. He was publisher of the *Beverly Hills Citizen*. A lifelong Democrat, he was very interested in politics and served one term as a California congressman before enlisting for overseas duties in World

Will in *Ah! Wilderness.*

War II. After government service in the Bureau of Indian Affairs, he retired to southern Arizona.

Mary was strictly show-business oriented. In July 1933 Will suddenly learned that Mary had been working under the assumed name of Mary Howard in a film at Fox Film, the same studio to which he was under contract. Will was pleased that she had managed to succeed without his help, but suggested that rather than start in films, she first get a good grounding of stage experience. Mary agreed and made arrangements for a stint at the famous Lakewood Summer Playhouse, in Skowhegan, Maine. She was a stunningly beautiful young woman and certainly had the talent for a successful future on the stage and in films.

Jimmy, the youngest, started in show business as a little boy, appearing in several of his father's silent films. Later, during World War II, he appeared in training films and shorts. Jimmy is the cowboy among his siblings. He is a fine polo player, raises and trains polo ponies, and is settled in southern California.

The fourth "child," the one by marriage, was incorrigible. He was usually given his way. It can be said that his leadership of the Rogers family was practically flawless, that most of his decisions were correct, that he was a faithful, loving husband and father, that he certainly provided well for his family, that he was the most generous contributor to many charitable causes, that he was an icon to a nation which needed one. Perhaps he was too awesome an example. Here he was, a half-century old and at the top of every endeavor he had attempted. He had arrived there not through nepotism or connections, but through unique talents, a superior innate intellect, and very hard work and persistence—an unbeatable combination.

And then there was Betty. Will repeatedly admitted in his writing that she was "the balance wheel" of the family. Betty was the perfect partner and mother, holding the family together despite the fact that Will was always so busy and traveled so much. Will was her husband, but he also belonged to the whole country, which made enormous demands on him. Betty was patient; she was his advisor, his critic when criticism was asked for. He would often run thoughts or scripts by her, and take her advice. It was definitely Betty who suggested that Will do verbal commentaries on the daily news. It was she who suggested that Will give his views on what he had just read in those numerous newspapers he was voraciously reading. Much of the credit for Will Rogers's success must be given to Betty. Will and Betty always remained kind, generous, decent people who were not changed by money and prosperity. Will had once put it into words and he lived by them:

> *I am just an old country boy in a big town trying to get along. I have been eating pretty regular and the reason I have been is because I have stayed an old country boy.*

In July, Will was working on a film called *Doctor Bull* while another American idol was adding to his own reputation. Aviation pioneer Wiley Post was on another round-the-world flight. This time he was alone. In the two years since he and Harold Gatty, his navigator, had completed such a flight, Wiley had heard many detractors claiming that while he, Post, had done the steering, the real brain had been Gatty, the navigator. Post was now out to prove that he didn't need a navigator; he could do it all by himself.

Will Rogers, already the country's foremost advocate of air travel, was very interested in his fellow Oklahoman. He liked his determination, his single-mindedness, which may have bordered on stubbornness. When Wiley not only completed his single flight successfully but broke the record set just two years earlier, Will sent him a congratulatory telegram.

In the Santa Monica hills, the New Year of 1934 was greeted with an all-night tropical cloud-burst. The Rogers ranch lay high above the dirt road leading to it, so it was in little danger of being flooded. But between the water running off the neighboring steep earth walls and the rain pelting on it for hours, the narrow wooden bridge forming part of the road soon gave way, creating a wide-open cut. There were no streetlights along the dirt road, and 1933 automobile headlights could barely penetrate the slashing rain. The very winding two-lane road was one

The cast of *Ah! Wilderness*, 1934.

of the few arteries connecting Los Angeles with the coast. While traffic on New Year's Eve would not be heavy, there was no way for it to move either way until the bridge was replaced. When Will was made aware of the great hazard in the middle of the night, he immediately alerted Emil Sandmeier, the ranch's factotum. The two men donned ponchos and stood in the battering downpour, waving lanterns to alert oncoming traffic of the danger. After the first hour, Will told Emil to return home and stay with his wife, Trudy, at the ranch, in case there arose some need there. For the rest of the night, until daylight and other help would arrive, America's number one film star stood solitary watch over a gaping hole in the road to keep motorists from killing themselves. Will Rogers never told the story.

When Will's latest film, *David Harum*, was finished, he, Betty, and Mary went to New York. They attended the theater and saw the great George M. Cohan appear in Eugene O'Neill's *Ah! Wilderness*. Then the three moved on to Washington, where they were invited to a formal dinner at the White House. And while still in town, Will and Betty were invited to tea at the White House, with Mrs. Eleanor Roosevelt pouring.

Friday, March 18, 1934, was the date on which the awards were to be presented by the Academy of Motion Picture Arts and Sciences. The annual dinner had always been a very staid affair. This year Will Rogers was asked to be the master of ceremonies, and the usual sober and serene evening was expected. But

Will (left) with Irvin Cobb (center) and John Ford (right) on the set during the 1934 filming of *Judge Priest*.

Courtesy of the Will Rogers Memorial Commission

Will was not one to follow precedent, and he changed the annual Oscar presentation forever:

> Will Rogers has never been known to pull his punches. At the recent Academy Awards dinner, the prophet of Fox Movietone City tossed big executives, stars, artists and whatnot on the griddle and roasted them to a turn. He even took a crack at the industry itself.
>
> "It's a racket," said Will; "if it wasn't we all wouldn't be here in dress clothes." And commenting on the fearsome sound of the Academy's full title, "Academy of Motion Picture Arts and Sciences," Will said: "If the movies are an art, I kinda think it'll leak out somehow without being told; and if they're a science—then it's a miracle."
>
> Will's wit changed the big affair from the customary ceremony of long winded speeches into a joyous riot.

Photoplay magazine could have quoted a lot more examples of Will's wit that evening:

> This is the day when the Academy hands out those little statues. They are lovely things. They were originally designed for prizes at a nudist colony's bazaar—but they didn't take 'em. They must be terribly artistic for nobody has any idea what it is. It represents the triumph of nothingness over the stupendousness of zero.

> Academy of Motion Picture Arts and Sciences. Boy, that's the highest sounding named organization I ever attended. If I didn't know so many of the people who belong to it personally, I would have taken the name serious.

> Academy of Motion Picture Arts and Sciences? You see, everything that gives pleasure and makes money is not an "Art" or a "Science." If it were, bootlegging would have been the highest form of artistic endeavor.

> You'll see great acting tonight, greater than any you will see on the screen. We'll all cheer when somebody gets a prize that everyone of us in the house knows should be ours. Yet we'll smile and take it. Boy, that's acting.

At the beginning of April 1934, a surprise announcement appeared in the *New York Times*. It said that Will Rogers would do *Ah! Wilderness*, Eugene O'Neill's only comedy. But Rogers had never done a straight play, where he had to give cues, and where there were no retakes, and where he certainly could not inject his own ad-libs. For once, had he bitten off more than even he could master? Will must have had the same thoughts. He called on his friend:

> Fred [Stone] was out here for awhile, and he helped me a lot on how to do the part."

When rehearsals began in earnest, Will felt fairly comfortable with the lines:

> *. . . been rehearsing with a show, I mean a stage show, that we are going to play out here at San Francisco and Los Angeles two or three weeks each, or till they get wise to us.*
>
> *And say, you have to learn lines, not my lines, but Eugene O'Neil's [sic] lines. He is that high brow writer, and I have quite a bit of trouble reading 'em, much less learning 'em. For instance, "So that's where you drive the Tumbril from and piled poor old Pierpont in it."*
>
> *Now that is a sort of saying in there from Carlyle's French revolution, but that word Tumbril, what you boys from the forks of the creek going to do with that? I couldent handle it. They say it means a kind of conveyance, a sort of an early day Ford, of the French revolutionary type. I imagine it's sorter like an old buckboard, with the slats out.*
>
> *Course this play "Ah Wilderness" is pretty sane outside of a few of those "Tumbrils." It's just a homely old family affair that's laid around New England in 1906. It's the play that is supposed to receive the Pulitzer Prize for the year. The Pulitzer Prize is the Kentucky Derby winner of the drama, and in the New York company Georgie Cohan made the hit of his life in it. . . .*

Will with Stepin Fetchit in *Judge Priest*.

Courtesy of the Will Rogers Memorial Commission

The show opened in San Francisco at the Curran Theatre for a limited engagement, and then moved for three weeks to Los Angeles at the El Capitan Theatre. Opening night in San Francisco, Rogers's entrance was greeted with applause that lasted for several minutes. When the curtain fell, there again was lengthy applause, and a curtain-call speech by Will that was pure Rogers. The next issue of *News-Week Magazine* wrote: "The shrewd, simple philosophy of Nat Miller might have been written for Mr. Rogers, so easily does he slip into the part and make it his own."

And the *New York Times* thought so much of the West Coast opening that it sent a reporter to cover it: "He [Will Rogers] made Nat Miller a delightful personage, and the father's scene with his adolescent son, Richard, he played with a simple sincerity that brought out handkerchiefs and made tears and smiles mingle."

And yet, it would be this touching scene which the *Times* had singled out that would cost Will Rogers his life. It is this scene in which the father explains that his teenaged son might someday have a relationship with a prostitute.

Advance sale in Los Angeles was extremely heavy, and attendance figures set records for West Coast theater audiences. The El Capitan Theatre seated 1,571, with top prices for matinees at $1.65, and for evenings $2.00. To accommodate the crowds, Will agreed to an extra matinee show during the third week, thus giving nine shows in one week. And still there continued this clamor for tickets. Will agreed to a fourth, a fifth and then a sixth week with still extra performances added. But it was in this sixth week that Will received a letter.

As Eddie Cantor explained it, the letter was written by a minister who had taken his teenaged daughter to the play, saw the scene in which the father explains about the prostitute, took his daughter by the hand and immediately left the theater, ashamed. The minister wrote that he had trusted Will's presence in a play to assure its purity. However, he had found the scene so disgraceful that since seeing it, he had not been able to look his young daughter in the face. The letter upset Will terribly. He had always made certain that his films were of high moral content, so that children could be sent to see them.

He had not felt as the minister did when he had first seen the performance in New York, nor had he felt

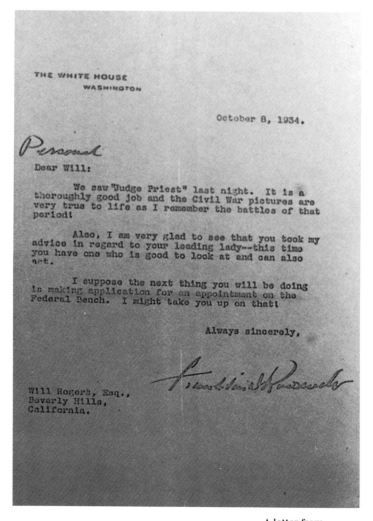

A letter from President Franklin D. Roosevelt commenting on Will's film *Judge Priest*, 1934.

that way when he played it now. But if there was just one spectator who felt that way, he would not continue in that play. There were constant pleas for just one more week, but Will remained adamant.

In fact, though Will had agreed to play the part in the motion picture, on loan from Fox to Metro-Goldwyn-Mayer, he now refused to do it and offered instead to do any other film for that company but this one. Lionel Barrymore would play the role in the motion picture. And as it turned out, in August 1935, when the cast of *Ah! Wilderness* left Hollywood for New England to film outdoor scenes, Will Rogers would be in Alaska with Wiley Post.

For the time, Will was working days on *Judge Priest*, directed by John Ford, while giving nine performances weekly. He also had his passport and those of Betty and the two boys renewed, for Will was planning another trip. Mary would not join them, as she was at the Lakewood Playhouse in Skowhegan, Maine. To see her before leaving, Will made another dash across the country. In Washington, D.C., he saw Secretary of State Cordell Hull, and called on Soviet Ambassador Alexander Troyanovsky about arrangements for flying the family across Russia from Vladivostok to Moscow. He was assured that a plane would be waiting for him and his family.

On Sunday, July 22, the SS *Malolo*, with four members of the Rogers family aboard, steamed out of San Francisco harbor. The family's first stop was Honolulu. They checked into the Royal Hawaiian Hotel, and then went out on a drive to see the city. Wrote Will:

> You don't have to be warlike to get a real kick out of our greatest army post, Schofield Barracks, and the navy at Pearl Harbor. If war was declared with some Pacific nation we would lose the Philippines before lunch, but if we lost these it would be our own fault.

That night Betty and Will were dinner guests of a vacationing President Roosevelt. Will reported the president's farewell wishes:

> The President told me, "Will, don't jump on Japan. Just keep them from jumping on us.'"

As if to confirm his own concerns, he had to report the next day:

> Japanese Naval Committee announced today it was going ahead with ship building. If allowed at the next conference they will have them. If not allowed they will have them, too. You can't beat logic like that.

The trip westward continued to Vladivostok, where the Soviets had promised to have a plane waiting. But there was none, nor had the local authorities been alerted or instructed to make any accommodations. Annoyed and disappointed, the family had to make arrangements on the Trans-Siberian railway, a trip which took days longer and threw their entire schedule out. Will had looked forward to getting his now-accustomed bird's-eye view of the landscape. The group was pretty tired and disheveled by the time the train reached the capital.

There was much to do—a visit to the opera, a talk with the *New York Times* correspondent and other local Americans to get background information, side trips to Odessa, then Leningrad—and of course, a visit to the Bolshoi. After that the family was off by plane via Estonia to Helsinki. The time lost in Siberia had to be made up, and the family rushed through Stockholm, went the next day to Oslo, then to England. But it was not over yet. It was on to Copenhagen, Vienna—and a visit to the opera there—on to Belgrade and Bucharest, back to Vienna, then to London for a Sunday broadcast back to the States. By September 20 the family was aboard the *Ile De France*, homeward bound and ready for a rest. Five days later they touched American soil again. The next commitment Will had was to report on October 19 in Sonora, California, to begin filming *The County Chairman*. Co-starring were Evelyn Venable and Kent Taylor, and there was a young boy part for Mickey Rooney.

Will was working during the early part of 1935, to get the year's films completed. By the beginning of May he was still in Monrovia, California, the home of the famous Santa Anita racetrack. The company was there filming scenes for Will's film, *In Old Kentucky*. By the third week in May, Will was in Sacramento, on the river where scenes of Will's next film, *Steamboat Round the Bend*, were being shot. Co-starring with Rogers was Anne Shirley, Stepin Fetchit, and Irvin S. Cobb. Will took the opportunity to look up his old companion of vaudeville days, Buck McKee, who ranched nearby. During the noon break, they sought out a cool, quiet place on the shady side of the upper deck of the steamboat, and just talked. There was a lot of emotional reminiscing and even a nostalgic tear or two shed. It had been many years since they had seen each other last, and looking back, even most of the hapless times had by now lost their sting.

While Will was busy with his various obligations, he was fully aware that Wiley Post was involved in experiments. Will had been following Wiley's attempts to learn more about high-altitude flying. By sheer accident, Wiley had discovered what has since become known as the "jet stream." On his round-the-world flights he had been furnished official Soviet maps and found them totally unreliable. What he thought was ignorance was admitted, years later, as intent. Not wishing to give information to possible invading enemies—such as the United States—the Soviets intentionally moved cities, misdirected streams and wrongly indicated the locations and altitude of mountains. In 1931, flying through inclement weather, Wiley became aware of the misinformation when he nearly plowed the *Winnie Mae* into the side of a mountain that did not even show on the map. After that he could not afford to rely on flying just above the altitudes indicated on the supplied maps. He had to fly much higher rather than risk collision with an unexpected peak. Flying at the higher altitude, he found to his amazement that his plane's speed exceeded specifications, at times by as much as 100 miles per hour. His conclusion was that at that higher altitude there had to be a very strong west-to-east tailwind. Post's deduction was prophetic: he foresaw, and so stated, that the future of aviation lay at 35,000 feet, where speeds in excess of 500 miles per hour would be the norm. To make more conclusive observations, Wiley knew that he would need oxygen, and insulated clothing against the freezing temperatures at that altitude. As the interior of the *Winnie Mae* could not be pressurized, as well as supplied with oxygen, Wiley reasoned that the pilot had to be encapsulated. He designed a flight suit based on a

Will, Betty, and Jimmy arrive in Honolulu on their trip around the world, 1934.

Will Rogers at the National Theatre in Washington, D.C., congratulating daughter Mary and Myron McCormick at the opening of their play *On To Fortune*, January 14, 1935.

**Will with Francis
Ford, in a movie
still from *Steamboat
Round the Bend*.**

*Courtesy of the Will
Rogers Memorial
Commission*

**Will with Irvin
Cobb, in a still from
*Steamboat Round
the Bend*, 1935.**

deep-sea-diver's gear, which became the forerunner of the extra-vehicular activity suit used by today's astronauts.

The Goodrich Tire and Rubber Company in Akron, Ohio, followed his specifications and finally came up with a working model. Having taken care of the pilot's major problem, Wiley rigged his plane with a landing gear that could be dropped immediately after takeoff to reduce air resistance. He next reinforced the plane's belly with a skid for landing without wheels. Now he was set to test his theory that the stratospheric wind he had observed could be used for high altitude flying. Four times he attempted transcontinental speed records; four times he failed. He did reach Chicago and other cities along his flight attempt at record-breaking speeds, which could not be accounted for except by Wiley's theory, but he never could fly coast to coast. On one occasion, after his engine was destroyed shortly after takeoff, metal filings had been detected in his oil. That was suspected to be an attempt on Wiley's life. Other mechanical failures could be rationalized as being due to the great heat being generated in the sub-zero temperatures of the altitude, which would intensify the deterioration of rubber and metal tubing.

Whenever there was an opportunity to boost Wiley Post and his heroic deeds, Will would do it, for he felt that Wiley needed help. Post was an unusual man and probably his own worst foe. He had few good friends, and made enemies easily. Because he was headstrong and contentious, the press disliked him and rarely cooperated. Thus, while others were capable of turning minor accomplishments into lifetime income producers, Wiley was unable to exploit his history-making feats. He could not even get a job on the strength of his achievements.

Wiley knew that his high-altitude-flying theory was correct, and he intended to prove it someday. What he needed was income. He approached Pan Am Airline with the idea of laying out an air route to Europe via Alaska and Siberia. This would be in line with that airline's pioneering traffic to the Far East and Japan, except that Post's route to Europe would be mostly over land, a far more confidence-inspiring trip. After all, a plane could set down on land, while there was little hope on water.

Wiley's price for such a search was the assurance of a pilot's job with the airline. Pan Am was one of the premier airlines of the day, a leader in both planes and service. Passenger service was still in its infancy, and considered perilous even with a pilot who had two eyes; imagine what timid passengers would think if they saw that they had to fly with a pilot who had only one eye? No passenger airline would ever take such a risk, and Pan Am refused to enter into such negotiations with Post.

The answer to Wiley was a definite "no," but . . . why didn't he go and see Will Rogers and have him support such a search? After all, hadn't Rogers written only this morning in his weekly column that he wanted to go to Alaska?

> *I never have been to that Alaska. I am crazy to go up there some time. . . . Wiley Post went back up there this last summer to visit. . . . Fred Stone and Rex Beach have been up there a lot but I never did get further north up that way than about a block north of Main street in Seattle.*

Post had realized that his *Winnie Mae* had served him well, but it was time to retire her and move on. As a matter of prudent economics, he looked for a secondhand plane. He found a Lockheed Orion, which until just a few days earlier had been part of the TWA fleet of passenger planes. There was nothing wrong with the plane. It had been made obsolete solely by an edict of the Department of Commerce. Washington had wisely decreed that henceforth any plane carrying passengers would have to carry a pilot and a co-pilot for safety. The Lockheed Orion, probably the best passenger plane of its time, could not be altered to allow space in the cockpit for a co-pilot, so it had to be sold. The Orion, a low-wing plane, had retractable wheels, which—once the plane was in the air—folded neatly into wells on the underside of the wing. Aerodynamically this was a great design, because it reduced drag, thus increasing speed while reducing fuel consumption. But this was not what Wiley wanted. He intended to have pontoons attached to an undercarriage and the Orion wing with those wells would not allow that. Charles Babb, America's foremost secondhand-plane dealer, had a Lockheed Explorer wing on hand. The sole survivor of its plane's crash in the Canal Zone some years before, it had gathered dust as an unwanted item. It was six feet longer than the Orion's original wing but it was solid and would serve Wiley's purpose—or so Wiley convinced himself.

Lockheed, the Orion's builder, refused to join the two unrelated parts or make any of the numerous other changes Wiley intended, calling them aerodynamically unsound and referring to the result as "a freak." Lockheed further warned that the plane, with so much alteration forward of the center of gravity, would be nose-heavy.

Wiley wanted numerous changes on this plane. As he intended to fly over Alaska and Siberia with their millions of summer lakes, he wanted pontoons—or as the pilots call them, floats—so he could land on any one of them. Should the need arise, those floats could easily be exchanged for skis for landing on ice. Further, he added extra fuel tanks for long flights, a heavier, more powerful engine, and a three-bladed propeller instead of the original two-bladed one. This was a necessity because a three-bladed propeller's blades are shorter. The plane on pontoons would sit lower than the original one on wheels; thus, the two original longer blades would have hit the water.

The work was done by a reputable California company and the workmanship passed inspection. After Post had taken the newly assembled plane up for a test flight, he told the government inspector that it was the easiest-handling plane he had ever flown. Without taking the controls, or even flying in it, the inspector issued a restricted airworthiness certificate for the "experimental" plane. Designated as "restricted" meant that no passengers would be allowed to fly in her, but up to three required technical personnel could. While Post officially praised the plane's performance, he told mechanics privately "that's the screwiest damn plane I ever flew."

The plane never was given an official name, but pilots and mechanics seeing the unusual configuration, which indicated its illegitimate birth out of unrelated components, dubbed it "Wiley's Orphan," or worse, "Wiley's Bastard."

Wiley intended to take Mae, his wife, along across Siberia, but he also asked well-known pilot Fay Gillis to come along. Fay was one of the early female pilots, and the first woman ever to be admitted to the Caterpillar Club. When her plane literally broke apart over Washington, D.C., she met the membership requirement of that exclusive club—her parachute saved her life. Having lived for years in Moscow, where her father was an American engineer, Fay spoke Russian and had contacts in flying circles. Wiley felt that she would be an excellent co-pilot and translator on his search for the best route into Europe.

Fay arranged for visas for the threesome, obtained maps, such as they were, and obtained landing permits in a number of Soviet cities. But then Fay eloped on April 1, 1935, with Lynton Wells, a famous foreign correspondent. When Lynton took the assignment to cover the Italian-Abyssinian war, Fay decided to accompany her new husband and bowed out of the trans-Siberian trip. Wiley Post had to decide between abandoning his plan, or try persuading Will Rogers to finance the enterprise.

Wiley, Mae, and Will arranged a short plane trip to Arizona, New Mexico, and southern Utah. It was never revealed as such, but it was a trial run, sort of a shakedown cruise, to see how the three would fare on a lengthy trip. After they returned to Pacific Palisades, Will agreed to cover their expenses—at least as far as Alaska—but Mae could not come along. There was not enough room, especially as all the weight had to be stowed in the very back to counteract the plane's nose-heaviness, and there was but a single short bench.

Will had finished his motion picture commitments for the year. The only thing left for him to do was to convince Betty that the trip was important. She, on the other hand, tried to persuade Will to travel elsewhere. She feared that the two men would be lost in the vastness of Alaska, with rescuers unable to find them. Will tried to reassure her again and again. Betty saw just how much Will wanted to go, and finally gave in.

Plans were made for the children. Will Jr. had taken a summer job on a tramp steamer headed for the Philippines; Mary and her chaperon, her aunt "Dick," were to be in Skowhegan, in the summer theater; Jimmy and his cousin would be traveling across the country by car and would end up with sister Mary. Betty, too, was leaving California and would spend the summer in Maine with her daughter and sister.

Wiley and Mae left Los Angeles for Renton, near Seattle, where the plane's wheels would be replaced by pontoons. Will, using the cover name of Mr.

Will and Wiley Post
at the opening of
W. C. Fields's film
David Copperfield.

From left: Will Jr.,
Will Rogers, Billie
Burke, Wiley Post,
and Fred Stone at
the Fox studio.

Williams, flew into Seattle. Mrs. Post told reporters that she would join her husband in a few days in Alaska, but later admitted that it had been Will Rogers who had made the decision that she not accompany them.

On August 7, the two men left Seattle in brilliant sunshine, but as forecast, ran into rain within two hours. Post skipped the planned landing for lunch in Ketchikan and kept on, about 50 feet over the water, along the coast into Juneau. There they were greeted by one of Wiley Post's few close friends, Joe Crosson, a famous bush pilot now in charge of Pacific Alaska Airlines [PAA], a subsidiary of Pan Am. The trip from Seattle had taken eight and a quarter hours. There was an official reception by the governor, a radio interview, and then a stay overnight in the governor's mansion.

After losing a couple of days to bad weather, Post and Rogers saw Skagway and the Chilkoot Pass, famous for the trek of the forty-niners in their hunt for gold. Then it was on to Dawson, in the Yukon Territory. The next day the pair flew to Aklavik, in Canada's Northwest Territories. Will visited an injured boy in the hospital and pressed a "substantial" check into the boy's hand when leaving. When refueling the plane's gasoline tanks, Will was told that it would cost $1.16 a gallon. He responded, "Well, you just go right ahead and fill 'er up. I ain't never ridden on no $1.16 gas before and I want to enjoy everything you got up here in the Arctic."

They flew around Herschel Island, where whalers used to winter, and returned south to Fairbanks, where Joe Crosson welcomed them again. Fairbanks was PAA's center and Crosson's home base. Wiley stayed with Joe and Lillian Crosson, while Will stayed at a local hotel. While dinner was cooking at the Crosson house, Wiley and Joe discussed the possible peculiarities of Arctic aviation. Above all, Joe tried to instill in Wiley's mind the Alaskan maxim: Never make your own weather! Always take the report of weather conditions as absolute truth, never try to interpret it to favor what you would like it to be. Will was in the kitchen, helping Lillian by mashing potatoes. The next day they all made a brief trip to Anchorage and visited the Matanuska Valley, where new immigrants from the Dust Bowl and drought areas tried to establish themselves.

The group returned to Fairbanks in time for supper, and Will treated Joe, Lillian, and Wiley to dinner at the Model Cafe.

Wiley and Will planned to fly to Barrow on the following day to interview Charley Brower, who had been commissioner there for many years and would have a lot of interesting tales to remember. Of course, it all depended on the weather. The day was absolutely perfect in Fairbanks, but the morning weather report from Barrow was "Zero, Zero," meaning zero ceiling, zero visibility. In plain words, there was no way to either locate the airport or see the ground. Landing would be impossible.

Another weather report was forthcoming at about 2 P.M. It might be better. After a short conference it was decided that the plane would be prepared for take-off, so that when the weather report indicated that all was well in Barrow, no time would be lost. Under no circumstances, so it was agreed, would Wiley fly into either clouds or fog.

Since the plane rested on the winding Chena River, which flows through the center of Fairbanks, it would be almost impossible to take off with a full load of gasoline. The heavy weight of the plane, fuel, and cargo would require great speed for liftoff, which the short straight sections of the river would not allow. Joe Crosson pointed out that Harding Lake would give Wiley plenty of space to gather speed while staying in a straight line. The experienced flyer suggested that Wiley and Will fly with almost empty tanks to Harding Lake, just 40 miles away. He would send a truck there with drums of gasoline to top all of the plane's tanks. The big lake would be infinitely safer. Wiley was instructed to telephone Joe from the lake to get the relay of the afternoon weather report from Barrow. While there were no telephones directly at the lake, the call could be made from one of two roadhouses within short driving distance. But Wiley did not bother to call; having his fuel tanks topped, he just took off.

When the afternoon report from Barrow was received in Fairbanks, it was unchanged from the morning's. It still meant that no plane could possibly land at Barrow. When no call came from the lake, Joe Crosson suspected the worst and sent a fast truck there to warn the fliers. By the time the truck reached the lake—a drive of about an hour on dirt roads—Post had taken off. There was no way to contact the plane in flight. The plane did have a radio, but Wiley was busy holding a nose-heavy plane level and on course, and could not possibly handle a receiver and Morse key.

From left: Lillian Crosson, Don Crosson, Will Rogers, Joe Crosson Jr., and Wiley Post.

The plane had enough provisions to sustain the two men for many days, had they chosen to set down and await a total change in weather. But Wiley opted to fly beyond the Brooks range of mountains that stretches across Alaska, dividing it. The southern part was clear; the North Slope was shrouded in fog near the ground, held in place by a layer of clouds.

Joe Crosson had instructed Wiley to approach Barrow the way bush pilots did: fly due north until one reached the northern coast on the Beaufort Sea, then turn west and follow the coastline into Barrow on the Chukchi Sea. But Wiley could see nothing. His calculations would have indicated that he must have reached the coast, but which one? Barrow was at the northernmost point of land on the North American continent and washed by two seas—one with an east-west coastline, the other with a north-south coast. The best Wiley could do was to circle, hoping for a break in the cloud and fog cover that would allow him to set the plane down. He circled leisurely, cutting back on the speed; when you are lost, there is nothing to be gained by speed.

It is known that Wiley circled for hours, because Inupiat Eskimos on the ground reported hearing his plane approach from the left, then disappear to the right, later to appear once again from the left. Consulting his watch, Wiley, the experienced pilot, must have realized that he still had enough fuel for two more hours of flight, when he spotted a lagoon below. He dropped rapidly, knowing that there were no mountains on the North Slope.

The Okpeaha family, Clair and Stella and the two daughters and three sons they raised, had been hunting during the short summer to lay in supplies for the dark winter. Now the Arctic summer was practically over and ice floes were thick on the sea. They were awaiting a motorboat to pick them up and take them back to their village of Barrow. When they heard the sound of an engine they thought at first that it was the boat. Then they saw the airplane set down on the lagoon, and coast until the floats ground to a halt on the beach. Two men got out, stretched,

Will, all suited up,
says farewell to
Betty.

Will, all suited up, says farewell to Betty.

and inquired about the direction and distance to Barrow. The man they spoke to was Clair Okpeaha, with his fourteen-year-old adopted son Patrick silently standing by. To the question of how far Barrow was, Clair did not know what to say. Distance was something he had never measured, never seen, and had no way of estimating. Though it was merely twelve miles, he answered "thirty," while pointing in a northerly direction.

Will and Wiley walked away and debated something. It probably was whether to stay on the ground and await the change in weather, or risk a return to the fog and clouds for the short hope of what they were told was 30 miles. The two men climbed back into the plane, waved farewell to Clair and his family, taxied across the lagoon and took off, banking steeply to line up with the coast pointing north.

At about 200 feet the engine backfired and quit. The plane was banking—making a diving turn to the left—and continued, diving nose-first into 3 feet of water. Clair was on his way back to the family's tent when the plane hit the shallow lagoon. He ran back to the water's edge and called out to the plane.

He called again, and then again, but his voice was the only sound breaking the Arctic silence.

Page 194, "As Will wrote . . . ," Daily Telegram #1664, November 22, 1931.

Page 194, "Crossing the International Date Line . . . ," Daily Telegram #1668, November 27, 1931.

Page 194, "We had a Lifeboat . . . ," "Letters of a Self-Made Diplomat to Senator Borah." March 5, 1932.

Page 194, "The Japanese say . . . ," Daily Telegram #1748, March 1, 1932.

Page 195, "We will drag along . . . ," *Saturday Evening Post*, April 30, 1932.

Page 196, "Had a fine day . . . ," Daily Telegram #1734, February 14, 1932.

Page 196, "After about the fourth . . . ," Daily Telegram #1749, March 2, 1932.

Page 196, " . . . but there was absolutely . . . ," Daily Telegram #1757, March 11, 1932.

Page 199, "I think he holds . . . ," Weekly Article #460, October 18, 1931.

Page 199, "Our world of 'make believe' . . . ," Daily Telegram #1862, July 24, 1932.

Page 203, "I am just an old . . . ," Weekly Article #90, August 31, 1924.

Page 205, "Will Rogers has never . . . ," *Photoplay*, June 1934.

Page 205, " . . . Academy of Motion Picture . . . ," Academy notes.

Page 205, "Fred [Stone] was out here . . . ," Weekly Article #597, June 3, 1934.

Page 206, " . . . been rehearsing with a show . . . ," Weekly Article #592, April 29, 1934.

Page 208, "You don't have to be . . . ," Daily Telegram #2495, August 1, 1934.

Page 208, "The President told me . . . ," Daily Telegram #2502, August 12, 1934.

Page 208, "Japanese Naval Committee . . . ," Daily Telegram #2503, August 13, 1934.

Page 211, "I never have been . . . ," Weekly Article #637, March 10, 1935.

Page 212, "While Post officially . . . ," Sterlings' interview with Warren Tillman, 1986.

Page 216, "Though it was merely . . . ," Sterlings' interview with Patrick Okpeaha, 1986.

This was Betty's favorite photo of Will.

Courtesy of the Will Rogers Memorial Commission

Postscript

Clair Okpeaha took the news to Barrow, from where Sergeant Stanley Morgan of the U.S. Signal Corps sent it to the world. Two boats went to the crash site to recover the bodies. Joe Crosson and Robert Gleason, Joe's radio operator, risked their lives the following day to fly from Fairbanks directly to Barrow, when weather conditions were still as hazardous as the day before. Experienced in the ways of the Arctic, they were able to make the trip there and back without incident. By the time they reached Fairbanks with the bodies, Charles Lindbergh had begun to make arrangements to return the bodies to California. America was stunned by the loss of two of its foremost heroes. Memorial services were held across the country, flags flew at half staff, motion picture theaters stayed dark, newspapers had special editions, CBS and NBC radio went off the air during the funeral services, and American newspaper editors considered this the number one American news story of 1935. America was in mourning as it had not been since the death of Abraham Lincoln.

An immediate investigation into the crash was announced by Daniel Calhoun Roper, secretary of commerce, responsible under the Air Commerce Act of 1926. There was enough guilt and negligence to cover everyone connected with the plane. To build it, Post combined unrelated parts simply because they were available. There was no official submission of plans for the structural changes, though that was a primary prerequisite under the law. Post took passengers—his wife, Will Rogers, and two teenagers—despite the dictates imposed by the plane's restricted license. There was no inspection for airworthiness, because of Wiley Post's self-serving, untrue statement to a criminally lax government inspector that this "was the easiest-handling plane" he had ever flown. Nor was there an inspection for airworthiness after the pontoons had been attached—which constituted another structural change. A plane that Lockheed had refused to alter because it would become "nose-heavy" should have been similarly diagnosed by any qualified inspector. The installation of six gasoline tanks without a single fuel gauge was inexcusable. The inspector in Seattle lied when he claimed that he had wanted to inspect the plane but that Post left town early on August 6; Post and

The crash scene
with bodies
wrapped in sleeping
bags.

*Courtesy of the
Stanley Morgan
Collection*

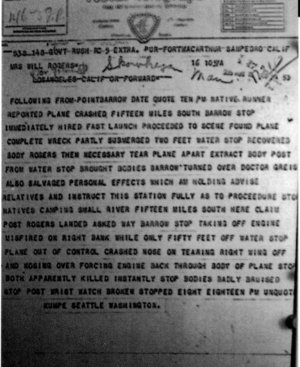

The telegram noti-
fying Betty Rogers
of Will's death.

Rogers left Seattle just before noon on August 7, almost forty-eight hours after the plane was ready. There was more than enough time to inspect the plane, had a conscientious inspector wished to do his duty.

The Department of Air Commerce issued an official report on the crash, though no official ever examined the wreck, no official looked at the engine, no official interviewed mechanics who serviced the plane, and no official sought a single eyewitness. But someone's head had to roll to make the investigation at least appear to be proper. America had lost two of its most admired men, and the public expected a guilty party to be identified. Under no circumstances could it be anyone close to the powers in Washington. The public's confidence in its all-wise and highly qualified leaders must never be allowed to waver. But where could an evildoer be found?

Finally, one was discovered. It was inspector Murray Hall in Fairbanks, Alaska. Of course he had no connection with the accident, but that didn't matter. Washington, D.C., appointed him the designated guilt bearer. All he had done was to lie in order to avoid having to go to Barrow and possibly become another crash victim. It was true that he had no plane of his own, but he could have gone with Joe Crosson and Robert Gleason when they flew there to pick up the bodies. So he lied a little, saying that he had tried to get a lift, but that Crosson did not have enough room for him. Crosson truthfully stated that he had offered Hall a lift to Barrow, but also told Hall that he would be unable to bring him back because of space and weight limitations. Hall further

California state
troopers move Will
Rogers's casket to
the Wee Kirk o' the
Heather Church.

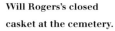

Will Rogers's closed
casket at the cemetery.

People lining up to
pass Will Rogers's
casket and pay their
last respects.

qualified as a guilt
bearer by being the far-
thest removed from the
bureaucracy in
Washington. Besides,
what punishment could
be meted out to some-
one who already had to
endure the fiery
Fairbanks summers and
the minus-40-degrees
winters?

Everyone connected with the Department had a reason to lie, because everyone was culpable. There had been a complete failure by inspectors to do their
duty, and there was no oversight to see that existing laws were obeyed. When dis-
cipline is lax, management is always at fault. It was as Will Rogers had said ten
years earlier in his article of October 4, 1925:

> . . . you can't believe a thing you read in regard to official Statements. The minute
> anything happens connected with official life, why, it's just like a cold night, every-
> body is trying to cover up.

In Washington, the Department of Air Commerce's first reaction upon hearing of the crash was to find out whether it could somehow dodge responsibility

The last remaining items from the ill-fated plane are on display at Mattie's Cafe in Barrow, Alaska.

Shirley Temple dedicating stage #8 at Twentieth Century Fox Studios to Will Rogers.

This oil painting of Will Rogers by Arnoldo Tambourini hangs in the North Gallery of the Will Rogers Memorial.

for the issuance of that plane's certificate of airworthiness. Eugene Vidal, the director, demanded an immediate internal search to determine whether, under existing laws, his department was supposed to have even inspected an "experimental" plane. Nobody in Washington knew. It took twenty-four hours to ascertain that the inspector in California had failed in his duties. He should indeed have tested the plane and made personally certain of the plane's airworthiness. Then there was the inspector in Seattle. He had lied because he wanted to cover up the fact that he did not inspect the plane after the structural change of installing the floats—a definite violation of regulation. Eugene Vidal signed a report that he must have known to be seriously flawed and definitely incomplete.

Why did no one want to tell the truth? There are several answers to that question. First, one does not accuse a national hero like Wiley Post. The Department of Air Commerce would not choose to be honorable enough to assume the guilt—the government rarely does. As for identifying guilty parties, nobody had a clean enough hand with which to point a finger at the real culprits. As we know, there were several.

And what was the cause of the crash? Since no one stepped forward to confess, guilt could not fall on any human. Therefore, it was conveniently shifted to the only possible one—Nature. It was Nature, they claimed, that caused clouds and fog and humidity and the cold which created tiny crystals of ice that supposedly blocked the fuel jets so no gasoline could reach the carburetor.

Issue of three-cent commemorative stamp, November 4, 1938.

That, of course, was just one more official lie. Most Alaskan fliers disagreed with that finding. They said that it was far more credible that Wiley Post did not know how much gasoline was still in the various fuel tanks without any individual fuel gauges. Leaving Walakpa Lagoon in an amateurishly steep, banking climb (described by eyewitnesses) on a near-empty tank made the fuel pump suck in air, causing the engine to quit and the nose-heavy plane to dive. At an altitude of only 200 feet, Post had no chance to pull the unbalanced plane out of its downward spiral.

At the time of the deaths of Will Rogers and Wiley Post, America mourned equally the loss of two of its idols. Headlines screamed their names jointly in bold letters; their pictures were side by side; their newspaper biographies were in glowing terms; their families' pictures and interviews were given equal space. Their funerals were even held simultaneously, though Post's was in Oklahoma and Rogers's was in California. Memorial services were held across the nation, and were broadcast as well. A rush began to memorialize both men.

But as time has gone by, a strange phenomenon has taken place. Though no voice was ever raised publicly accusing Post of lying or heedlessly rushing into trouble or needlessly endangering Rogers's life, history seems to have assumed the role of judge. Wiley Post has been relegated into the dark recesses of American chronicles. Few, if any, outside of aviation even recognize his name today. In 1986, when Americans Richard Rutan and Jeana Yeager flew nonstop around the world in their spindly craft Voyager, they were justly hailed. Famous aviators of the past were recollected. Amelia Earhart and Charles Lindbergh were frequently mentioned. Yet nobody recalled Wiley Post. There is a statue of Wiley in Oklahoma City, and an airport is named for him there. A minor office building in the same city bears his name and displays mementos, which gather dust. The navigational beacon atop the eastern support of the George Washington Bridge spanning the Hudson River between New York City and Ft. Lee, New Jersey, is called the Will Rogers-Wiley Post Beacon, but most likely only fliers know its proper name. And then there is a plaque on the observation deck at the Newark, New Jersey, airport

An informal studio photo of Betty Blake Rogers, Will Rogers's widow, circa 1940.

honoring both men, but rarely does anyone ever read it. Post's family home in Maysville, Oklahoma, his hometown, is unmarked, and the main store does not have even a single postcard to sell in his remembrance.

Wiley Post's grave in Memorial Park Cemetery at Edmond, Oklahoma, is inconspicuous and hard to find. When in November 1979 the United States decided to remember Wiley Post with postage stamps, their denomination was twenty-five cents, but such stamps were rarely needed and rarely used. Had history delivered some final verdict on the man who, if at all, is best remembered not for his exploits and achievements, but for the fact that he died with Will Rogers?

The death of Will Rogers, by comparison, created a groundswell of public fervor to create memorials and reminders of a man beloved by most. A major office building, streets, parks, schools, churches, theaters, turnpikes, a beach in California—all were named in his honor. The Rogers family ranch in Pacific Palisades become a state park, and the house is kept as if the family were to return in minutes.

Even Congress moved swiftly. A bill to authorize the interment of the remains of Will Rogers in Arlington National Cemetery was passed, though vetoed by President Roosevelt. He agreed with the sentiment, but correctly pointed out that the cemetery was reserved for those who had served in the armed forces.

On November 4, 1979, the centennial observation of his birth, this fifteen-cent stamp was issued in Will Rogers's honor.

Will Rogers's last resting place, at the Will Rogers Memorial in Claremore, Oklahoma.

Congress passed joint resolutions designating U.S. Highway 66 as the Will Rogers Highway, and in joint resolutions also passed the coinage of a memorial medal and the issuance of a postage stamp. Another stamp in Rogers's honor was issued on the occasion of the one hundredth anniversary of his birth. The state of Oklahoma commissioned world-famous sculptor Jo Davidson to create two statues of Rogers, with one being placed into Statuary Hall in the nation's Capitol in Washington, D.C. In keeping with instructions that Will gave when such a possibility was mentioned in his lifetime, the statue faces Congress. Will had said that he wanted to "keep an eye on those birds that are stealing this country blind." The other statue stands in the center hall of the Memorial in Claremore, its toe rubbed shiny from those who swear that Will brings them kindly thoughts and luck.

Schoolchildren collected pennies, in the midst of the Depression, in order to erect a memorial. An immediate commission of 230 top civic and industrial leaders of the land was formed under the leadership of Vice President John Nance Garner to determine the proper memorial to crystallize "the nation-wide sentiment calling for some tangible expression of the regard in which Will Rogers was held by people in all walks of life." Among those eager to serve were former President Herbert Hoover, Henry Ford, former Vice President Curtis, Vincent Astor, Bernard Baruch, Evangeline Booth, Admiral Byrd, James Doolittle, Marshall Field, Judge Kenesaw M. Landis, Alice Roosevelt Longworth, Mrs. Adolph S. Ochs, William S. Pailey, General J. Pershing, Mary Pickford, Eddie Rickenbacker, Nelson Rockefeller, Elliot Roosevelt, James Roosevelt, Igor Sikorsky, Alfred E. Smith, and Mrs. Woodrow Wilson.

As the "memorial" was to be a living remembrance, the money collected was distributed in three funds for scholarships. The Universities of Oklahoma and California at Los Angeles shared $250,000, while the University of Texas received $60,000.

Betty Rogers donated the land Will had bought for their retirement home to the state of Oklahoma, which built an impressive memorial and museum on that site. A dignified area for Will's and Betty's final resting places is set aside on the grounds.

Hundreds of thousands have streamed through the galleries and grounds of the Memorial, for even though almost three generations have passed since that August day in Alaska, visitors still interrupt their travel to get off the new Interstate 44—the Will Rogers Turnpike—for a short spin on old Route 66, the Will Rogers Highway, and drop in on Will and Betty at Claremore, in Rogers County, Oklahoma.

Will Rogers will be remembered because his wisdom and philosophy appealed to folks. His humor made them laugh—and think. When he spoke, he spoke the language of the people; when he wrote, he wrote so that everyone could understand him. He showed that a high school dropout could walk with princes, be the top star in motion pictures, become the most widely read newspaper columnist in the country, wed the girl he loved and stay happily married, raise a family, and with all that success still remain the modest fellow next door.

There has not been another man like Will Rogers. Every so often a momentary flash appears and newspapers are quick to call him "another Will Rogers," but it never lasts. None of them excels in all the fields Will did, none of them will spend their talent, time, and energy to go single-handedly on a tour to raise money for those in terrible need. Will gave away much of his own money, and never even reported it to the Internal Revenue Service to save on his taxes. None of those new ones will ever stand all night in the dark beside a washed-out bridge in a torrential downpour, holding a lamp aloft to stop traffic so that no one gets hurt. Clem Vann Rogers, the onetime despairing father, would have to agree that Will did indeed ride his own horse. And even better than that, Will left America a legacy which will bear fruit for many generations yet to come. For Will, in his own words, left a view of an age as seen through the eyes of a kindly, unbiased humorist and philosopher, who was loved in his own land and in his own time. America was fortunate to have had a role model who has withstood the harsh scrutiny of time. There are not many in our history who were pure in thought, pure in character, and pure in his actions—well, Will did get a few speeding tickets!

And while the Jo Davidson statue has inscribed in its marble base Will's most famous words—"I never met a man I didn't like"—should you, welcomed visitor, rub that shiny toe, don't be surprised if you think you hear Will drawl: "Don't take things too serious; least of all yourself. Just live your life so you wouldn't be ashamed to sell the family parrot to the town gossip."

Will Rogers (1879-1935)

He loved and was loved by the American people. His memory will ever be in benediction with the hosts of his countrymen who felt the spell of that kindly humor which, while seeing facts, could always laugh at fantasy. That was why his message went straight to the hearts of his fellow men. . . .

Will Rogers's star at 6401 Hollywood Boulevard on the Hollywood Walk of Fame. Will also has a star for broadcasting, at 6608 Hollywood Boulevard.

President Franklin Delano Roosevelt, August 16, 1935, when the news of Rogers's death reached the White House

We pay grateful homage to the memory of a man who helped the nation to smile. And, after all, I doubt if there is among us a more useful citizen than the one who holds the secret of banishing gloom, of making tears give way to laughter, of supplanting desolation and despair with hope and courage. For hope and courage always go with a light heart.

There was something infectious about his humor. His appeal went straight to the heart of the nation. Above all things, in a time grown too solemn and sober he brought his countrymen back to a sense of proportion.

With it all his humor and his comments were always kind. His was no biting sarcasm that hurt the highest or the lowest of his fellow citizens. When he wanted people to laugh out loud he used the methods of pure fun. And when he wanted to make a point for the good of mankind, he used the kind of gentle irony that left no scars behind it.

President Franklin Delano Roosevelt, November 4, 1938, at the dedication of the Will Rogers Memorial

Page 225, "An immediate commission . . . ," *New York Times*, September 22, 1935.

Works Cited

Newspapers

Akron Times-Press, Akron, Ohio
Alaskan Empire, Anchorage, Alaska
Anchorage Times, Anchorage, Alaska
Associated Press, New York, New York
Chelsea Reporter, Chelsea, Oklahoma
Claremore Weekly Progress, Claremore, Oklahoma
Daily Oklahoman, Oklahoma City, Oklahoma
Detroit Evening News, Detroit, Michigan
Fort Worth Star-Telegram, Fort Worth, Texas
Houston Chronicle, Houston, Texas
Juneau Daily Empire, Juneau, Alaska
Kansas City Star, Kansas City, Kansas
London Daily Mail, London, England
London Times, London, England
Los Angeles Chronicle, Los Angeles, California
Los Angeles Examiner, Los Angeles, California
Los Angeles Herald-Express, Los Angeles, California
Los Angeles News, Los Angeles, California
Los Angeles Post-Record, Los Angeles, California
Los Angeles Times, Los Angeles, California
Maysville News, Maysville, Oklahoma
Muskogee Times-Democrat, Muskogee, Oklahoma
News-Miner, Fairbanks, Alaska
New York American, New York, New York
New York Evening Post, New York, New York
New York Herald, New York, New York
New York Herald Tribune, New York, New York
New York Journal, New York, New York
New York Mirror, New York, New York
New York News, New York, New York
New York Post, New York, New York
New York Sun, New York, New York
New York Tribune, New York, New York
New York Times, New York, New York
New York World Telegram, New York, New York
Ponca City News, Ponca City, Oklahoma
Richmond Times-Dispatch, Richmond, Virginia
Rocky Mountain News, Denver, Colorado
Seattle Post-Intelligencer, Seattle, Washington
Seattle Times, Seattle, Washington
Tulsa Daily World, Tulsa, Oklahoma
United Press International, New York, New York
Variety, New York, New York
Ventura Free Press, Ventura, California
Washington Evening Star, Washington, D.C.
Washington Herald, Washington, D.C.
Washington Post, Washington, D.C.
Washington Star-News, Washington, D.C.

Magazines

Academy Magazine
Alaska History, Anchorage, Alaska
Motion Picture Classic, Chicago, Illinois
Motion Picture News, New York, New York

News-Week, New York, New York
Oklahoma Today, Oklahoma City, Oklahoma
Photoplay Magazine
The Pilot, Southern Pines, North Carolina
Review, New York, New York
The Saturday Evening Post, Indianapolis, Indiana
TIME, New York, New York

Interviews with the Sterlings

Ayres, Lew—Motion picture star
Blahuta, Renee—Historian, University of Alaska, Fairbanks
Brower, Thomas—Son of Charley Brower
Brown, Tom—Motion picture star
Butler, David—Motion picture director
Carey, Harry Jr.—Motion picture star
Carey, Olive—Motion picture star
Collins, Dorothy Stone—Stage star
D'Orsay, Fifi—Motion picture star
Doolittle, Jimmy—Aviation pioneer, Army Air Force General
Farley, James A.—U.S. Postmaster General
Ford, John—Motion picture director
Gaynor, Janet—Motion picture star
Gershwin, Ira—Lyricist
Gleason, Lt. Colonel Robert J. L.— Communications director for PAA
Holloway, Sterling—Motion picture star
Jarman, Lloyd—Airplane mechanic in Alaska, writer
King, Henry—Motion picture director
Leavitt, Rose Oklahomapeaha—Housewife
Loy, Myrna—Motion picture star
Marshall, George—Motion picture director
McCrea, Joel—Motion picture star
Millbrooke, Dr. Anne—Historian, archivist, author
Mohr, Hal—Cinematographer
Morgan, Barrow—Son of Sgt. Stanley Morgan
Oklahomapeaha, Clair—Eyewitness of plane crash in Alaska
Oklahomapeaha, Patrick—Adopted son of Clair Oklahomapeaha
Rich, Irene—Motion picture and radio star
Roach, Hal—Motion picture producer
Rogers, James B.—Son of Will and Betty Rogers
Rogers, Mary A.—Daughter of Will and Betty Rogers
Rogers, Will Jr.—Son of Will and Betty Rogers
Sandmeier, Emil—Factotum on the Rogers ranch
Sandmeier, Trudy—Wife of Emil Sandmeier
Stephenson, Patricia Ziegfeld—Only child of Florenz Ziegfeld Jr. and Billie Burke
Tillman, Warren—Airplane mechanic in Alaska
Venable, Evelyn—Motion picture star
Wells, Fay Gillis—Pioneer aviatrix, correspondent
Wood, Peggy—Stage and screen star
Wynn, Keenan—Motion picture actor

Books

Convention Articles, by Will Rogers, © 1976, Oklahoma State University Press, Stillwater, Oklahoma
Daily Telegrams, by Will Rogers, Vol. 1, © 1978, Oklahoma State University Press, Stillwater, Oklahoma
Daily Telegrams, by Will Rogers, Vol. 2, © 1978, Oklahoma State University Press, Stillwater, Oklahoma
Daily Telegrams, by Will Rogers, Vol. 3, © 1979, Oklahoma State University Press, Stillwater, Oklahoma
Daily Telegrams, by Will Rogers, Vol. 4, © 1979, Oklahoma State University Press, Stillwater, Oklahoma
Ether and Me or *"Just Relax"* by Will Rogers, © 1929, G. P. Putnam's Sons, New York City, New York
Goldwyn, by A. Scott Berg, © 1989, Alfred A. Knopf, New York City, New York
The Illiterate Digest, by Will Rogers, © 1924, Albert & Charles Boni, Inc., New York City, New York
Letters of a Self-Made Diplomat to His President, by Will Rogers, © 1926, Albert & Charles Boni, Inc., New York City, New York
More Letters of a Self-Made Diplomat, by Will Rogers, © 1982, Oklahoma State University Press, Stillwater, Oklahoma

My Cousin Will Rogers, by Spi M. Trent, © 1938, G. P. Putnam's Sons, New York City, New York

The Papers of Will Rogers, November 1879–April 1904, by Arthur Frank Wertheim and Barbara Blair, © 1996, Will Rogers Heritage Trust, Inc., Claremore, Oklahoma

Radio Broadcasts of Will Rogers, © 1983, Oklahoma State University Press, Stillwater, Oklahoma

Rogers-isms, The Cowboy Philosopher on the Peace Conference, by Will Rogers, © 1919, Harper and Brothers, New York City, New York

Rogers-isms, The Cowboy Philosopher on Prohibition, by Will Rogers, © 1919, Harper and Brothers, New York City, New York

There's Not a Bathing Suit in Russia & and Other Bare Facts, by Will Rogers, © 1927, Albert & Charles Boni, Inc., New York City, New York

Trails Plowed Under, by Charles M. Russell, © 1943, Doubleday, Doran & Company, Inc., Garden City, New York

W. C. Fields, by Himself, © 1973, W. C. Fields Productions, Inc.

W. C. Fields, by Robert Lewis Taylor, © 1949, The Haddon Craftsmen, Inc., Scranton, PA

Weekly Articles, by Will Rogers, Vol. 1, © 1980, Oklahoma State University Press, Stillwater, Oklahoma

Weekly Articles, by Will Rogers, Vol. 2, © 1980, Oklahoma State University Press, Stillwater, Oklahoma

Weekly Articles, by Will Rogers, Vol. 3, © 1981, Oklahoma State University Press, Stillwater, Oklahoma

Weekly Articles, by Will Rogers, Vol. 4, © 1981, Oklahoma State University Press, Stillwater, Oklahoma

Weekly Articles, by Will Rogers, Vol. 5, © 1982, Oklahoma State University Press, Stillwater, Oklahoma

Weekly Articles, by Will Rogers, Vol. 6, © 1982, Oklahoma State University Press, Stillwater, Oklahoma

Will Rogers, by Betty Rogers, © 1941, Bobbs-Merrill Company, New York City, New York

Will Rogers & Wiley Post: Death at Barrow, by Bryan and Frances Sterling, © 1993, M. Evans & Co., New York City, New York

Will Rogers at the Ziegfeld Follies, by Arthur Frank Wertheim, © 1992, University of Oklahoma Press, Norman, Oklahoma

Will Rogers in Hollywood, by Bryan and Frances Sterling, © 1984, Crown Publishers, Inc., New York City, New York

World of Flo Ziegfeld, The, by Randolph Carter, © 1974, Praeger Publishers, Inc., New York City, New York

Ziegfeld Follies, The, by Marjorie Farnsworth, © 1956, G. P. Putnam's Sons, New York City, New York

Ziegfeld's Girl, The, by Patricia Ziegfeld, © 1964, Little, Brown & Company, Boston, Massachusetts

Broadcasts

Will Rogers, January 4, 1928
Will Rogers, April 27,1930
Will Rogers, May 11, 1930
Will Rogers, October 21, 1931
Will Rogers, January 28, 1934
Will Rogers, April 14, 1934
Will Rogers, May 19, 1935

Research Centers

Academy of Motion Picture Arts & Sciences, Los Angeles, California
Alaska Historical Aircraft Soc., Anchorage, Alaska
British Film Institute, London, England
Cal. State University, Northridge, California
Fed. Aviation Administration, Oklahoma City, Oklahoma
Fed. Aviation Administration, Washington, D.C.
Library of Congress, Washington, D.C.
Los Angeles Public Libraries, California
Museum of Flight, Seattle, Washington
Museum of Modern Art, New York, New York

National Archives, Washington, D.C.

National Cowboy Hall of Fame, Oklahoma

National Museum of American History, Washington, D.C.

National Press Club, Washington, D.C.

New York City Public Libraries, New York

Oklahoma Historical Society, Oklahoma City, Oklahoma

Oklahoma State University, Stillwater, Oklahoma

Public Libraries, London, England

Seattle Public Library, Seattle, Washington

Smithsonian Institution Library, Washington, D.C.

Toronto Public Libraries, Toronto, Ontario, Canada

Twentieth Century Fox Library, Los Angeles, California

University of Alaska, Anchorage, Alaska

University of Alaska, Fairbanks, Alaska

University of California, Berkeley, California

University of California, Los Angeles, California

University of Southern California, Los Angeles, California

University of Michigan, Ann Arbor, Michigan

University of Oklahoma, Norman, Oklahoma

Westminster Research Library, London, England

Will Rogers Memorial and Birth Place, Claremore, Oklahoma

Will Rogers Ranch, Pacific Palisades, California